**VICKI FORD** is a counsellor and psychosexual therapist working in private practice. She is accredited by the British Association for Counselling and Psychotherapy (BACP) and the British Association for Sexual and Relationship Therapy (BASRT). Vicki is also registered with the United Kingdom Council for Psychotherapy (UKCP) and has taught for many years in Further and Higher Education on counselling programs. She currently offers supervision to other therapists both privately and for Relate North Wales.

## DATE DUE

| | | | |
|---|---|---|---|
| 13/1/17 | | | |
| | | | |
| | | | |
| | | | |
| | | | |
| | | | |
| | | | |
| | | | |
| | | | |
| | | | |

Demco No. 62-0549

The aim of the **Overcoming** series is to enable people with a range of common problems and disorders to take control of their own recovery program. Each title, with its specially tailored program, is devised by a practicing clinician using the latest techniques of cognitive behavioral therapy – techniques which have been shown to be highly effective in changing the way people think about themselves and their problems.

The series was initiated in 1993 by Peter Cooper, Professor of Psychology at Reading University and Research Fellow at the University of Cambridge in the UK whose original volume on overcoming Bulimia Nervosa and binge-eating continues to help many people in the USA, the UK and Europe. Many books in the **Overcoming** series are recommended by the UK Department of Health under the Books on Prescription Scheme.

Other titles in the series include:

Bulimia Nervosa and Binge-Eating

Overcoming Anxiety

Overcoming Panic

Overcoming Depression

Overcoming Social Anxiety and Shyness

Overcoming Low Self-Esteem

Overcoming Traumatic Stress

Overcoming Childhood Trauma

Overcoming Anorexia Nervosa

Overcoming Mood Swings

Overcoming Anger and Irritability

Overcoming Your Smoking Habit

Overcoming Weight Problems

Overcoming Obsessive-Compulsive Disorder

Overcoming Relationship Problems

Overcoming Chronic Fatigue

All titles in the series are available by mail order.
Please see the order form at the back of this book.
www.overcoming.co.uk

# OVERCOMING SEXUAL PROBLEMS

A *self-help guide using*
*Cognitive Behavioral Techniques*

Vicki Ford

ROBINSON
London

Constable & Robinson Ltd
3 The Lanchesters
162 Fulham Palace Road
London W6 9ER
www.constablerobinson.com

First published in the UK by Robinson,
an imprint of Constable & Robinson Ltd 2005

A copy of the British Library Cataloguing in
Publication Data is available from the British Library.

**Important Note**
This book is not intended as a substitute for medical advice or treatment.
Any person with a condition requiring medical attention should consult a
qualified medical practitioner or suitable therapist. Every effort has been
made to ensure that information concerning government schemes and
benefits for the US and UK are correct at the date of publication.

ISBN 1-84529-069-0

Printed and bound in the EU

1 3 5 7 9 10 8 6 4 2

# Contents

# Acknowledgments

My thanks go out to all my colleagues, my supervisor, and my clients. Without knowing you all I could not have written this book.

Thanks also to my children, Isobel, Tim, and Caroline; all my family, especially my sister Marian and also Ruby, Kathryn, and Alan; and my friends (you know who you are). Special thanks go to my husband, Dr David Ford, and Dr Garry Potter, whose discussions over dinner in the Canadian Rockies allowed me to think writing a book was not an impossibility.

# Introduction

## Why Cognitive Behavior Therapy?

You may have picked up this book uncertain as to why a psychological therapy such as cognitive behavioral therapy could help you overcome your sexual problems. Problems with sex are physical problems, you might think. Cognitive behavioral therapy is for people who have psychological problems, and that's not me. In fact, although CBT was developed initially for the treatment of depression, the techniques this therapy uses have been found to be extremely effective for a wide range of problems including anxiety disorders, eating disorders and drug and alcohol addictions. So what is CBT and how does it work?

In the 1950s and 1960s a set of techniques was developed, broadly collectively termed 'behavior therapy'. These techniques shared two basic features. First, they aimed to remove symptoms (such as anxiety) by dealing with those symptoms themselves, rather than their deep-seated underlying historical causes (traditionally the focus of psychoanalysis, the approach developed by Sigmund Freud and his followers). Second, they were techniques, loosely related to what laboratory psychologists were finding out about the mechanisms of learning, which could potentially be put to the test, or had already been proven to be of practical value to sufferers. The area where these techniques proved of most value was in the treatment of anxiety disorders, especially specific phobias (such as fear of animals or heights) and agoraphobia, both notoriously difficult to treat using conventional psychotherapies.

After an initial flush of enthusiasm, discontent with behavior therapy grew. There were a number of reasons for this, an important one of which was the fact that behavior therapy did not deal with the internal thoughts that were so obviously central to the distress that patients were experiencing. In particular, behavior therapy proved inadequate when it came to the treatment of depression. In the late 1960s and early 1970s a treatment was developed specifically for depression called 'cognitive therapy'. The pioneer in this enterprise was an American psychiatrist, Professor Aaron T. Beck, who developed a theory of depression which emphasized the importance of people's depressed styles of thinking. He also specified a new form of therapy. It would not be an exaggeration to say that Beck's work has changed the nature of psychotherapy, not just for depression but for a range of psychological problems.

The techniques introduced by Beck have been merged with the techniques developed earlier by the behavior therapists to produce a therapeutic approach which has come to be known as 'cognitive behavior therapy'. This therapy has been subjected to the strictest scientific testing; and it has been found to be a highly successful treatment for a significant proportion of cases of depression. However, it has become clear that specific patterns of thinking are associated with a range of psychological problems and that treatments that deal with these styles of thinking are highly effective. So, effective cognitive behavioral treatments have been developed for anxiety disorders, like panic disorder, generalized anxiety disorder, specific phobias and social phobia, obsessive compulsive disorders, and hypochondriasis (health anxiety), as well as for other conditions such as compulsive gambling, alcohol and drug addiction, and eating disorders like bulimia nervosa and binge-eating disorder. Indeed, cognitive behavioral techniques have a wide application beyond the narrow categories of psychological disorders: they have been applied effectively, for example, to helping people with low self-esteem, those with marital difficulties, those who wish to give up smoking, and people with sexual problems.

The starting point for CBT is that the ways we think, feel, and behave are all intimately linked; and changing the way we think about ourselves, our experiences, and the world around us changes the way we feel and what we are able to do. So, by helping a depressed person identify and challenge their automatic depressive thoughts, a route out of a cycle of depressive thoughts and feelings can be found. Similarly, addressing the way people with sexual problems think about their bodies and their own and their partners' sexual feelings and responses, opens the way to solving these problems.

Although effective CBT treatments have been developed for a wide range of problems, they are not widely available; and when people try to help themselves they often make matters worse. In recent years the community of cognitive behavior therapists has responded to this situation. What they have done is to take the principles and techniques of specific cognitive behavior therapies for particular problems and represent them in self-help manuals. These manuals specify a systematic program of treatment which the individual sufferer is advised to work through to overcome their difficulties. In this way, the cognitive behavioral therapeutic techniques of proven value are being made available on the widest possible basis.

Self-help manuals are never going to replace therapists. Many people will need individual treatment from a qualified therapist. It is also the case that, despite the widespread success of cognitive behavioral therapy, some people will not respond to it and will need one of the other treatments available. Nevertheless, although research on the use of cognitive behavioral self-help manuals is at an early stage, the work done to date indicates that for a very great many people such a manual will prove sufficient for them to overcome their problems without professional help.

Many people suffer silently and secretly for years. Sometimes appropriate help is not forthcoming despite their efforts to find it. Sometimes they feel too ashamed or guilty to reveal their problems to anyone. For many of these people the cognitive behavioral self-help manual will provide a lifeline to recovery and a better future.

Professor Peter Cooper
The University of Reading, 2005

# *Preface*

## The Rationale behind this Book

Why another book on sex? Bookshops and libraries are filled to overflowing with all sorts of books, videos, and magazines telling us all how to do it, and do it well. That is fine for all those enjoying a satisfying and fulfilling sex life, but what about when things go wrong? Where can we turn for help? There are, of course, trained therapists who deal with such issues. However, not everybody has the time and resources to consult a specialist. Nor will everybody need the services of a trained therapist. This book is specifically aimed at those people who recognize that they have a problem but feel they would like to try to sort it out for themselves. It is also for people who may feel daunted at the prospect of disclosing their intimate lives to a stranger. It is not easy to share personal problems, especially if they are linked to such emotions as embarrassment, fear, or even shame.

As in embarking on any self-help guide, it is important to recognize that there *is* expert help available should it be needed. This book might turn out to be the first step in acknowledging that your particular problem is more complicated than you had realized. However, even if you do decide to seek further help, it is good to feel that you have done everything in your power to solve the problem yourself first. After all, learning to cope with problems is part of our life experience.

Most people problem-solve every day, sometimes in small ways, sometimes on a larger scale, in response to the situations that constantly arise connected to family, work, hobbies, interests, or other areas. Sometimes things go wrong for very obvious reasons – a breakdown in communication, for example. In most cases, things work themselves out and life goes on, even after the most testing experiences.

This book is a starting point for coming to terms with your sexual problems. We all need to make sense of things. First recognizing, then understanding your problems are the necessary first steps towards sorting things out for yourself. The book explores some of the many reasons and causes of sexual difficulty and offers easy-to-follow self-help methods to help you take control of your sexual life. This may be the first step you take in *overcoming sexual problems*.

## The Structure and Content of the Book

The book is separated into two distinct parts. Part One is about understanding the range and nature of sexual problems within a framework of cognitive behavioral therapy. Part Two sets out a program of self-help by which both single people and couples can work towards overcoming their own particular sexual problems.

Chapter 1 begins by explaining the main sexual dysfunctions, with brief case studies to illustrate them. They include erectile dysfunction (impotence), premature ejaculation (coming too quickly), male orgasmic dysfunction (failing to ejaculate or taking a long time to do so), vaginismus (inability to have intercourse due to muscle spasm), dyspareunia (pain during sex, for a variety of reasons), orgasmic dysfunction (lack of orgasm during intercourse, masturbation or both), and loss of desire (which can affect both men and women, both single people and those in a relationship).

The chapter then goes on to consider the many external factors that can affect your sex life: for example, the environment in which you live, or a particular situation in which you find yourself. Sexual problems don't usually occur in isolation, and having an awareness of your own particular circumstances can often help to take away some of the pressure.

Chapter 1 concludes with a section on how cognitive behavioral therapy (CBT) can help in tackling sexual problems. As Peter Cooper's introduction to this book explains, CBT is a well-established and highly regarded form of treatment applied to many conditions that have a psychological basis. It concentrates on changing behavior and negative thinking patterns that impinge on the way you act and respond, and has long been acknowledged as a valuable tool in the resolution of sexual difficulties.

Periods of transition and change are particularly likely to affect how you feel about yourself. Chapter 2, which looks at a wide range of life stages and situations in which sexual problems can arise, begins by examining life as a single person. This can be invigorating and fun, but for some it spells loneliness and frustration. Lack of confidence about sex can be a problem in itself. Both men and women are constantly bombarded by images in the media of what being single means and, crucially, what they may be missing out on. For women, images such as Bridget Jones and the girls from *Sex and the City* can have a very powerful impact on their thinking, often prompting them to ask: 'Why isn't sex like that for me?' Sitcoms such as *Men Behaving Badly* and some of the most popular soap operas portray men in some very negative ways: selfish, domineering, even abusive. While these programs may bear little relation to real life overall, elements in them often strike a chord with viewers, and for those struggling with a sexual problem they can send mixed messages. But above all it is the *real* world around you, your social environment and your particular experiences within it, that dictates how you feel about sex. Many people find themselves on their own for many different reasons, and not always by their own choosing. Adjusting to single life can be very daunting, especially after a relationship breakdown. Coping with this new stage of life and the challenges it brings can be a testing time.

# Preface

Couples experiencing major upheavals and changes in their lives often find that sex slips to the bottom of their list of priorities. They often lack energy and enthusiasm under the weight of problems bearing down on them. Money, children, work, coping with ageing parents: these are just a few of the issues that can affect your sexual life, whether you are coping alone or with a partner. It is not difficult to see why sexual problems may arise in these conditions. A clear understanding of this can help you to realize that you are not alone.

People are also living longer, and as a consequence sex and ageing is worthy of special consideration. Having a sexual relationship later in life is no longer considered unacceptable. In fact, it is to be encouraged. Sex is a very positive way to use your body. It keeps you fit and supple and gives enormous pleasure at any stage of life. One fairly common problem experienced by older people is coping with a new partner after losing a long-term spouse or companion. Adjusting to life with another person can create its own problems. Feelings associated with bereavement can resurface, often from guilt at being happy again. Sometimes a sense of disapproval, especially from family members, can make starting again very difficult. Physical constraints can also impinge, with the onset of age-related aches and pains and other disabling conditions.

Disability itself covers a huge range of physical, mental, and emotional problems. Some people are born with a disability; others become disabled as a result of illness or accident. However, even the most severely disabled person can enjoy a level of physical contact, and they deserve to be encouraged and helped to do so. I remember well a man I worked with who had had a stroke. He was concerned about whether he would ever have a normal sex life again. On asking his consultant, he was told that he was lucky to be alive and shouldn't give it another thought. Insensitive responses like this are, unfortunately, fairly typical and yet can be extremely hurtful and discouraging.

Another area often overlooked is that of sexual orientation. Gays, lesbians and bisexuals are all vulnerable to the same sexual problems as the rest of the population – and in addition, worrying about sexual orientation in itself can cause a lot of distress and confusion. Sometimes it may be worth considering speaking to a trained professional or contacting a gay helpline (suggestions are offered in Appendix 1). Cross-dressing and transgender issues will also be sensitively addressed in this book. These topics are often regarded as taboo, leaving many people feeling isolated from mainstream society.

Issues around infertility, pregnancy and childbirth are also explored, as these can have a huge impact on your sexual relationship. Quite often sex gets left on the back burner during pregnancy, or seems to be taken over by the medical profession when conception fails to occur. Bereavement, abuse, addiction and medication are other highly significant areas that are addressed. A discussion around unusual sex completes the chapter.

The whole of Chapter 3 is devoted to contraception. Contraception can be the saviour of sexual activity and also its worst enemy. Condoms and safe sex can help lessen the fear of sexually transmitted disease and unwanted pregnancy. However, it must be said that many couples and individuals find condoms rather unappealing, and many people find them difficult to use. Nonetheless, times have changed and extensive health promotion has made condoms not only more accessible to the public, through the media, stores, and family planning clinics, but also more interesting. Different colours and different flavours can spice up your love life. With good communication and an element of fun, condoms can be incorporated into sex play with minimal embarrassment, fuss and effort. Of course, condoms are not the only option, and finding the right type of contraceptive device is vital to a good sexual experience. All forms of contraception have both positive and negative aspects to their use, and this chapter looks at the pros and cons of all the main methods.

Chapter 4 takes a sober but unalarmist look at one of the main dangers associated with sex: that of sexually transmitted diseases (STDs). STDs are unfortunately on the increase at present, causing widespread concern. The high incidence of chlamydia is especially worrying, as this disease is often symptomless, and yet in young women can lead to infertility. This causes untold distress to many couples who, having failed to conceive after years of trying, seek help only to be told that chlamydia is the cause. It is important to be aware of the dangers connected to a wide range of STDs and the importance of safe sex. It is also important to check out your sexual health if you are at all concerned.

In recent years the Internet has become a part of everyday life for many of us. At its best the World Wide Web can provide hours of fun talking to new people. For people on their own this can be extremely liberating, offering a whole new and exciting world where we can be whoever we want. This can lead on to experiences and situations that are not available in real life close to home. Many friendships and indeed permanent relationships have been forged through this relatively new medium. But it also has its downside, and should be used with caution, as Chapter 5 shows. Surfing the net can be compulsive, and in some instances the time spent doing this has undermined existing relationships. Anyone using the net for sexual purposes needs to think about who may be affected. I have heard both men and women complain about a decline in their real sexual relationships as they have become more involved in what is now known as 'cyber-sex'.

Part Two of the book focuses on self-help techniques. The first step (Chapter 6) is setting your goals. This chapter is designed to help you think about what you are hoping to achieve, who is involved in working on the problem, and how to establish a positive environment for your efforts. Will you be working on the problem on your own? Are you in a relationship with a partner willing to work with you? Are you living together? If so, what are your circumstances? Do you have children to consider? Getting the right environment for any self-help work is vital. Setting the scene and providing the right atmosphere could make the difference between success and failure.

Chapter 6 also helps you to assess your motivation for change. This may not be necessary in all cases, but can be a useful exercise to help you focus your thinking. I have had the experience of working with someone on a short program who, in response to my question, 'Do you really want to do this?' replied 'No!' Overcoming sexual problems can only be achieved with motivation, time and effort. A three-stage exercise to tackle negative thinking is provided that may be helpful if you are unsure of your degree or motivation and/or your ability to change.

Chapter 7 then moves on to relaxation and its central importance to good sex. Help is given here in the form of a relaxation program that is easy and straightforward to follow. Feeling relaxed is a key part of feeling good. It is hardly surprising that people experience sexual problems when you stop to consider the circumstances in which so many of us live. Certain lifestyles are simply not conducive to good sex. For example, if you are getting up at the crack of dawn to drive many miles, or catching a train prior to a 12-hour day of intensive work, or spending 2 hours at each end of the day crawling through the rush hour, sex is probably going to be the last thing on your mind by the time you get home. Stress management techniques can help you to recognize that some aspects of your lifestyle may need to change if you are to overcome your sexual problems.

In Chapter 8 the self-help program gets under way in earnest with exercises to help you to relearn how your body responds in order to enable it to work well. 'Sensate focus' is designed for couples to work through together. Other techniques can be done individually. 'Body awareness' is a four-part exercise for both men and women that can help you to think more positively about your body. Pelvic floor exercises for both men and women are designed to improve and strengthen the muscles important to sexual activity to enhance arousal. Fantasy can be used to enhance couple sex as well as to improve your sex life while on our own. All these exercises are designed to reduce stress and build up a repertoire of positive behaviors that can be beneficial even beyond the primary objective of improving sex. One busy manager I worked with commented that if he failed to do anything else ever again, he would always make time for massage!

Chapters 9 and 10 focus on specific areas of sexual difficulty for single people and couples respectively: Chapter 9 is for those of you on your own, or those wanting to work on a problem by themselves, while Chapter 10 looks at the same problems but is designed for couples. All exercises are set out in an easy-to-follow format. Just follow the instructions given for your particular sexual difficulty. At this stage it is *you* who decides which aspect of the program is most likely to be helpful.

This book has been written as a self-help guide in overcoming sexual problems. However, self-help techniques will not prove to be the answer in all cases; for some people, and in some situations, professional help will be needed. The final part of the book, Chapter 11, looks at what you can do if it still isn't working. This section includes some suggested further reading and some useful names and contact details of relevant organizations through which you can seek further help.

Good luck!

PART ONE

# Understanding Sexual Problems

Sex is part of life and should be the most natural thing in the world. Like moving and breathing, sex is a source of energy that can revitalize you and contribute to that wonderful sense of well-being that we all seek. Giving and receiving pleasure are among the most rewarding and satisfying experiences anyone can have. But if it is so natural, why does it sometimes go wrong?

Most people will experience sexual difficulties at some point in their lives. This could be because of stress and overwork, a result of being in the wrong relationship, or simply down to technical reasons. This part of the book is designed to help you to identify what your sexual problem is and how you can help yourself to put the problem right.

# 1

# Sexual Problems Explained

So what is a sexual problem? Usually it means that something in your sex life is not happening in the way you want it to. This can lead to a variety of emotions and feelings, ranging from minor frustration to severe distress. It is important to recognize that, just as there is a range of responses, so there are many different levels of severity in sexual problems themselves, with mild symptoms at one end of the spectrum and very serious difficulties at the other, with all kinds of gradations between. Also, each person is unique and will try to deal with a sexual problem in their own way. What is apparent across all these variations is that sexual problems are upsetting and require help.

*The breakdown of his marriage left 41-year-old Gary lacking in confidence, not helped by a disastrous one-night stand during which he lost his erection. Meeting Louise, who was kind and sympathetic, helped to restore his confidence, and his erection.*

*Ralph (32) lived at home with his parents. He never felt comfortable masturbating there, so he would come as quickly as he could. Ralph only took his girlfriend home when his parents were out, but still found he was ejaculating quickly, usually after a few thrusts inside her. This was frustrating for both of them and was beginning to affect their relationship. They chose to seek help together.*

*Liz had been married to Don for five years but they had never had penetrative sex. Liz had vaginismus, a condition that causes the vaginal muscles to go into spasm, and tensed up every time Don tried to get inside her. Talking to their doctor helped Liz and Don understand the problem and to look at ways of overcoming it.*

The following are the most commonly experienced problems regularly treated by psychosexual therapists.

*Male sexual problems:*

- erectile dysfunction (the inability to sustain or maintain an erection);
- premature ejaculation (coming too quickly);
- orgasmic dysfunction (failing to ejaculate or taking a long time to do so).

*Female sexual problems:*

- vaginismus (inability to have intercourse due to muscle spasm);
- dyspareunia (painful sex, for one or more of a variety of reasons);
- orgasmic dysfunction (inability to reach orgasm during intercourse, masturbation, or both).

In addition, both men and women can suffer loss of desire.

## Male Sexual Problems Explained

### Erectile Dysfunction (ED)

An erection is achieved by the flow of blood into the penis and the blocking of the small blood vessels, making the penis hard. The process is somewhat similar to pumping air into a tyre. The inner tube holds the air, while the outer tyre protects the tube and keeps the tyre hard. If the air is released from the tube, the tyre will go down. It will also go down if there is a slow puncture, and if there is insufficient air in the tyre the wheel will not perform well. Much the same happens with penises. The problem could be partial, where the penis will become semi-erect (the half-full tyre) but not hard enough for sexual intercourse. Alternatively, it could be a total inability to achieve an erection (flat tyre). In some cases the erection is hard enough at the beginning of sex play but then is difficult to maintain (slow puncture).

It is a fact that most men will suffer erectile problems at some point in their lives: research indicates that currently one in ten British men are suffering erectile dysfunction. The causes are many and varied, and the circumstances in which the problem occurs – in any of the variants mentioned above – are of crucial importance to a proper understanding of the problem.

> *Sam (28) had no trouble in obtaining an erection but he had started to lose it halfway through intercourse. Sam's problems stemmed from his focusing on quantity rather than quality. He wasn't interested in many of the girls he bedded, and his penis was simply responding to that indifference. With help and encouragement Sam was able to reflect on his sexual behavior and identify what he needed for good sex, and as a consequence his sex life improved.*

There could also be medical reasons for erectile problems.

> *Jim (73) had prostate surgery resulting in a loss of erection. The doctor prescribed Viagra, and Jim is now enjoying a full sex life again.*

It is important that you see your doctor if you have any concerns about your general health. Research has indicated that erectile dysfunction can be an indication of various medical disorders, including heart problems, high blood pressure, or a high cholesterol level.

## Premature Ejaculation

Premature ejaculation (PE), or coming too quickly, is the result of an inability to identify the 'point of inevitability'. The 'point of inevitability' is where you will orgasm no matter what. Men have a unique response mechanism that enables them to achieve orgasm much more readily than women. It occurs in two stages – emission and ejaculation. Emission is where fluid leaves the seminal vesicles and enters a point at the base of the penis. Once this has occurred, ejaculation is inevitable. Ejaculate (seminal fluid and sperm), once released, must leave the body and will do so via the end of the penis.

Women, in contrast, do not have a point of inevitability. They can reach the point of orgasm, be on the verge and lose it. This frustrating experience is sometimes due to a loss of concentration, but more commonly to momentum being lost through a change in position or stimulation. Men do sometimes experience difficulties achieving orgasm, but in these instances the point of inevitability is not reached.

For those of you experiencing premature ejaculation, this book will help you learn to control when the point of inevitability is reached, as part of learning about your body and how it works. Faulty learning takes place when orgasm is achieved quickly and the connection is not made between the brain (telling you what you want to happen) and the body (physically responding to the brain's message). Taking time to focus on what your body is doing and how it feels immediately before ejaculation is vital to understanding and gaining control. Obviously, on occasion it may suit a person to come quickly, and in such cases it will not be a problem, especially if you are in control when you need to be. However, if it is happening all of the time and affecting your relationship, then learning to gain control of your point of inevitability is a necessary part of improving your sex life.

Erectile dysfunction can be a distressing side effect of PE. Lack of confidence in your own ability to avoid PE can lessen your desire for sexual contact and undermine your erection. This can in some instances lead to the avoidance of sexual situations altogether.

*Josh was getting tired of losing girlfriends. He was starting to realize that his anxiety about coming too quickly was now making*

6

*the original problem worse. He also recognized that he was so busy trying to get it right that he was no longer enjoying sex for himself at all. This situation caused Josh so much stress that he lost the confidence to go out and meet girls. Josh withdrew into himself and so effectively avoided the problem: a drastic and highly unsatisfactory solution to an entirely resolvable difficulty.*

Defining the level of PE is useful when establishing whether a problem exists or not. The following case is an example of a wrongly diagnosed sexual problem:

*Adam's girlfriend complained about him coming too quickly and asked him to seek help. On further investigation Adam said that he often ejaculated after about 10 minutes; though this was leaving his girlfriend frustrated, it was clearly not PE. When a therapist saw them together and talked things through with them, it became apparent that the problem was not Adam's speed of ejaculation but his girlfriend's inability to have an orgasm. With help and support she learned first to bring herself to orgasm, and later to experience orgasm with Adam.*

In general terms, a diagnosis of PE can be made on the following criteria: ejaculation prior to insertion, ejaculation on entry to the vagina, or ejaculation after a few thrusts. However, the best diagnosis for PE is self-diagnosis, where a man decides for himself that he is ejaculating involuntarily before he wants to. Most men will experience problems of PE occasionally when stressed or anxious, or after a period of abstinence (no sex with a partner). This is quite normal and usually rectifies itself. However, if the problem is constant and continuing, it can be remedied.

## Orgasmic Dysfunction

This could be described as the opposite of PE. Instead of coming too quickly, a man finds that he is unable to ejaculate or takes a long time to do so. Again, the reasons are many and varied; but whatever the reason, the frustration this causes is often very bad for relationships. Some women blame themselves for not being attractive enough or fear that their partner has gone off them. Of course, in some cases this could be true, and in such instances relationship counselling may be the order of the day. However, ejaculation also has associations with 'letting go' or 'losing control', and so may be difficult or impossible for someone with psychological problems connected to a fear of loss of control. For example, your body may simply be responding to protect itself from unpleasant memories or experiences.

Failing to ejaculate is clearly a problem if you are hoping to have a child.

> *Pete and his wife Sue wanted children. Pete had never been able to come inside a partner, yet he was able to masturbate successfully on his own. Exploration into Pete's background revealed a sad story of childhood sexual abuse by an older female relative. Pete went for help with a counsellor who was able to work through the trauma of his past. With the help of his wife he learned to relax and was soon able to masturbate in her presence. Eventually he progressed to ejaculating successfully during intercourse with her.*

Taking a long time to ejaculate or not ejaculating at all can sometimes be a normal consequence of getting older, as the desire to ejaculate decreases with age. This can be of benefit for those couples where PE has been a problem, as the ageing process can assist in slowing things down.

However, it is possible that you may have developed a physical problem. This could be due to a hormone deficiency, or the onset of a condition such as diabetes or a heart problem. Failure to ejaculate can also be caused by 'retrograde' ejaculation, a symptom of which is cloudy urine that appears opaque rather than clear. This could indicate that seminal fluid, instead of being ejaculated in the usual way, through the end of the penis, may be leaking back into the bladder. If you think this may be happening in your case, it is best to consult your doctor for further investigation, as it may possibly indicate a health problem such as diabetes or bladder dysfunction.

## Female Sexual Problems Explained

### *Vaginismus*

Vaginismus is caused by the involuntary spasm of a group of muscles surrounding the vagina, called the pubococcygeal muscles. The response is similar to when your eyes close in response to something coming towards your face very quickly. This is an *involuntary* response: your brain does not have time to tell your eyes to close. A somewhat similar process can happen in the muscles around the vagina when penetration is attempted. A spasm causes the vagina to close in such a way that it can be impossible to put anything inside at all, or even have an internal examination. Vaginismus, like all of these problems, is a very distressing phenomenon. It is one of the main causes of unconsummated relationships (where intercourse has never successfully taken place).

Primary vaginismus is where a woman has never been penetrated, has never used a tampon, and has never been able to have an internal examination. Some women find it impossible even to think about putting something into their vaginas, and clam up immediately at the thought of anything inside them. Nonetheless, many couples cope very well with the problem and have fulfilling sex lives without penetrative intercourse. The problem of primary vaginismus can often come to light when a woman or couple want a baby. It is the desire for a child that forces them to confront their problem and seek help. In other cases women learn to adapt to the symptoms, sometimes as a result of the demands of the jobs they do.

*Nina (25) is a fitness instructor. She had suffered from primary vaginismus as far back as she could remember. She needed to overcome her fear because she could not afford to keep taking days off work when she had her period. Her solution was to start by using the very smallest tampon available. Once she was able to insert this comfortably she gradually went up in size until she was able to accommodate the size of tampon she needed. Nina was soon able to run her exercise class during her period – a huge achievement for her. Her solution also reduced the stress she was under at work by avoiding potential problems with her employers.*

Secondary vaginismus is where a woman has in the past been able to have sexual intercourse but now, perhaps because of a traumatic experience, her body is now saying no to sex.

*Theresa's second child was born in the breech position (facing the wrong way). She needed to have a caesarean section but unfortunately the baby was too far down the birth canal for this to be carried out. The result was a prolonged labour and considerable pain, not helped by her baby being eight and a half pounds in weight. The resultant damage to her body left her feeling traumatized and suffering from vaginismus.*

*Sara (19) was raped at a party by two men she knew. She didn't feel able to report the assault as she felt ashamed and blamed herself for drinking too much. Subsequently her body froze when she found herself in a sexual situation. She was unable to be sexual again until she had fully confronted the horror of what had happened to her.*

## Dyspareunia

Dyspareunia, otherwise known as 'painful sex', is often associated with vaginismus, the spasm occurring in this case in response to pain experienced during intercourse. This can make further attempts at penetration very difficult. Painful sex has many different origins. Often women try to persevere with intercourse, hoping that it will be better next time. This can

10

lead to the development of psychological problems, particularly when sex doesn't get any better. Some women may avoid sex altogether, or blame their partners for the problem.

Sometimes the cause is an infection or bacterial disease such as thrush. These lie dormant within the body, and when they manifest themselves can be very unpleasant and at their worst extremely painful. The pain can often be experienced even in the absence of visible symptoms, and it can be very distressing to visit the doctor for help, only to be told on examination that there is nothing there, when you still feel pain.

Painful sex can also be the result of other treatable conditions.

*Vivienne (28) suffers from endometriosis. This is where the lining of the womb comes away and establishes itself outside the womb cavity. These cells stick to other organs of the body and bleed at regular intervals in response to hormonal changes in the body during the monthly cycle. This in turn causes pelvic pain and discomfort, especially during intercourse. Recent laser treatment has given Vivienne some respite from the pain, and her consultant is hopeful that with more treatment things will improve still further.*

Another painful complaint is vulval vestibulitis, often referred to as the 'burning vulva syndrome'. The causes of this, and its related condition vulvodynia, are as yet not fully understood. The symptoms of both conditions include burning, itching, and soreness, particularly during sex. Sufferers have been found to have a heightened sense of touch, and pain and stress are known to exacerbate the problem in some cases. Complementary therapies, as well as mainstream medication, can help alleviate symptoms.

There are many other causes of painful sex, among them lack of natural lubrication (sometimes a symptom of the menopause), pelvic inflammatory disease, and various untreated sexually transmitted diseases. The Vulval Pain Society has been set up to help women who continue to experience pain on intercourse despite their treatments (for contact details see Appendix 1).

11

## Orgasmic Dysfunction

Like vaginismus, orgasmic dysfunction may be categorized as either primary or secondary. Primary orgasmic dysfunction is where a woman has never experienced an orgasm. Secondary orgasmic function may take a number of forms. In some cases a woman may have an orgasm with a partner during intercourse, but be unable to experience one through manual stimulation (using the hand) or oral stimulation (using the mouth). In other cases a woman may experience orgasm through masturbation and/or through manual or oral stimulation, but be unable to reach orgasm through intercourse. Being unable to experience an orgasm in one situation or another can be frustrating and upsetting, and for some may even challenge their nature as a woman. Nearly everyone wants to feel 'normal', however that may be defined.

> *Carole (31) was very upset when she came to see me. She didn't think anyone could possibly understand what she was going through. She felt like she was the only woman in the world who wasn't having orgasms, but worst of all she felt that not being orgasmic made her less of a woman. Carole's distress was very real, and her deep-seated fear of not being 'normal' took time to treat.*

A significant feature of the female body is the hidden nature of the genital area. In contrast to a man's penis, the vagina is tucked away from direct view. This could well explain why so many women are unfamiliar with the way they look and why some women don't touch themselves 'down there'. Problems can arise from this lack of familiarity with your own body. If you don't know what you look like when healthy, can you be sure you would know if something were wrong? It also follows that if *you* don't know how to stimulate yourself or what your body enjoys, it cannot be assumed that a partner will know either.

Girls are not generally encouraged to explore their bodies.

*Paula (21) distinctly remembers being told by her mother to take her hand out of her knickers when she was idly touching herself at about 4 or 5 years of age. She also remembers feeling surprised at her mom being cross. However, she got the message that she shouldn't touch herself there in future. In fact, touching 'down there', Paula believed, was something that only your partner should do to you. Paula was surprised to learn that friends at her college not only touched themselves but experienced orgasms as a consequence.*

*Rose (55) had never had an orgasm during her first marriage. In fact, she had found the whole business of sex rather unpleasant and had tolerated it only to please her husband. When her marriage broke up and she met Tony she was surprised to find herself experiencing feelings she had never had before. Tony was an experienced lover and soon taught Rose how to really let go and enjoy their love-making. Very soon Rose had her first orgasm, and she hasn't looked back since.*

## Loss of Desire

Men and women can experience the problem of loss of desire equally. Many people find at some time that, irrespective of whether or not they have had good sex in the past, they have 'gone off it'. Loss of desire can cause relationships to break down in cases where one partner no longer feels sexually turned on by the other. No matter how much a partner is told 'it's not you, it's me,' the other person is bound to experience feelings of concern, anxiety, and rejection.

It can be hard to pin down why people lose desire for sex. Sometimes there are clear reasons; sometimes you really don't know what has caused this to happen. Sometimes loss of desire is a slow process, with sex gradually happening less and less often. This can go unnoticed by the other person, perhaps due to long working hours or stress. In such cases the acknowledgment of the problem comes as a shock and its onset is perceived as sudden.

*Alex, a 45-year-old businessman, said, 'One minute things were great, the next she wasn't bothered any more.' However, his wife said Alex was always too busy for sex. At first she had minded, but she had since got used to abstinence and now didn't fancy having sex any more.*

*Anita went off sex after her twin girls were born. All she had ever wanted was a family, and she had strongly associated sex with trying to become pregnant. For Anita, sex didn't seem quite so important once she had the girls. She had also been very sore after the births and this had reduced her desire to be sexual. Anita was busy with the children, especially as they grew up. Simon felt left out and lonely, but had not been able to tell her how he felt. Sadly for them both, they drifted apart. Simon talked to a woman at work who was very understanding. The affair that followed brought Anita and Simon into counselling.*

None of these sexual problems occur in isolation. Many factors contribute to the unique conditions and circumstances of every individual's sexual difficulties. What these factors are, and how they can influence what is going on for you sexually, are the focus of the next section.

## Other Factors Affecting Sex

### Social Factors

Social pressure is all around us with regard to sex. We are bombarded by programs on television showing beautiful men and women with perfect bodies. This can be very hard to cope with – along with the magazine articles, videos, and books all telling you about how your sex life should be. This can be pretty daunting, especially if you are having difficulty getting an erection or are scared to have penetrative sex. Friends often seem to be having such a wonderful time, appearing to have sex without a care in the world. This can make it difficult to confide in anyone about how *you* feel about sex. It can feel especially isolating if your social life is not all it might be.

---

### Questions to Ask Yourself

Am I influenced by what I see in the media?
Do my friends' opinions matter more than my own?
Do I bow down to peer pressure?
How do I behave in social settings?

---

Change is a constant factor in all of our lives. Often it is not possible to stay where you are known and loved. Losing a job, relocation, or starting a new job often means huge upheaval: not only the sadness of leaving familiar places, friends, and family behind, but the stress of finding a new home and settling into a new position. Going away to university can be an exciting prospect to some, but for others it can mean loneliness and/or new demands, both academic and social.

All these kinds of social pressure can affect how you feel about sex, and can be harder to cope with in the absence of family and friends. Even if you stay in your home town, it may be difficult to find similar, like-minded people. When considering sexual problems it is useful to take into account the wider social landscape surrounding you.

*Carrie (17) was enjoying going to college as she had not been able to make many friends at her local school. She found herself in a circle of very outgoing girls and boys who loved socializing. They appeared to her to be very free and easy about sex. Carrie had never had a boyfriend, let alone sex, yet she desperately wanted to fit in. Her new friends started putting pressure on her to join in. Carrie became very anxious and fearful of losing her newly found status as part of the crowd, yet didn't feel ready to have sex.*

*Ada (71) has met Fred (69) at the local dance club. Fred is an excellent dancer and flirts with all the women there. Ada is aware that he would like their friendship to become closer. Ada has been widowed for many years and likes Fred's attention but hasn't had sex since her husband died. She is very nervous of how Fred will feel about her body, especially after surgery 2 years earlier left her with a very visible scar.*

## Physical Factors

Having taken into account social factors, it is important to link these to physical factors and the role these play in sexual problems. How you feel about yourself is a crucial aspect of being a sexual person. Everybody is conscious of how they look, even if they are not particularly concerned about it. If you consider yourself unattractive, too tall, too short, overweight, underweight, breasts too big or too small, penis not big enough, you will inevitably feel less confident in a sexual situation. Accepting yourself as you really are and being happy within yourself plays a huge part in being attractive to others. If you like yourself, the chances are other people will like you too.

It is also important to know what you can and can't change about your physical appearance. Losing weight can really make a difference in how you feel about yourself. For some it can bring fresh confidence and a new wardrobe. Other people may be happier with their size yet feel the pressure to fit in, to conform to society's view of how a person should look. Bowing down to this pressure is not helpful if it makes *you* feel unhappy. As long as you lead a healthy and happy life, size should not matter. Certainly you can do little about being too tall or too short. At any rate, who is to say what is *too* tall or *too* short? Fortunately, men and women are so diverse in their likes and dislikes that whether you are blonde, brunette, or auburn, a size 10 (US size 8) or a size 24 (US size 22), a 1.8 metre (6-foot) hunk or a couch potato, life often has a way of sending you the person you want to be with. You may meet a lot of frogs and toads on the way, but that's part of the challenge and a lot of the fun. Remember, we come in all shapes and sizes, and all shapes and sizes are capable of enjoying a happy and fulfilling sex life.

---

### Questions to Ask Yourself

Am I really happy with the way I look?
What can I realistically change?
Do I really want to change?
How motivated am I to change?
Can I accept myself exactly the way I am?

---

Sometimes, however, an individual's physical appearance or capabilities are changed as a result of illness or accident. This can be particularly hard to cope with if you are already established in a long-term relationship.

*Danny (33) suffered serious injuries in a road traffic accident. He will never walk again and uses a wheelchair. Danny and Diane had only been married for two and a half years and sadly Diane could not cope with this huge change in their marital circumstances. Danny was lonely and unhappy for several years after Diane left him, but the story has a happy ending. Danny met Pam, a carer at a physiotherapy centre he was attending. They fell in love and have since married, and they manage a full sexual relationship together.*

Many people face problems of altered body image after a serious illness or accident. Fortunately, with help most come to terms with the changes and adjust to their new status well.

*Robyn (45) could not face showing her partner her mastectomy scar. Sensitive help from hospital staff enabled Robyn to share her fears with her partner, who was then able to discuss his concerns with her as well.*

*Sylvia (35) talked to the stoma nurse about how to cope with sex after her colostomy operation. Detailed information provided by the nurse gave Sylvia the reassurance and help she needed.*

## Psychological Factors

Psychological factors play a huge role in sexual problems. How you feel inside your head can make the difference between having good sex and not. Many sexual problems originate in the mind. The mind is very powerful, and once you find yourself in a negative frame it can be very hard to change it. Factors affecting you psychologically can include

- upbringing (how, when, where);
- your family attitude to sex;
- cultural and religious beliefs;
- whether or not you were taught about sex at home or at school (sex education);
- first awareness of sex;
- first experience of sex.

Inevitably, your thoughts, beliefs, and values about sex will impinge on your sexual experience, whether positively or negatively.

---

**Questions to Ask Yourself**

What is your earliest sexual memory?
What was the family attitude to sex?
When did you become aware of the opposite sex?
How and when did you learn where babies come from?
What was your sex education?
What was your early experience of periods/wet dreams?

---

Sexual arousal is stimulated by hormones released as a result of messages sent to the body from the brain. Sometimes these messages – for instance, 'I feel really turned on' or 'Wow, this feels so good' – are psychologically good messages that contribute towards sexual feelings building up until tension is released by way of orgasm. However, sometimes these messages from the brain can spell doubt: for example, 'Am I going to keep my erection?' or 'Will he get bored if I take too long to come?' Too many negative messages result in a loss of sexual arousal. For men this may mean loss of erection, for women it may mean loss of vaginal lubrication.

Some individuals experience psychological problems stemming from childhood experiences, and will require expert help in order to move on. Childhood sexual abuse, for example, can adversely affect how a person responds sexually in their adult life. This is extremely sad and distressing for the person themselves and for their partners.

*Melanie (29) had never told anyone about an incident that occurred when she was a child. She had successfully blocked it out of her mind and had established a very happy and varied life. Successful at work, popular with men, she was never short of a partner to go out with and have fun. Since meeting Colm (31) things had changed. Colm said he was in love with her and wanted the relationship to develop sexually. This was further than she had gone with anyone else before. Subsequently, Melanie found herself tensing up whenever Colm started to get close to her. She knew he wanted more than the kisses and cuddles they had shared so far. She started having vivid dreams and the disturbing memories returned. The sexual incident from her childhood had come back to haunt her. After one particularly traumatic evening Colm had asked her what was wrong. Melanie struggled to find the courage to tell him what had happened because she feared rejection. Fortunately, in this case, Colm genuinely cared for her and was prepared to do whatever he could to help her through.*

Psychological states such as anxiety and anger can have a negative effect on sexual behavior. It can be very difficult to feel sexually attracted towards someone when you are feeling resentful or hostile. Resentment is not conducive to sexual activity, especially if the feeling cannot be expressed and openly shared. Good communication is essential for good sex. For some people, having a good row can clear the air and sex will follow. As the old song says, 'The best part of breaking up is when we're making up.' When this doesn't happen, or when relationships are strained beyond the point of being able to talk through the problems, sex will often be the first thing to disappear. Giving the cold shoulder takes on a more literal meaning.

*Jenny (35) works full-time and is married to Jack (37). They have three children at school. Jenny resents the fact that when Jack comes home from work he does nothing to help her organize the evening meal and sort out the children. Jack has noticed that Jenny is rejecting him in bed, saying she is too tired for sex. Jack has not connected this with his lack of support and is unaware of her growing anger and resentment. Jenny is assuming that Jack should know why she is behaving in this way, but she is wrong. Jenny needs to ask Jack directly for more help around the house and with the children, rather than withholding sex as a punishment.*

## Environmental Factors

The environment in which you live often gets overlooked when considering factors that could be affecting sex. That is because most people don't think of the environment in relation to sex. However, if you are stuck in a one-bedroom apartment with children you may need to think again. For sex to be enjoyed, most people need privacy and time to be alone together. Sharing a space with children, especially young children, can seriously affect the quality of sex between you and your partner. Similarly, you may find living with parents a happy arrangement; however, knowing that your parents are in the next room may seriously affect your partner. Alternatively, it may be you who feels embarrassed at making love, knowing that your parents are next door.

---

**Questions to Think About**

Is the environment I am in conducive to good sex?
Is privacy an issue?
Do my children/parents/pets affect my sex life?

---

*Martin and Karen were noisy lovers and were horrified when their 8-year-old son asked whether Daddy was hurting Mommy. Fortunately, Martin and Karen were members of the Caravan Club. Their solution was to take their sex life out of the bedroom and into the caravan.*

Not everyone is fortunate enough to have a caravan. However, most problems of this kind can be solved or improved. What is generally needed is some lateral thinking in order to work out the best solution for your particular problem.

*Julie and Mike couldn't seem to stop their children walking into their room at night. They didn't want to deny them access, especially if they were upset. What they needed was some kind of delay mechanism. Putting a small bolt on the top of the door prevented the children from coming in while Julie and Mike were making love.*

*Jane (38) didn't like bringing men home as her two young teenage children made her feel uncomfortable. As a single mom she felt responsible for them, yet at the same time Jane had a healthy sexual appetite and wanted to enjoy her body. Jane's solution was to speak to her ex-husband. She arranged for the children to stay overnight with their father on a regular basis. This would allow her to enjoy some freedom within her own home. Initially the children protested, especially as Mom had not wanted them to stay over before, but Dad and his new wife were able to make the arrangement as much fun as possible and a routine was established.*

## Situational Factors

As with environmental factors, most people rarely question the situations in which they find themselves. Yet asking yourself the question, 'Am I happy with this situation?' is important when considering your sex life. It is not uncommon for a person to find themselves in a situation that they feel unhappy with, but unable to do anything about.

> *Mary (25) was regretting going back to John's flat. She liked him well enough at work but didn't really fancy him. Now she was feeling very uncomfortable and wasn't sure what to do.*

> *Matthew's girlfriend was away on a course. Linda had invited him out for a drink after a long and dreary meeting. He knew he should have refused as he was aware that Linda liked him. Now he was in her flat and she was taking her clothes off.*

It's all too easy suddenly to find yourself in a situation not of your choosing purely because you have not been thinking far enough ahead and asking yourself where a particular chain of events may be leading. Unfortunately, not thinking a situation through at the beginning can have painful consequences later on. Take care not to allow alcohol to cloud your judgment and take away your sense of what is right and wrong for you. If Matthew had accepted a drink, but not the invitation home, all would have been well. If Mary had been more open with John and told him she saw him as a friend and nothing else, she might well have been able to have a drink with him in his flat without fearing the worst.

Some situations can be really frightening.

> *Danielle (20) made the mistake of leaving her friends at the end of the evening and walking home alone. She heard footsteps behind her and froze. Her heart was beating faster and faster until the person behind overtook her. It turned out to be another woman hurrying home. Danielle used her cellphone to call for a taxi, even though she had no money with her. She got home safely.*

---

**Questions to Think About**

Do I think things through before I do them?
Do I take unnecessary risks?
Have I ever put myself in danger?
Do I worry about what others might think in certain situations?

---

You may well recognize some of the situations mentioned above. Some you may have experienced personally, some you may be aware of through friends and family. What is important is that you open your mind to all the wide range of issues that can have an impact on your sexual life. Remember, *sexual problems do not occur in isolation*. Considering some of the questions posed here will help you to identify important factors that can affect not only your sex life but your overall happiness and future well-being. The road to self-discovery can start here – and the method to help you with this is cognitive behavioral therapy (CBT).

## How Cognitive Behavioral Therapy (CBT) Can Help with Sexual Problems

Various psychological therapies have been used in counselling and psychotherapy for many years, and all have their own particular way of looking at problems. Peter Cooper's introduction to this book (see pages vii–x) has explained how CBT has developed and become established as a very effective way of treating various disorders and problems. The particular advantage of CBT over other approaches is that it unites two very important elements, combining 'thinking' and 'doing'. Thinking (and perhaps talking) about and understanding why you have a problem can be very helpful; but you will need to go a bit further than this, and take action. This book is designed to help you to do just that. CBT offers a down-to-earth and practical way of dealing with sexual problems. A further advantage of CBT is that you can set your own goals and work towards them at your own pace. In other words, *you* take control.

Let's look at how CBT can help in a real situation.

*Tom has premature ejaculation. Basically, he comes too quickly for Anna to take pleasure from their lovemaking. As it happens, a lack of privacy earlier in their relationship had meant that their lovemaking had always been hurried. However, now that they have a home of their own, what had been quite OK has suddenly became a problem. Looking at this outcome from a purely behavioral perspective, what Tom had previously learned needs to be unlearned. Tom needs to gain control. Through graded tasks and with Anna's help, Tom has begun to identify with his bodily sensations and recognize his point of no return.*

Tom's case is a very straightforward example of how behavior that is problematic can be altered. Also, the couple were in agreement about what the problem was and jointly wanted to resolve it. But life is rarely so uncomplicated. Let's look at the same basic scenario again, but in the context of a different couple's relationship.

*Lee has premature ejaculation. Due to lack of privacy his lovemaking with Maria had always been hurried; not that Maria had seemed to mind. She had always said that Lee shouldn't worry. Lee wanted to spend more time loving Maria and giving her a good time. Maria found this difficult and just wanted Lee to 'get on with it!' She wasn't able to tell Lee how she felt. As a consequence, when they moved into their own home Lee was very disappointed, as Maria seemed uninterested in sorting out what he clearly perceived as a problem. This resulted in a very unhappy and confused time for this young couple, who in lots of other ways had everything to look forward to. Maria and Lee sought help. It soon emerged that Maria had very negative feelings about sex. Her upbringing had been very strict, and sex was not only disapproved of but also actively described as 'dirty 'and 'only what men want'.*

> *CBT helped Maria to challenge this negative way of thinking and to focus on what their lovemaking was really about – showing their love for one another and enjoying each other's bodies in this intimate way.*

In this case the couple needed to improve not only their sexual performance (behavioral change) but their sexual communication as well. Maria's negative thinking needed to be shared with Tom and changed (cognitive change). CBT not only focuses on changing behavior but looks at the thinking patterns and motives underlying our behavior. CBT considers how we think and feel about any given situation. Using a selection of practical skills, self-awareness, and exercises to combat negative thinking can help to cut through some of the difficulties associated with sexual problems. It is this combination of the two elements of 'doing' and 'thinking' that make up the essence of cognitive behavioral therapy.

Sexual problems can seriously harm even the closest of relationships, often leading to arguments or withdrawal, sometimes even to separation and divorce. They can also indicate disaster with respect to the forming of new relationships. Having considered what sexual problems are and introduced the approach we shall develop later in the book to deal with them, we now need to identify and explore the range of issues relating to sexual problems.

# 2

# Specific Issues Affecting Sex

## Sex and the Single Person

You may well be questioning at this point what could possibly be said on the subject of sex and the single person. You might even go so far as to think, 'Do single people have sex?' Sex usually happens between two people, and in certain situations with more! You don't have to be in a permanent relationship in order to have sex (although some would argue that it helps); you just need a willing person. Sexual activity in the form of self-loving (masturbation), on the other hand, does not require anyone else to be present. Sex for one works too!

Being single conjures up many images, most of which are shaped by how you see yourself in relation to others. Couples often view single people with sympathy: 'Poor fellow, he doesn't have a partner'. Others will view singles with envy: 'How I wish I had the freedom to do what I want'. Certainly some people prefer to be single. Some relish it because they enjoy their own company and are happy to spend time alone. Others like the freedom to come and go as they please, opting in and out of relationships as and when they choose without having to consult others.

Although being single is commonly linked to being young, it is not age-related any more. Changes in society and moral attitudes, with more women seeking higher education and independent careers, have led to many young people putting off settling down until much later. The old concept of being 'left on the shelf' doesn't mean much today. Very few men and women feel pressure to marry, or even to live together. As a consequence, people are leaving it much later to start their families. Also, people nowadays are less likely to tolerate living within unhappy relationships, so that more marriages are ending in divorce and cohabiting couples are more likely to split up. These trends have further increased the number of single people within society. Furthermore, adult children are staying in the family home for longer. For some this is down to economics but for others it is actually a lifestyle choice, especially among young men. It is not at all unusual today to find men and women in their thirties living with their parents.

Being single does not preclude a sex life. Sex can be a positive part of your life, an activity that you can enjoy without censure, shame or guilt. However, if you are single by choice you may be in a better position than someone who has it inflicted upon them. One woman who found herself on her own after her husband had died felt guilty at her sexual feelings and disloyal to her husband when she masturbated, as this had not been part of their life together. Once she overcame this feeling she was able to relieve her sexual tension without guilt. Many people choose to live alone, and being happy with sex for one can be part of that.

Many 'single' people, of course, have children, and this can have profound effects on feelings about sex.

*Alice found bringing up her three children after her husband left very difficult – so hard, in fact, that sex went completely out of the window. However, as she regained her self-esteem and her confidence she began to go out with other single friends and have some fun again. At this point her lust for life, and sex, returned.*

*Gavin was widowed and left with two teenage daughters. Coping with their combined grief took a long time. Gavin felt lonely. He missed his wife but had found his daughters unable to cope if he took a female colleague out for a drink. Gavin was devoted to his girls and so he made the best of time alone, or late at night, to remember his wife and enjoy himself sexually. Gavin's choice was to devote himself to his daughters while they needed him. He felt he had plenty of time in the future to look for a new relationship. In the meantime, his thoughts and memories of his beloved wife were enough to sustain him.*

Being aware that you have a sexual problem can in itself prevent you from getting out and meeting people. Knowing that your erection has been failing, or that you are frightened of penetrative sex, can be a real issue. So what do you do? Go out anyway and hope for the best, or stay at home and wonder what to do? The difficulty here is that if you meet someone who really turns you on, especially on a first date, how on earth do you tell him or her that you have a problem? A message constantly given to couples is that for good sex you need good communication. This is very hard when you have just met the person concerned. Often people will make excuses at this point in order to avoid embarrassment in a sexual situation: 'I'm sorry but it's that time of the month', or 'I really like you and want to get to know you better'. This can feel all right at first but can rapidly become very rejecting, especially if the other person is responding positively and indicates that they want sex. Most people will accept such avoidance in the very early stages of a relationship, but if it continues it could spell the end of what might have been a good partnership. How many people would want to go into sex therapy when they have just met? Not many! Recognizing that you have a sexual problem and doing all you can to resolve it on your own before you embark on a relationship could make all the difference.

*Toby had been having erectile problems for some time. He met Suzie at a party and they really hit it off. As the party wasn't up to much they decided to leave early and go back to Suzie's apartment. There, things got really heated until Toby said he had an early start the next day and had to go. Suzie was not only disappointed but surprised. She felt sure that she had received the message that Toby really liked her as much as she liked him. Over the next few weeks Toby wined and dined Suzie and she began to fall in love. However, he always seemed to avoid situations where they could be alone together. Suzie finally got Toby back to her apartment to resume what they had started on the first date. This time Toby didn't have a reason to leave. When his erection failed neither knew what to say or do. This situation might have been avoided if Toby had felt able to talk about his problem to Suzie openly. Of course, this could have put her off and stopped the developing relationship in its tracks, just as Toby's avoidance tactics might well have done. On the other hand, if Suzie really liked Toby she might have been willing to explore the problem with him.*

Clearly there are always risks involved in embarking on any relationship, and each situation needs to be considered with great care.

## Sex in Established Relationships

Relationships can be enhanced by the experience of a satisfying sex life. The joy of an intimate sexual partnership can help overcome many other more general problems in a couple's relationship, just as a poor sexual life can harm an otherwise good relationship. Falling in love is one of the most deeply emotional states that you can find yourself in. If it is reciprocated then that feeling increases tenfold.

For couples, whether married or not, the key to good sex is communication. In the first flush of being in love sexual problems often go unnoticed. For example, rushing into each other's arms and ripping your clothes off in a fit of passion can sometimes mask premature ejaculation, especially if you are somewhere you shouldn't be and it needs to be quick! Good communication about what you like and don't like is crucial after the initial 'lust' phase begins to settle down. As couples get to know each other better, lovemaking often improves and deepens into something really special. However, many couples find it hard to talk about sexual techniques and/or behaviors that don't have the desired effect. Such awkward issues are likely to persist in the absence of good communication. Not being able to tell each other how you like things done can lead to frustration and disillusionment. Putting up with a practice that you don't enjoy will soon lead to ways to avoid such acts, often to the consternation of your partner.

*James loved the idea of Jeanne giving him oral sex (her mouth on his penis), but in practice Jeanne's technique caused him discomfort. Jeanne, believing that this was a very special way to please James, was surprised when he moved her away from his penis to do something else. James was unable to tell Jeanne the real reason for avoiding this form of sex play and eventually it was dropped from their sexual repertoire. Jeanne would have been horrified to know she had been hurting James, but instead of talking about it and improving her technique she concluded wrongly that James didn't like her giving him oral sex.*

There are many pressures on couples today. More women are working full-time and experiencing the same stresses as men. Working long hours and getting home late can put a strain on a relationship. Also, shift patterns or travelling can make it hard for couples to be at home at the same time.

*Laura was a nurse married to Ed who drove a truck. Their sex life was practically non-existent as they never seemed to be home at the same time. Laura wanted to start a family but Ed was constantly on the road and very tired when he did come home. No sex, no baby! Very sensibly, neither of them felt that they could start a family living the way they did. Clearly, Laura and Ed needed to rethink their careers and their lifestyle.*

*Bill and Astrid were both bankers. They earned a lot of money between them but never had time for each other. They realized they were losing sight of one another and that something had to change. Knowing that the only way they could do this and continue to do their jobs efficiently was with careful time management, they started to book appointments with each other. This not only*

*allowed them quality time together but put some of the spark back
into their relationship, especially when they booked an evening out
together. This would often re-energize them sufficiently for sex to
happen when they got home.*

Couples bringing up children often find that their sex lives
dwindle. Many parents feel too tired for sex. The constant pressure of being on call 24 hours a day combined with jobs outside
the home can be a killer for sex. Having a baby in bed with you
is not conducive to a passionate roll in the hay! Nor is sleep
deprivation. Having a helping hand at such times, perhaps
family or friends taking over the children for a few hours, or a
night, can make all the difference as to whether you feel like
sex or not. Parents of young children often relish the time to
be together after the children go to bed. They can relax, talk
about the day, watch some television together, and have some
time as a couple rather than just as Mommy and Daddy. As
children grow, and begin to stay up later, so this 'couple time'
gets eroded. When the children are old enough to get themselves to bed, one way of getting over this problem is for you to
go to bed first, making it clear that your bedroom is your private
space for that evening. You can then make love without fear of
interruption or disturbance.

*Belinda and Felix used to say they had to practise their yoga tech-
niques in the evening three times a week. The children became
accustomed to this and left their parents in peace.*

Couples can also be overwhelmed by problems beyond their
control. Money worries affect couples deeply. How do you pay
the mortgage and feed and clothe the children on low incomes
or state benefits? This can put tremendous pressure on families.
If you live with the constant fear of losing your home, this can
compound an already difficult and stressful situation. Worry
can cause depression and ill-health, and your sex life is liable
to become a low priority under such circumstances. Sometimes
it can be very hard even to retain a sense of humour. Yet despite
the many problems that surround couples it is surprisingly

heartening to see how well many cope, remaining cheerful and optimistic against all the odds. Staying close and affectionate during adversity is a way of giving each other the support you both need.

## Sex and Ageing

Can you remember how you felt when you discovered that 'old people' had sex? Certainly, the recognition that your parents have sex can be very off-putting to a young person. Sex has always been portrayed as a young person's activity. We are constantly seeing young, usually good-looking, people having sexual relationships on television, in movies, and in books and magazines. Fortunately this has recently been challenged by positive images of older people in sexual situations. Some recent advertising on television shows older people flirting, or suggests they are having sex behind closed doors. One advert for a certain brand of butter included four ladies, all in the senior age bracket, having lunch and clearly enjoying a discussion on the merits of sex.

One reason underlying such attitude change is that as a nation we are an 'ageing population'. As a result of better living conditions and improvements in health care, people are living much longer. Also, greater awareness of the importance of physical fitness and healthy diet has seen an increase in people not only living for longer, but living *more actively* for longer. Today, many people in their eighties and nineties are still living independently and taking care of themselves. Even those who have moved into community housing, sheltered housing, or retirement homes are much more alert and alive than in the past. It is not uncommon nowadays to hear of romance in a retirement home.

*Ivy (81) and Charlie (80) met when Ivy moved into the care home where Charlie was already living. Their romance blossomed over the Scrabble board. Both were very alert and active, even if a little challenged physically. When the news of Charlie's marriage proposal spread through the home, everyone was thrilled. The staff helped organize the wedding, and family and friends attended. Ivy and Charlie were very lucky to be in a good care home where people really did matter. Joint accommodation was prepared for them so that they could be together on their return from their honeymoon.*

So what are the implications of improving physical fitness and longevity? For one thing, you are likely to be sexually active for a lot longer than your grandparents. That is not to say that all older couples years ago gave up on sex. However, it was not unusual in times past to hear older people say, 'We've given up on all *that*.' Today, older people are not giving up on sex, especially those who were young adults at the time of the sexual revolution of the 1960s. The contraceptive pill changed the world for ever by giving women greater control over their sexuality. Those sexually liberated ladies of the 1960s are now in their sixties and seventies, many of them more aware of their own needs and desires. Why would they want to stop having sex now? Another social factor is later remarriage. Men and women no longer feel obliged to remain single after losing their partners, or after divorce. It is now not unusual for couples to be getting together in their sixties or later in life. It is also a fact that men are fertile for much longer than women. There has been a recent spate of celebrity older men having children in their sixties and beyond.

Obviously, physical effects associated with ageing can be problematic. It really is a case of 'Use it or lose it!' People who remain sexually active, even in periods when they are not in a relationship, will be in better shape to carry on a sexual relationship in later life. For women, it is important that they still lubricate (or use a good quality lubricant); for men, that they can maintain and sustain an erection. In both instances this may take a little longer to achieve than it once did.

One of the most common physical side effects of ageing on men is related to the refractory period. This is the period of time a man needs to recover from ejaculation before he is physically able to ejaculate again. In young men it can be minutes, but in older men this period of time increases, to maybe hours, days, even weeks. It's a very individual thing. The recovery period is also likely to be shorter for those men who have been more sexually active in the past. However, an extended refractory period need not be a disadvantage, especially if the couple are aware of this physical change and can talk about it. Most older men are happy to have intercourse even if they don't always experience ejaculation and orgasm. To be physically close can be just as good. After all, lots of woman have intercourse without the release of orgasm and don't mind. Often, for both, it is the quality of the relationship in later life that matters most. However, it might be a problem if you have always experienced a fulfilling sexual life and suddenly this becomes harder to achieve. Knowledge is key here. If you are aware of the effects of ageing on sexual activity, you can prevent age-associated issues becoming more of a problem than they need be.

*Frances (69) thought that Ted (77) was losing interest in her. Frances was aware that her sex life with Ted wasn't quite the same as it used to be. This coincided with Frances not feeling good about her forthcoming seventieth birthday – was Ted finding her less attractive as she got older? She finally found the courage to confide in her doctor, who questioned her about the quantity of their sex life. It was still very regular, and for Frances very satisfying. She was only concerned that Ted wasn't getting much out of it as he no longer always ejaculated. The doctor explained about the change in the refractory period as part of the ageing process, and, reassured by this information, Frances was able to relax and believe Ted when he told her that sex was as good for him as it had ever been.*

The natural 'wear and tear' on the body as it ages can give rise to heart problems, hypertension (high blood pressure), and diabetes. Late onset diabetes is a well-known cause of erectile problems in some men. Fortunately there are drugs that can treat erectile dysfunction caused by diabetes, for example

34

Viagra or Cialis. All of these problems, and others such as rheumatism and arthritis, affect sexual activity in older people. For some women painful sex and lack of libido (desire) are attributable to the menopause, along with other typical symptoms including hot flushes, vaginal dryness, and night sweats. Not all women experience all these symptoms, and fortunately there is a great deal of help available for menopausal women. Happily for the sexually active older woman, the ending of the menopause can trigger new interest and vigour in sexual contact. This can, of course, also be good news for older men!

Sexual activity is good for the health of both sexes. It helps keep you physically fit, mentally alert, and emotionally satisfied. It will also contribute to your feeling good about yourself and others. Being able to share your physical self, or even to practise sex for one, will contribute to your leading a longer and healthier life. Exercise is frequently recommended today: walking, swimming, sport or joining a gym. These activities can keep the body healthy and in shape. Sexual exercise will also keep your muscles in trim and your blood circulation moving. It can also aid movement and agility by the adoption of positions not normally associated with other types of exercise.

## Sex and Disability

Disability is an umbrella term for a vast array of physical and mental difficulties that can be present at birth or brought on by illness, disease, or accident. Disabled people are often made to feel invisible: for example, wheelchair users have experienced questions directed at their carers rather than themselves. It is as if they do not exist. Fortunately, there are many highly qualified people dedicated to promoting the needs of the disabled, including disabled people themselves. This has enabled disabled people to live independently, and find work and employment that accommodates their particular difficulties. However, even today sex can be a major problem if you are dependent on others to care for you. Some able-bodied people take the attitude that disabled people do not want or need sex. Of course, this is complete nonsense. Just because you may not be fully functioning in certain areas does not mean that you do not have sexual feelings and needs. Sexual problems for the disabled can be tackled with a bit of help, support, and encouragement from others. Sometimes the help of a sympathetic carer is necessary to enable the disabled person to enjoy a sexual experience.

Workers in the field have identified sexual problems as sometimes being not so much a problem for the disabled person as a problem for the carer. If a carer has not had proper training in this area, or has never experienced giving help to a disabled person with regard to sex, they may be embarrassed and in some cases disapproving. However, even a sympathetic carer will need supervision and support. Involvement in another person's sexual life has to be governed by sensitivity and firm boundaries, as this type of help can be open to abuse.

Disability takes many forms, and in most the effects may range from mild to severe. When mental or physical handicap is part of the disability it is extremely important to make sure that the disabled person is as fully aware as possible of what is happening to them.

*Adrian has cerebral palsy and as his speech is affected this is very difficult to understand. When he came into therapy it was because his carer thought he needed to talk to someone about his sexual needs. It became very clear that Adrian had no difficulty with what he wanted sexually, but that he was very upset by the lack of help and support he received in relation to his desire to masturbate. He often experienced bad treatment in his care home when staff discovered he had been masturbating. They made it very clear to him that they did not enjoy cleaning up 'his mess'. There was little Adrian could do, as he needed and enjoyed this sexual activity. This issue was brought to the attention of the home and discussion with the staff followed. It was agreed that Adrian didn't have a problem at all, but that the staff did. For practical purposes Adrian was given small bags and tissues to help reduce the 'mess' element, and staff were encouraged to accept that this was part of the job, and that it was not acceptable to make an already difficult situation worse. Most people enjoy their sexual selves in private. Adrian's sexual behavior became public knowledge, and so the attitude of staff was of paramount importance in enabling him to express himself sexually without fear of censure.*

Disability can also be the result of accident, whether on the roads, at work, in the home, or on holiday. It is a sobering thought that just one such event – a fall, lifting something heavy in the wrong way – can change a person's life for ever. Also, the very fact that these events happen suddenly and unexpectedly can add to the stress of coping with change. Some of you may have had such an experience and recovered fully; others may be living with permanent injury and disability.

*Jeff (52) was lifting a heavy box into his garage when he felt his back go. He was initially told by his doctor to lie flat, which he did. However, this actually led to the problem being exacerbated and to a permanent back injury from which he would never fully recover. Jeff has never worked again, and as a consequence lost his business and his home. Under such circumstances it is easy to become depressed and apprehensive about your sex life. Jeff's wife has become his full-time carer and both of them have shed many tears over the loss of their previous life together. However, while they now have a much more limited sexual relationship they are nonetheless able to give and take pleasure to and from each other.*

Not only do things change physically in such circumstances, but life also becomes a challenge emotionally. This is especially true if the injured party has suffered head injuries and is prone to mood changes.

*Jessie (29) was finding life very hard since Luke's motorbike crash. Although he had been wearing his helmet and protective clothing, he had suffered severe head injuries. He was not the Luke she had fallen in love with and she was finding this very difficult to cope with. She did not want to let Luke down or be disloyal, but the reality of the situation frightened her, as she could no longer see a future in which she felt safe and happy.*

Illness and disease can also place a tremendous strain on those involved, especially when a condition is life-threatening. Living with cancer puts huge pressure on the individual as well as on their family and friends. Better treatment and advances in medical knowledge have increased survival rates to the extent that cancer is no longer necessarily a death sentence. However, surgery does alter body image and can effect how you feel about yourself.

*Shelley's double mastectomy operation affected her deeply. She felt self-conscious in front of her husband and was reluctant to have sex. Fortunately, Shelley's surgeon gave her 'the breasts of an 18-year-old' and her confidence was restored.*

*Clare (36) had had treatment for cervical cancer, and although her doctor reassured her that her vagina was robust enough for sex, the bleeding she experienced after intercourse with her husband put her off. She felt unwomanly and unconnected to her sexual self. Discovering she had cancer had been a huge shock to Clare, who needed help not only to regain her sex life but to understand what cancer meant to her.*

*Lawrence (57) had had major heart surgery. His sex life before his operation had been non-existent, much to the distress of both Lawrence and his wife. The surgery was successful and sexual activity resumed.*

In each of these cases the role of medical professionals proved vital in being willing and able to respond to questions, not only about treatment but about life after surgery. A consultant who understands that sex is an important part of life, and that patients need good advice and guidance about sex after major surgery, is worth his or her weight in gold.

Remember, whatever your disability, sex is there to be enjoyed. Thinking creatively and doing what works is the best way forward.

*Rob was very worried about hurting June during sex. June had osteoarthritis and suffered pain and stiffness after sex. What Rob needed to hear was that June thought it was worth it. She loved having sex with Rob. It made her feel alive and, more importantly, 'normal'. They found ways of using cushions and extra support to make sex more comfortable, and experimented with different positions to learn for themselves what worked best.*

This willingness to overcome the obstacles that disability may have placed in the way of your sex life is essential to sexual fulfilment.

## Sex and Sexual Orientation

Sexual problems experienced by gays, lesbians and bisexuals are generally no different from those experienced by the rest of the population. However, in the context of this particular book it is important to look at the role sexual identity or orientation can play in sexual behavior.

*Kathy (19) was finding it difficult to relate to boys. She had been out with several boys since leaving school and attending college, but had never enjoyed intimate contact with them. A girlfriend had recently suggested they go to a gay bar for a laugh. Kathy found herself enjoying the atmosphere and feeling very comfortable with the women she met. However, Kathy knew her family were homo-phobic (disapproving and hostile towards homosexuality) and she realized that as a consequence she had been avoiding the awareness that she herself was gay. She had never really been interested in boys at all but had been going along with the crowd for the sake of family harmony. Kathy needed to talk to someone about her feelings and her anxiety about revealing her sexual orientation to her parents.*

*Will (34) had been married for 10 years before he accepted that he was gay, realizing that he couldn't go on living a lie. It was seeing men behind his wife Janice's back and putting himself into some risky situations that in the end forced him to come out. This caused great pain and heartache for Janice, who had wanted to start a family and had been puzzled by Will's reluctance. He was so wonderful with their nieces and nephews. Janice now understood that Will had been struggling with his sexuality and concluded that their marriage was over. Will hoped they could remain friends, but only time would tell.*

For those of you concerned about your sexual orientation, some sources of help and guidance can be found in Appendix 1: Useful Organizations and Resources.

Another issue concerning sexual identity is cross-dressing (also known as transvestism). This is not such an uncommon phenomenon as you may think. Many men and women enjoy dressing in the clothing of the opposite sex, though there is no full explanation as to why someone may choose to behave in this way. Cross-dressing often begins at a very early age. For some it is no big deal and may happen rarely, while for others it is a real compulsion. Some, in order to cross-dress on a regular basis, may join a club or group of like-minded people. For others, it is a shameful and secret activity that is kept for times when they are sure they are alone and unlikely to be found out.

In this situation, the attitude of a partner or spouse can make all the difference. Individuals' responses to the knowledge that their partner, husband, wife, or lover is a cross-dresser vary hugely. Some prove to be very supportive. They may even like dressing up themselves. I know of a couple who went shopping together to buy clothes, shoes, wigs, and make-up. Unfortunately, for many others the shock of discovering the man or woman they have been living with, often for many years, is a cross-dresser can destroy a relationship. Typical responses include, 'It's disgusting/embarrassing/shameful,' and 'Who is this person? I don't know them any more.' One woman told me she was unable to have sex with her husband in case he wanted to dress up. She could not bear the idea of being in bed with him dressed as a woman. She felt that to do so would be tantamount to declaring herself a lesbian.

In some cases marriages and partnerships can survive through the spouse or partner learning to accept that the cross-dresser is essentially still the same person they were before the revelation. Although some men and woman who cross-dress do like to dress up during sex, it isn't always the case. Some people like to keep these activities very separate. Also, you mustn't confuse your husband/wife enjoying wearing your silk boxer shorts/panties as indication that he/she is a cross-dresser. Information on transvestism is available through the Beaumont Society in London (for contact details see Appendix 1).

'Transpeople' is the term used to describe men born female-bodied and females born male-bodied ('transsexual' is another term meaning the same thing). For some transpeople, living as a member of the opposite sex is sufficient. For others, nothing less than a complete sex-change operation will do. This is very different from the cross-dresser who is often happy with their sexual orientation and has no desire actually to be of the opposite sex. Transpeople believe themselves to be in the wrong kind of body, and suffer greatly from what they feel was a mistake at birth.

Changing sex is a very courageous thing to do. While some do embark on this process, many who would like to cannot, fearful of what others would think, or what they might do, should they find out. Some live isolated, locked into a secret that they cannot share for fear of reprisal. Others become depressed and even suicidal, often unbeknown to their loved ones. Those who do disclose their desire to change sex risk losing the support of their families, in many cases including long-term partners, and in some cases their children.

A sex-change operation is anything but an easy option. Psychological testing, the taking of hormones and living in the world as a member of the opposite sex are all parts of the process of change that must be gone through long before an operation is undertaken to transform physical appearances. It is not easy for any family to come to terms with what a sex-change operation will have in store for them; but their support is invaluable to anyone embarking on this daunting path, as is support from friends, colleagues, and the local community in which the person lives. Many trans men and trans women continue to suffer from ignorance and prejudice after their decision to make the change. In some cases they experience violence and abuse from individuals or groups who cannot even begin to understand what a person is going through in order to become the person they long to be, and indeed feel they have the right to be.

Inevitably, sex change affects sexual relationships. While some transpeople will continue to live with their partners, not all these couples will have sex together. For partners of trans men and trans women there are many different possible outcomes. It is very hard to generalize, as every such couple is unique and their problems very individual. Again, the Beaumont Society can help anyone who wants more information or guidance in this area (for contact details see Appendix 1).

## Sex and Religion

Religion can play a big part in sexual acceptance and sexual difficulty.

*Siobhan, a Roman Catholic, told me she had spent so many years saying no to sex that now she couldn't say yes. Once married, instead of giving herself to Patrick as she romantically expected, she was shocked to find her body continuing to tense up to reject her husband. Fortunately, Siobhan and Patrick were able to talk openly about the problem and work on relaxing and taking time to get to know each other sexually.*

*Anil and Leena were introduced by their families in their mid-thirties. Both had separately experienced previous relationships outside their own Hindu culture. However, as none had resulted in the per-*

42

*manent partnership they were looking for, they had each agreed to let their parents arrange a potential match. They trusted and respected their parents' wishes, and yet knew it would be hard to marry someone they didn't know. Leena and Anil were both virgins, and Anil was very shy. None of Anil's previous relationships had included intercourse, though some had involved heavy petting. Anil was aware of his inexperience and this awareness, combined with Leena's own concerns about her body, made their early attempts to consummate their relationship very difficult. On top of this, none of the advice they had been offered had been at all helpful. Basically, Anil and Leena had to start from scratch, not only sexually but as a couple. They had to get to know one another and learn to communicate openly about all sorts of things, including sex.*

While it may be important to you that you observe the rules of your religion, it is also good to enjoy sexual behavior. Some religions regard male masturbation as taboo, seeing it as 'wasting the seed'. If this is the case for you in your religion, it is important that your partner understands and accepts this as part of your sexual relationship. Alternatively, you may have converted to a different religion on marriage or entering into a partnership without being fully aware of the sexual rules that are applicable. Understanding what is acceptable and what isn't at the start of your relationship can avoid all sorts of misunderstandings later on.

*Rubin and Esther had very different thoughts on the use of fantasy. Rubin had regarded this as harmless and erotic. Esther, on the other hand, could not cope with the thought of Rubin having sexual thoughts, especially about others. She felt betrayed within the context of her marriage, and more specifically her marriage vows. Discussing this issue openly and in a safe environment enabled Esther to engage in thoughts and situations that they could both share. This shared use of fantasy opened up a whole new world for them. It allowed Rubin not to feel guilty about fantasy, and gave Esther lots of scope for enhancing her relationship with Rubin in a non-threatening way.*

43

## Sex and Infidelity

Having sex with someone outside an established relationship can be fun. It can sometimes improve a stale or diminished sexual relationship, and it can also add variety and excitement. However, these statements are true *only* if both partners are in agreement and a conscious decision has been made about opening up your sexual relationship to another or others. Without this agreement, sex with someone outside your relationship can have devastating effects, the precise consequences varying from couple to couple.

Discovering that your partner is having an affair, or has had casual sex, or sex with a prostitute, or with a work colleague at an office party, can come as a terrible shock, or a dawning realization; either way, it is not something most people want to have to confront. Not wanting to see the signs – to question yet another late night, or unexplained numbers on a telephone account – is evidence of wanting your relationship to be OK. Occasionally an erring partner will leave signs that cannot be overlooked or missed. Often this is unconscious, but sometimes the partner actually intends to bring into the open a situation that has perhaps moved beyond their control. Naturally, it is very easy to blame the other man or woman rather than the person actually responsible, i.e. your husband, wife, or partner. However, affairs usually mean something. Perhaps the straying partner is fed up with the same routine or bored with a long-term relationship? Perhaps they are angry for some reason, or feel that life has passed them by and they haven't had much sexual freedom or fun?

*Cameron and Annabel had met at school when they were both 14. They had married six years later, and by their late twenties had three children. Annabel felt that she had achieved nothing in her life, so when Cameron suggested she go to university she jumped at the chance. As Cameron had done well at university and subsequently in his job, he was more than happy to take care of the children while Annabel studied. Annabel did really well. She enjoyed meetings with other like-minded students and quickly helped set up a self-help group. This led to her being invited to run a study group by her tutor. It was during a summer school that things went wrong for Annabel and Cameron. As a thank-you her tutor invited Annabel out. Annabel accepted and after a meal and plenty of wine went back to the tutor's room and had sex with him. An affair followed which carried on until her course was finished. However, the tutor only wanted a casual affair and Annabel was devastated when he stopped answering her calls. It was during a tearful episode that Cameron confronted her with his suspicions.*

Whether or not a relationship can survive such a situation depends on the two people involved. You might think infidelity is instant justification for divorce, but this is not always the case. If you love someone and have invested a huge amount of time and energy into the relationship, it isn't easy to simply walk away. There are important factors to consider, such as children and/or the home you may have created together. Family and friends, and even the pet or pets you share, can make walking out a difficult decision. It is also important to remember that it isn't only you who may be affected, either by the affair itself or by a subsequent split. The ripple effect of infidelity and relationship breakdown spreads widely and invariably has consequences well beyond the three main participants.

Couples can and do learn from infidelity, and many renegotiate their relationship. Some partners can be very forgiving. If you know why you or your partner had the affair and can talk openly and honestly about it, you can start to rebuild your lives. However, once broken, trust often takes a long time to mend. It often depends on what course the relationship takes once an affair has been discovered. Sometimes the wronged partner can behave in ways that cause the wrongdoer to think that their punishment will go on for ever. Not a prospect to relish!

All of this turmoil inevitably affects sex. The 'guilty' party may be extra-attentive, and sex can sometimes be better than before. Alternatively, sex may happen less often, and in some cases it ceases completely.

While sexual unhappiness is not the main cause, infidelity can clearly be an indication that all is not well in a couple's sex life. Seeking help or discussing problems openly can sometimes avert an affair before it happens. Indeed, any relationship in which difficult issues can be explored is less likely to be vulnerable to affairs.

The topic of infidelity inevitably raises that of sexual jealousy. There's no harm in being aware of the potential attractiveness of your partner to others: it can keep you on your toes and make you aware that you can't take your relationship for granted. At its worst, however, jealousy can seriously damage a relationship.

*David had always felt jealous of other people. He remembered feeling jealous of his older brother at a very early age, and of schoolfriends. This feeling came from a basic insecurity and lack of trust in others. David's early relationships all ended because his girlfriends got fed up with his constant checking up and questioning. Somehow, he could never quite believe a girl really wanted to be with him. When he met Melissa all of this changed. She was obviously smitten by him and wanted to spend every spare minute of her time with him. They married and had two children. Melissa was happy to stay at home and take care of David and the children. However, all that changed when David was made redundant. Things got very tight financially. A friend of Melissa's suggested she work part-time in the local bar just until David got back on his feet. At first David was happy with the situation, but after a few weeks of Melissa working in the evenings all his old worries and insecurities returned. He started asking about the men who came into the bar. Melissa was happy to chat about her customers, but soon the questions became more personal and made her feel uncomfortable. This previously happy couple soon found themselves arguing and shouting. Melissa was hurt, confused, and angry. After all, she was only working to help out. David felt guilty for upsetting Melissa. Deep down he knew he could trust her, but somehow he just couldn't help feeling the way he did.*

## Sex and Abuse

Abuse comes in many guises and is carried out, and suffered, by both men and women. Abuse can be separated into physical, sexual, and emotional/verbal abuse, but in practice these three types often overlap to a lesser or greater degree. You may be more familiar with the term 'domestic violence' when thinking or talking about abuse. However, abuse doesn't only happen within the home. It can happen at work under various guises, including bullying, harassment, and sexual discrimination. Nonetheless, all abuse, wherever it occurs and in whatever shape or form, can be devastating to individuals, relationships, and families. Taken to its extreme it can result in severe distress, serious injury, and even death. Victims of abuse are often silent on the subject of what is happening to them in the belief that it is their own fault.

The impact of child sexual abuse on adult sexual relationships can be devastating. As a result of the conspiracy of silence that so often attends it, this form of abuse is in many cases kept secret until the victim meets a significant partner. Fear of the consequences of sharing the secret of the abuse can manifest itself in sexual problems, often to the confusion of the partner. In some cases disclosure leads to the individual who has been abused seeking help with the support of their partner. For some, though, it can lead to unexpected rejection as the partner is unable to cope with the knowledge, thus exposing the victim to further hurt and feelings of betrayal.

*Tessa was regularly criticized for her poor sexual performance in bed, so much so that she blamed herself for not satisfying her husband. It never occurred to her that his behavior might have something to do with how she felt. On reflection, he had always commented negatively on her looks and dress. Somehow she never ever got it quite right.*

*Lorraine was constantly on edge. Her boss was always picking on her and belittling her in front of other staff members. This was starting to affect her work. She had been extremely competent and up for promotion before this new guy had arrived to take over from the woman she used to work for. The treatment he meted out eventually undermined Lorraine's confidence completely. At home she was always tired and unwilling to go out. She couldn't even summon up enough energy for sex, and now this was causing rows between her and her husband. It was only when she finally plucked up courage to visit her employer's Human Resources officer that Lorraine was able to tell someone what was going on.*

If you are experiencing any kind of abuse, you may need to seek specialist help. Appendix 1 provides some useful information on sources of support and guidance.

## Sex and Infertility

Childlessness is a very sad and emotionally painful state that puts tremendous strain on couples. The unanswered questions 'Why us?' or 'Nothing's physically wrong, so why isn't it happening?' can be overwhelming. This distressing condition affects many couples each year. Usually a visit to the doctor starts a process of finding out whether pregnancy is possible and how to achieve it. There are many causes of inability to conceive, among them a low sperm count in the man and damaged fallopian tubes in the woman; many are treatable, but sometimes, sadly, no solution can be found. Whatever the specific reason, infertility affects couples in many different ways.

*Wes and Mandy had been trying for a child for more than 3 years before it started to affect their relationship. Damaged fallopian tubes were the cause and IVF treatment was recommended. Luckily Wes and Mandy were able to finance IVF privately. The treatment was successful and baby Troy was born. However, working to temperature readings and having sex by the clock had played havoc with their sex life. Also, Mandy's sexual problems predated IVF as she had started to see sex as only about baby-*

*making. This led to frustration and anguish every time her period arrived. Aware of this, Wes felt he had lost Mandy and that their sexual relationship didn't mean anything to her beyond creating a child. As a consequence, Wes had found it hard to bond with Troy. In her new-found happiness, Mandy had failed to notice how Wes was feeling; in time, however, she realized that something was wrong. Now they were able to talk about things and work together to get their relationship back on to an even keel.*

For some couples the reality is that they will never be parents. This realization will mean different things to different people. For some adoption, or fostering, is an option. Others throw themselves into their careers or even their pets. Sadly, a few will part. Most couples do return to enjoying sex for pleasure again after infertility problems, but this can take time.

## Sex after Childbirth

Having a baby can be one of the most rewarding experiences any couple can have. The miracle of a new life, and the fact that you have created it, can bring a couple closer together than any other life event. Unfortunately, the opposite can also be true, and in these cases, rather than being a blessing, the baby can create tension and unhappiness. Either way, getting back your sex life after childbirth can be problematic. As a new mom, or dad, you may be anxious and nervous about your new role. Sharing your fears with your partner can help take the stress out of the situation and avoid excluding him or her. The baby's individual character also makes a big difference: how good-humoured he or she is, how inclined to sleep, whether there are problems feeding. Also, tiredness is no friend of sex, and you will never be so tired as after the arrival of a new baby. Getting up in the night, not just to feed but often to try to calm a crying baby down, can really take its toll on new parents. And all of this seems as if it will last for ever! Fortunately it does not. Usually the baby will settle once some sort of routine has become established. Then more normal sleep patterns return, to the relief of all concerned. However, if you have any concerns about the health or welfare of your baby it is always advisable to speak to your doctor or health visitor.

For a woman, making love again after having a baby can sometimes feel a little scary. Your body has gone through a tremendous change, and you may feel a little alienated from it. It usually takes between 6 and 8 weeks for your womb to go back to its normal position and size, although breastfeeding can reduce the time through the release of the hormone oxytocin. It is usual to have a postnatal examination at around 6 weeks, and some couples wait for this checkup before resuming their sex lives. For other couples (and particularly for those women who did not have stitches after the birth), sex can resume much earlier. In fact, as soon as you feel ready and able to have sex, it should not be a problem. However, if you find it unpleasant having sex during a period you may like to wait until your post-childbirth discharge has finished. This is slightly different from a normal period as it is the result of the placenta coming away from the side of the womb. The discharge is initially bright red in colour but then becomes a reddish-brown colour as it reduces before disappearing altogether.

If you experience pain during intercourse in the early weeks after delivery you may need to seek help. The vagina can be sore; this may cause you to tense up, which in turn will stop you lubricating naturally and exacerbate the problem. Also, tearing, or an episiotomy requiring stitches, can make sex more uncomfortable to start with. A caring partner and good lubrication can help you over this, as it can many other physical and emotional problems. You will also need to think about contraception. It is not unusual to hear of new mothers rapidly finding themselves pregnant again because they believed breastfeeding would prevent it. (For more information, see Chapter 3 on contraception.)

It is not uncommon for a woman to experience 'baby blues' within a few days or weeks after giving birth. You may feel tearful or get easily upset. The reality of what having a baby means can be daunting, especially after all the excitement and fuss that surrounds the birth of a child. Finding yourself alone with this new bundle of life places a huge responsibility on you, not helped by feeling tired and needing to adjust to huge changes in your lifestyle. These feelings are quite normal and usually pass quickly; however, for some new moms this phase can turn into postnatal depression, a condition that needs expert attention. Again, your midwife or doctor can help.

Under these circumstances sex can be the last thing on your mind. Partners can also feel neglected and shut out after the baby arrives. Making love can help them to feel special and significant again. Also, being close to your partner and loving them can often help you feel you are yourself again – not just a mom, but still a woman too! In intimate moments it is possible to recapture your 'pre-parenting' feelings for each other. Couples who love each other and show it often make the best parents, as babies are sensitive to mood and atmospheres. Taking care of each other at this very special time of adjustment is really important.

## Bereavement

No one who has not experienced this awful tragedy can ever really know what it is like to lose a child. You can only imagine, because words cannot adequately express the pain and heartache such a loss causes. The death of a child can occur at any stage in the life cycle between the early weeks of pregnancy and adulthood. How you cope as a parent is a very individual thing. Some couples take solace from each other and remain very close and loving. Others withdraw from life, and sometimes from their partners. Whatever the situation, help is available. Talking to your doctor or health visitor can help you to get in touch with the right people in your area. Contact details of some useful organizations are given in Appendix 1 of this book.

Losing a child is a particularly terrible event, but any bereavement can have a very real impact on your relationship with your spouse or partner and your sex life.

*When Nicola's mom died she was inconsolable. Bob did not know what to do or how to comfort her. Everything fell apart. He tried his best to organize the children and the house, but a very demanding job made it difficult for him to take time off. This led to huge resentment on both sides that finally brought this couple to crisis point. Fortunately, a close family friend was able to intervene and put them in touch with appropriate helping agencies.*

## Sex and Medication

If you are taking medication, the specific effects and implications for your sex life are things you will need to check out with your own doctor. However, it is important to note here that most medication has side effects and some medication can affect your libido (sex drive). Being aware of this general point can help avoid unnecessary worry that your partner has gone off you, or that you are no longer able to find them sexually appealing. Some antidepressants can affect the ability to have an orgasm in both women and men. Unfortunately, drug information leaflets rarely state in their lists of 'contra-indications' that the medication can affect your sex life. They will tell you that you might feel sick, tired, or dizzy, but sex is rarely mentioned.

## Sex, Addiction and Compulsions

Addictions and compulsions comes in very many guises and can range from relatively harmless to being risky and dangerous to yourself and/or others. Most of you will be aware of what constitutes addictive and compulsive behaviors, either from your own experience or through knowing someone else with such a problem, maybe with some well-known addictions, including alcohol, drugs, smoking or gambling. There are many debates on the causes of addictions and compulsions, which may range from behavioral problems or chemical dependence to psychological disturbance. Whatever the cause, these problems do affect sexual relationships. If your partner is spending all your money on retail therapy you are unlikely to be happy with him or her. Further, if your partner's golf handicap becomes more important than your relationship, you are less likely to be responsive in the bedroom. More seriously, being married to or living with an alcoholic, drug or sex addict, or compulsive gambler can cause irreparable damage to a relationship or family.

Sex itself can be compulsive to some people. Saying this to other people often prompts laughter or mindless comments such as 'good for you'. Anyone who suffers from such a compulsion, or lives with someone who does, will know that it is not good, and certainly not fun. Needing constant sexual gratification can lead to very risky behavior, including visiting prostitutes and/or areas where you may be in danger, and using the workplace as an arena in which to act out sexual behavior, including perhaps using the employer's computer for sexual gratification while at work.

Underlying all addiction is deep unhappiness, low self-esteem, and a sense of worthlessness.

*Andrea had been bulimic for most of her teenage and young adult life. When she met Sean she was so happy that her need to binge and throw up seemed to disappear. However, once they were married all her old anxieties returned and her need to overeat came back to haunt her. Sean began noticing the very large amounts of food that were disappearing from the refrigerator and cupboards. For some time now Andrea had been suffering mood swings, and the couple's sex life had become non-existent as the tension between them generated a state of almost constant arguing. After one night out with the boys Sean returned home earlier than usual to find the kitchen like a bomb site and Andrea with her head over the toilet seat. Andrea, fearing an absolute rejection, found the courage to talk to Sean about her long struggle with bulimia. Sean was indeed very shocked, but remained supportive while Andrea finally sought help.*

*Phil's drinking was getting out of hand. What had started as a beer or two after work with clients and colleagues had turned into* all-night sessions. Phil was getting home later and later, much to the disgust of his wife Tricia. The last thing Tricia then wanted was sex, especially given that Phil could be quite aggressive and argumentative when drunk. It was only when Tricia threatened to leave that Phil began to face his problem. The truth was that Phil was not coping with pressure at work. Tricia suggested couple counselling and a visit to their doctor to see what help was available.

## . . . And Finally, Unusual Sex

Unusual sex? You may well be asking: What does that mean? Paraphilia (literally 'unusual love') is the term to describe sexual acts, practices and behaviors that lie outside the normal range. It includes dressing up in rubber or leather, acting out bondage scenes (tying up), engaging in S&M (sado-masochism: the voluntary infliction or receiving of pain), fetishism (the enjoyment of certain objects that have acquired erotic value), and voyeurism. These are just a few behaviors that you may have heard of. There are others that constitute criminal acts. These include indecent exposure (revealing your genitalia in public), rape and paedophilia (child sexual abuse).

The important point here is that the enjoyment *between two consenting adults* of sexual behavior in ways that may seem unusual to others is not a problem. What *is* a problem, however, is if one person's preference for such practices leads to another person not enjoying sex – or, worse, being upset or harmed by it.

*Nick wanted to spice up his sex life with his partner and invited an old friend round for the evening to discuss a threesome over a few drinks. Unfortunately, they did not consult Nick's partner first. The three of them ended up in bed together, Nick having plied his partner with drink so that she was only half aware of what was going on. She was in no doubt the next morning when they all woke up together. As a consequence she walked out. Nick was horrified, and ultimately heartbroken to lose her.*

*In retrospect he wished he had told his partner that he wasn't happy with their sex life so they could have discussed options together.*

As mentioned earlier, when sexual boredom sets in the thought of an affair, or getting others involved, can seem pretty exciting. However, the reality often doesn't match up to expectations. Furthermore, relationships can struggle to survive in such circumstances, even when consent is given in the first place. It really depends on what you want or are looking for. It's all too easy to find yourself in a situation from which you can never go back. Too often people regret decisions they took which resulted in their relationships ending. Sometimes the search for excitement can be very costly.

Instead of looking elsewhere for excitement, why not reappraise your own sexual relationship? Discuss it together and explore what has happened to you both. Why has the sparkle gone? Look back over the factors affecting sex and see if you can identify at what point sex became less frequent or less fun. Maybe the specific problems and issues highlighted in this chapter have encouraged you to think about what is going wrong for you. If so, there is much you can do to improve your sex life. Part Two of this book will help you to begin this exploration. First, however, we need to consider the very important issue of contraception.

# 3

# Contraception: A Guide to Methods

The last thing you might want to think about while in the throes of passion is contraception. I often hear people say, in response to the question 'Why didn't you use something?', 'We got carried away', or 'It spoils the moment', or even 'I like sex to be spontaneous, I can't be bothered with that'. However, being fully aware of what is available and finding a contraceptive method to suit you is one of the most important aspects of being able to enjoy sex in a light-hearted and spontaneous way. Being caught short, risking it, or throwing caution to the winds will not be any consolation if you find yourself suffering from a troublesome infection or, worse still, an infection that cannot be cured but only managed, for example HIV or herpes (see Chapter 4). Then, of course, for women there is the other tragedy – an unwanted pregnancy.

It only takes as long as it takes to have sex (and it doesn't have to be penetrative intercourse) with an infected partner to become infected yourself. It takes less time to become infected than it does to use a condom. For those of you engaging in casual sex, condoms are an absolute must. They are the only sure-fire way of preventing the nasty consequences of sex, including a wide variety of infections. Fortunately, you can get them absolutely free from family planning associations, sexual health clinics, and some family doctors (see Appendix 1 for further details). In order to practise safe sex it is advisable that girls and women carry condoms in their handbags and men keep a couple in their wallets. That way nobody need panic in the heat of the moment. In fact, a 'belt and braces' approach is probably best, using condoms alongside some other type of contraception, for example the pill. For those of you in steady relationships, where the likelihood of infection has passed and you are sure that neither of you is going to put the other at risk, alternatives to condoms may well be more appropriate.

The right type of contraception can make the difference between good sex and not so good sex. Which is the right contraceptive for you will depend on a myriad of factors. If you are concerned about getting pregnant, for instance, you will want as high a level of protection as you can get. This might be especially true if you have completed your family.

*Georgia and Mac had four children and felt their family was complete, especially as neither baby Molly nor their second child Ellie had been planned. They decided that the best option for them was for Mac to have a vasectomy operation (surgical sterilization) to free them both from the possibility of further unplanned pregnancies.*

*Howard and Olivia had had a scare as Olivia hadn't realized that being sick could interfere with the pill. When she missed her period and she and her partner were told how a sickness bug might have made her contraceptive ineffective they were both horrified. Neither of them felt ready to have a child and they went through several bad days until Olivia started her period. Furthermore, Olivia hadn't been terribly good at remembering to take her pills and had resorted to emergency contraception (the 'morning after' pill) on more than one occasion. After a really helpful discussion with the family planning doctor, Olivia decided to have Depo-Provera, a contraceptive injection. This suited them both. It only needed to be repeated every 12 weeks, and as thoughts of children were many years ahead, the fact that it might take a while for Olivia's periods to return to normal after she stopped taking it wasn't an issue.*

If you are thinking about what form of contraception to use, or just want more information on what is available, check out the following.

## Condoms

Condoms are available for both men and women. The male condom is usually made of very thin latex (rubber) or polyurethane, and fits over a man's erect penis. A female condom (often called a Femidom, the brand name of the only one currently available) is made of very thin polyurethane (plastic) and is inserted into the vagina to line it. Both these condoms form a barrier to stop sperm meeting an egg. They can also protect you from sexually transmitted diseases. Both types of condom are available free of charge from the family planning associations, sexual health clinics and some doctors' surgeries. You can buy condoms through a variety of outlets, including mail order, vending machines in public facilities, service stations, supermarkets and pharmacies. Male condoms come in a variety of different shapes, sizes, colours and flavours. Individuals and couples should try both the male and female versions to see which type of condom works best.

### Effectiveness of Condoms

Male condoms, if used correctly, are 98 per cent effective. The Femidom is 95 per cent effective. Instructions for use are included in all packets of both types and should be read before any sexual contact takes place. Check the 'use by' date, and always use a new condom every time you have sex.

To ensure the condom is used most effectively, be aware of the following possibilities:

- If the penis is in contact with the area around the vagina before fitting a condom, sperm may enter the vagina.
- Care must be taken *not* to use oil-based lubricants such as Vaseline or body oils with latex condoms (this does not

apply to polyurethane condoms and Femidoms), as these can damage the latex and make the condom more likely to split. A water-based lubricant is best for latex condoms.
- Condoms can be damaged by sharp or uneven fingernails or jewellery (including studs used in body piercing), so care needs to be taken when putting a condom on.
- It is also possible for the condom to slip off without you being aware.
- Sometimes the penis can enter the vagina outside the female condom by mistake.
- Alternatively, the female condom can get pushed too far into the vagina.

Avoiding these problems will help keep you safe.

---

### Using Male Condoms

Open the pack carefully and avoid tearing or damage through nails or jewellery. Always put a condom on before any penis/vagina contact takes place. Squeeze the teat at the end of the condom to remove any air that may be trapped inside (if you don't, you will find the teat will begin to swell like a balloon). Put the condom over the glans, or tip, of the erect penis and gently unroll the condom over the penis. If the condom doesn't roll all the way down to the base of the penis, it probably isn't on correctly. Remove and start again with another condom (as sperm could already be on the first one).

Once you have ejaculated it is important to remove the condom while the penis is still partially erect. Hold on to the end of the condom and withdraw slowly, making sure that no semen can leak out. When you have taken the condom off, wrap it in a tissue or piece of toilet roll before disposing of it in a convenient bin. Do not flush condoms down the toilet as you could block the system.

For those of you using condoms for the first time, it makes good sense to practise prior to sex until you feel

---

confident you know what you are doing. This applies to both men and women. Courgettes (zucchinis) and cucumbers make good substitutes for beginners in the absence of a penis! Alternatively, some vibrators can help you get the right idea.

## Using Female Condoms

You can put the Femidom inside you any time before you have sex, but be sure always to fit it before the penis touches the vagina. You may need to experiment first of all to find out the easiest way to insert the Femidom. Some prefer to lie down, others to squat, or stand with one leg up on a chair. Those of you who use tampons may like to insert the Femidom in the same position. Check your fingernails are not too long or too sharp, as they could damage the condom or indeed hurt the inside of the vagina. Take hold of the inner ring of the Femidom and squeeze it between your thumb and middle finger. Keep your index finger on the inner ring to help you keep control of the Femidom. Put the Femidom inside your vagina and push it up as far as you can. Next, put your finger inside the Femidom until you can feel the inner ring and again push the Femidom up as far back into the vagina as you can. It should then be lying just above your pubic bone (which you should be able to feel if you curve your finger forward slightly). The outer ring should cover the area outside the vagina (the vulval area). It is helpful if you assist your partner by guiding his penis to make sure he is inside the Femidom. The Femidom is loose-fitting (unlike the male condom), so it will move during intercourse. This isn't a problem as long as the penis stays inside it.

To remove the Femidom, all you need do is twist the outer ring to keep the semen inside and then pull the condom gently out. Discard in the same manner as male condoms.

## Good Points about Condoms

- They are easy to obtain.
- You only need them when you have intercourse.
- They offer protection from infection.
- There are no side effects.
- Condoms come in all shapes, sizes and flavours. You can always find one to suit your personal preference.
- For women, the Femidom can be inserted at any time before sex, thereby taking away the need to interrupt lovemaking.

## Bad Points about Condoms

- The male condom interrupts sex.
- The male condom can slip off without you being aware.
- They can split occasionally.
- Condoms must be removed carefully to avoid any spillage of semen.
- The Femidom is not so widely available, and can be expensive to buy.
- Although this is rare, some people have an adverse reaction to latex or the spermicide that is used in male condoms (female condoms do not contain spermicide). If you find you are allergic, you can use polyurethane condoms or condoms without spermicide. You may find it helpful to discuss this with a sexual health practitioner.

## Other Points about Condoms

Despite the possible drawbacks, condoms offer excellent protection when used properly and have none of the side effects of other methods. Many people still find condoms initially difficult to use, in spite of the excellent leaflets available from the family planning associations and the instructions for use enclosed in every packet. This is quite often the result of a reluctance to use them in the first place. Common complaints are that they are awkward or fiddly, or that they interfere with the natural flow of sex. However, there are some positive aspects to condom use: for example, many men find it very arousing having their partner put the condom on. Also, fun condoms or flavoured ones for oral sex can add that extra sparkle. Have condoms ready by the bedside or nearby, so they are within easy reach at that moment when things are hotting up and penetration is close. Even with the best knowledge and information things can go wrong, so practise to build confidence. (Read the section on emergency contraception on pages 77–9 so you know what to do should a condom fail for any reason.)

## The Contraceptive Pill

There are two types of pill for women: the progestogen-only pill (POP) and the combined pill (which contains oestrogen and progestogen). Both rely on your ability to remember to take it! POP also requires you to remember to take it at the same time each day.

### POP

Expert advice is required before taking POP. Your medical health needs to be assessed first, to check whether POP can be prescribed and, if it can, which type is most appropriate for you. POP is not suitable in certain situations, for example, if you have had an ectopic pregnancy (this is where the fertilized egg implants itself in the fallopian tube instead of the womb – a very dangerous condition) or have had breast cancer, heart attack, or stroke. POP prevents pregnancy by thickening the mucus produced from the cervix and so making it difficult for sperm to reach an egg. It also makes the lining of the womb thinner and less hospitable to any egg that does manage to get fertilized, and it can sometimes stop ovulation (your ovaries releasing eggs).

*Effectiveness of POP*
POP is 99 per cent effective if used properly. However, if you are over 70 kg (154 lb) it may be less effective.

If you forget to take even one pill you will not be protected. If you are more than 3 hours late, continue to take subsequent pills as usual, but you will also need to use a condom for the next 7 days. If you are less than three hours late, take it as soon as you remember, and be sure to take the next one at the specified time. If you are sick within 3 hours of taking the pill, or have severe diarrhoea, continue to take the pill as usual but use a condom for the following 7 days.

## Good Points about POP

- There are no serious side effects.
- It doesn't interfere with sex.
- It can be taken at any age.
- Breastfeeding is not affected.
- It may help with PMT (premenstrual tension) and painful periods.
- If you cannot take oestrogens like those found in the combined pill, this could be the pill for you.
- It can be taken by smokers over age 35, for whom the combined pill is not suitable.

## Bad Points about POP

- It gives no protection against sexually transmitted diseases.
- Periods may become lighter, or stop altogether (this will not be a problem to everyone). Periods can also become irregular and/or more frequent. These symptoms usually settle down, but you may find it difficult to start with and worry that you may be pregnant. Speaking to a sexual health professional should reassure you; if not, a change of pill may be called for.
- Temporary side effects can include sore breasts or acne, but these usually go away fairly quickly.
- A small risk of an ectopic pregnancy exists: although this is very rare, the condition is dangerous if it does occur.

## Other Points about POP

POP should be taken on the first day of your period in order to start protecting you against unwanted pregnancy immediately. If you start later than this you will need to use additional contraception, usually a condom, for 7 days. Remember, the pill must be taken each day at the same time. This may not be convenient if your lifestyle or work pattern means you don't have a regular daily routine. Using an alarm or reminder on your cellphone can help with timing. Once you have established yourself on the pill, you should take your pills without a break, even during your period.

> *Grace wanted to breastfeed her new baby for as long as she possibly could, so when her health visitor recommended POP she went to her local family planning clinic to discuss this method further. After discussing her medical history and general health the doctor was happy to prescribe it for her.*

Always mention you are taking POP if prescribed any other medication, in case this interferes with the workings of the pill.
For further advice or information on POP consult your local family planning clinic or doctor's surgery.

## The Combined Pill

The combined pill contains two hormones, oestrogen and progestogen. The combination of these hormones prevent you from ovulating (releasing an egg each month). Unlike POP, this pill is taken on only 21 days of each monthly cycle, leaving seven days for breakthrough bleeding (corresponding to a normal period).

### Effectiveness of the Combined Pill

Like POP, the combined pill is 99 per cent effective if taken correctly. It can be taken within a wider time-frame than POP, so you don't have to take it at exactly the same time every day. However, it will not be effective if taken over 12 hours late. As with POP, if you are sick or have severe diarrhoea you should use extra precautions for 7 days. Always tell your doctor you are on the pill if you are prescribed any other medication, as some prescribed drugs can stop the pill working.

## Good Points about the Combined Pill

- It can ease the pain of periods and reduce the amount of blood lost each month.
- It can help reduce the effects of PMT.
- It provides protection against cancer of the ovary and womb, and some pelvic infections.
- If you are a healthy non-smoker you can use this pill up until the menopause.

## Bad Points about the Combined Pill

- It does not protect against STDs.
- There can be minor side effects such as nausea, tiredness, headaches, and feeling bloated. These are usually temporary.
- Some women gain weight.
- Although rare, serious side effects can include thrombosis (blood clots), cervical cancer, and breast cancer.
- It is not recommended for smokers aged over 35.

*Lucy was studying for her A-levels (high school diploma) but was really suffering each month with severe period pains which forced her to go to bed as she felt faint and sick. Her doctor recommended the combined pill. Lucy was surprised but delighted when she had her first pain-free period. It also improved her sex life. Richard and Lucy had always used condoms and now they were able to enjoy their sexual relationship in what they felt to be a more spontaneous way.*

## The Contraceptive Patch

Like the combined pill, the patch offers good protection from unwanted pregnancy through the gradual release of oestrogen and progestogen. The patch is placed on your arm, buttock, or stomach once every 7 days for 3 weeks. The fourth week is patch-free, and this allows for a withdrawal bleed or period. The patch works in the same way as the combined pill, but is much better suited to those who find pill-taking difficult.

## Effectiveness of the Contraceptive Patch

The patch is as effective as the combined pill if used correctly.

## Good Points about the Contraceptive Patch

- It's easy to use and doesn't interfere with sex.
- Periods are lighter, regular, and usually pain-free.
- You are less likely to experience the nausea or diarrhoea that are sometimes associated with the pill.
- You only have to remember to replace the patch once a week.

## Bad Points about the Contraceptive Patch

- It offers no protection against STDs.
- The patch can cause skin irritation in some women.
- Depending on where you stick the patch, it may be visible.
- Side effects can include headaches, nausea, breast soreness, mood swings, and some fluctuations in weight. For some women there is breakthrough bleeding. All these side effects usually diminish after the first few months of use.

*After talking through the various options Sonia choose the patch as it gave her the same protection as the pill without the hassle of having to remember to take it. The patch suited her lifestyle and gave her the freedom and control she wanted.*

## Contraceptive Injections

These can be ideal for those of you who have difficulty remembering to take pills or put on patches. There are two brands currently available: Depo-Provera and Noristerat. The injection is quick and relatively painless, and you only need to top up every 11 or 12 weeks – excellent for those with a busy lifestyle. The injection releases the hormone progestogen very slowly into the body. This stops you from ovulating (releasing an egg); it also thickens the mucus in the cervix to prevent sperm and egg meeting.

## *Effectiveness of Contraceptive Injections*

This method is 99 per cent effective.

## *Good Points about Contraceptive Injections*

- Depo-Provera lasts for 12 weeks. Noristerat lasts for slightly less long: 8 weeks.
- The injection may provide protection against cancer of the womb and offers some protection against pelvic inflammatory disease (PID).
- You don't have to think about contraception for as long as the injection lasts.
- Could be considered an excellent method for those of you who have completed your family.

## *Bad Points about Contraceptive Injections*

- Periods often become irregular or stop. (Some may find this an advantage!)
- Regular periods and fertility may take a year or more to return after stopping the injections.
- Some women experience side effects such as headaches, acne, sore or tender breasts, mood swings and bloating.
- Some women gain weight.
- Unlike the pill, if you are suffering side effects you cannot just stop using it; also, side effects may continue for some time beyond the 8- or 12-week time period covered by a single injection.

## *Other Points about Contraceptive Injections*

Many women find that they become used to the injection and it takes all the stress out of contraception. You are free to live your busy life without worry.

> *Natasha works in the theatre. Depo-Provera not only sorted out her contraceptive needs but the fact that she stopped having periods was an added bonus, especially as hers had always been heavy and painful.*

## Implants

These are ideal for women who want long-term contraception but do not want the finality of sterilization. Implants and work by a steady release of progestogen into the bloodstream. The implant itself is a small flexible tube placed under the skin of the inner upper arm.

### *Effectiveness of Implants*

Implants are 99 per cent effective.

### *Good Points about Implants*

- A single tube works for 3 years.
- You don't have to think about contraception during this time period.
- They are good for those who may yet want to have children, because when the implant is taken out a woman's normal level of fertility will return immediately.

### *Bad Points about Implants*

- They give no protection against STDs.
- Periods are often irregular during the first year with some bleeding in between, or may be missed altogether.

- Side effects can include headaches, mood changes, and breast tenderness.
- Some women gain weight.

## *Other Points about Implants*

Implants are usually put in under a local anaesthetic and no stitches are necessary. The area may feel tender for a few days with bruising and some swelling. Although most women can feel the implant under the skin, it can't be seen. Removal can sometimes be difficult.

*Victoria decided to have an implant as she hated taking tablets and injections every 12 weeks didn't fit in with her changing work schedule, which took her out of the country regularly. With an implant Victoria wouldn't have to think about contraception for the next 3 years.*

## Intrauterine Device (IUD)

An IUD (formerly known as a coil) is a small plastic and copper device that is put into the womb. It prevents sperm meeting an egg, and may stop an egg settling in the womb. Many women choose this particular method of birth control because it puts them in control of their fertility. The IUD has no long-term side effects such as interfering with your normal menstrual cycle. When it is removed, you are immediately fertile again. The IUD is often considered a useful method in between pregnancies.

## *Effectiveness of the IUD*

The IUD is 98–99 per cent effective, depending on the type you choose.

## *Good Points about the IUD*

- It is effective immediately after it has been inserted.
- You can keep it in place for 3 to 10 years depending on the type, but you can have it taken out at any time.

- You don't have to think about contraception while it is in place.
- If you are over 40 the IUD can stay inside you until the menopause.

## Bad Points about the IUD

- If you are at risk of getting an STD an IUD is not a suitable method.
- The IUD is not usually suitable for women with heavy and painful periods, as it can make your periods heavier, longer, and more painful.

## Other Points about the IUD

Not everyone can use an IUD: you will need to speak to your doctor or nurse about your family medical history before the decision is made. The IUD will usually be put in towards the end of your period or a few days later. They come in different types and sizes. You are examined to ascertain the position and size of your womb before the IUD is fitted, so that a suitable one can be chosen. You must be sure you are not pregnant and that you have no infections.

It can be uncomfortable having an IUD fitted, but you can take a painkiller or ask for a local anaesthetic to help with this. You may get a period-type pain and some bleeding for a few days after the IUD is fitted, but again painkillers can help with this. You are taught how to check the IUD is in place by feeling for the threads high in the vagina.

*Val is a young single mom of two boys. She recently met and fell in love with Ozzie, who wants to marry her. They would both like a child within the next couple of years. Val decided to come off the pill to restore her cycle. The IUD seemed like the best option in this situation as Val knew her fertility level would return to normal immediately after removal.*

## Intrauterine System (IUS)

This can be a better option than the IUD for women who suffer from heavy and painful periods. It works in a similar way to the IUD. A small plastic device is put into the womb and releases the hormone progestogen. Like the IUD, it stops sperm meeting an egg and the egg settling inside the womb. As with the IUD, you need to check the IUS regularly by feeling for the threads high up in the vagina.

### *Effectiveness of the IUS*

This method is 99 per cent effective.

### *Good Points about the IUS*

- Periods will be much lighter and shorter.
- It works as soon as it is placed inside.
- It works for 5 years, but can be removed at any time.
- As long as it is in place you don't have to think about contraception.

### *Bad Points about the IUS*

- It gives no protection against STDs.
- Irregular light bleeding is common for the first 3 months or so.
- There can be side effects such as breast tenderness and acne, but these are usually temporary.

*Cindy was approaching 50 and it was recommended that she stop using Depo-Provera in order to allow her menopause to progress normally. The IUS, with its slow release of the hormone progestogen, could stay in place until her menopause was complete.*

## Caps and Diaphragms

Caps and diaphragms, like condoms, are 'barrier methods' of contraception that put a physical barrier between sperm and egg. They fit inside the vagina and cover the cervix. They come in different shape and sizes, but generally cervical caps are smaller than diaphragms. Both are circular domes made of thin rubber with a flexible rim. They work by covering your cervix and stopping sperm reaching an egg. Extra protection is needed in the form of a spermicidal cream or jelly. Caps and diaphragms need to be fitted by a qualified family planning practitioner, as your cervix needs to be measured to ensure a correct fit. It is also important to have your cap or diaphragm checked once a year, or if you lose or gain more than 3 kg (7 lb) in weight.

## Effectiveness of Caps and Diaphragms

These are not as effective as some other methods, the percentage being somewhere between 92 and 96 per cent, if used correctly.

## Good Points about Caps and Diaphragms

- They may protect against cervical cancer and some STDs.
- There are no serious health risks or major side effects.
- You use it only when you have sex.
- There are several types to choose from.

## Bad Points about Caps and Diaphragms

- It takes time to learn to use them properly.
- Some women find it messy using spermicide.
- Cystitis can be a problem for some women.
- They can interrupt sex if not put in place earlier.

## Other Points about Caps and Diaphragms

This method can be impractical if you have any disability in your hands. However, if you can insert a tampon you should be able to manage a cap. While they are a bit fiddly to start with, the nurse will show you how to put it in, and you can practise at home before deciding whether it is right for you. Although it may feel like a lot of work for some, it has the advantage that you can put it in any time before you have sex (although if this is longer than 3 hours you will need to add extra spermicide). This can help to create a more spontaneous situation when having intercourse. You also need to leave it in place for at least 6 hours after sex. This may not be inconvenient if you have sex at night, and with added spermicide you can have sex again in the morning without having to remove it first (you mustn't leave it in for more than 30 hours). You can also use your cap or diaphragm during a period.

*Deirdre is a career girl who works long hours. She chose a diaphragm because it fitted in with her lifestyle and her long-term relationship. Deirdre feels happier being in control of her own fertility without having to worry about possible side effects.*

Not every woman can use this method of contraception. It is not suitable for you if you have an unusually shaped cervix or poor vaginal muscles, or have ever suffered toxic shock syndrome. Repeated attacks of cystitis (a urinary infection) can occasionally be a problem; however, changing to a different type of cap or diaphragm can often prevent cystitis from recurring.

## Male and Female Sterilization

This is the most effective and permanent solution for both sexes once you are sure that you no longer want children or have completed your family. Reversal is not usually an option or recommended, although this has been carried out successfully for some.

Because it is permanent you do need to be certain this is the right decision for you (and your partner, if you are in a relationship). For this reason counselling is often recommended before any sterilization operation (male or female).

## Effectiveness of Sterilization

The failure rate for vasectomy is 1 in 2,000, for female sterilization 1 in 200. In both cases this is most commonly because tubes rejoin (see below).

## Good Points about Sterilization

- It doesn't interfere with sex.
- It is permanent, so you don't have to think about contraception again.
- A vasectomy is a quick and simple operation.
- There are no serious side effects, long- or short-term.

## Bad Points about Sterilization

- You are not protected against STDs.
- Female sterilization usually requires a general anaesthetic.
- It takes time for sperm to disappear from the tubes, so another form of contraception is needed until two semen tests have proved clear.
- Although it is not common, the tubes can rejoin, in both men and women.
- Sterilization cannot be easily reversed.

For women, the fallopian tubes are cut, sealed, or blocked so that eggs cannot travel down them to meet sperm. This method is suitable for women who want to be in complete control of their own fertility. While the fallopian tubes can rejoin, this is not very common. You also need to use another form of contraception until you have your first period after the operation. A day in hospital is usually all the time it takes, depending on the method chosen, although you will need to take things easy for a few days afterwards.

*After giving birth to her fifth child by caesarean section Beth opted for sterilization. She later concluded it was the best thing she had ever done.*

For men, a vasectomy operation is more straightforward. The process only takes about 10–15 minutes and can be done at the local doctor's surgery or clinic. The tubes (vas deferens) that carry sperm are cut and tied. This means that sperm is no longer present in semen. It takes a while after the operation for sperm to clear. As a consequence two negative sperm tests are needed for confirmation. Clearly it is important that condoms or another form of contraception are used until the all clear is given. As with female sterilization, the tubes can rejoin, but this is very unlikely.

After the operation you may experience some swelling or bruising and some slight discomfort or pain. This usually passes very quickly, and after resting for 24–36 hours you should feel completely fine again. Sport or exercise should be avoided for at least a week. However, depending on the type of work they do men are less likely than women to need time off.

*Brian had no trouble deciding on a vasectomy. He felt it was the least he could do for Wendy, since her last pregnancy had resulted in twin girls. Their family was large enough and, as he felt that Wendy had done most of the hard work, a vasectomy seemed a small price to pay. He was able to have his operation at his local doctor's surgery and returned to work the very next day.*

## Natural Family Planning

This is an option that is available to anyone who may have difficulty with other forms of contraception. It revolves around avoiding intercourse at the fertile period of the woman's menstrual cycle, and so being aware of this fertile time is the key to success.

Obviously you need to become familiar with the method, and so patience will be needed while you are learning over a 3- to 6-month period. You need to work out exactly how long your cycle lasts and watch out for natural signs (temperature, bodily secretions) and record these each day.

75

This method can be useful in preventing pregnancy, but can also be used to plan one.

## Effectiveness of Natural Family Planning

A fertility device is available that can help you to monitor changes in temperature, urine, or saliva. This is currently named 'Persona'. When used correctly, it is said to be 94 per cent effective at predicting fertile (and infertile) times. Improved devices are being developed and will become available in due course.

## Good Points about Natural Family Planning

- There are no side effects at all.
- You are in control of your own fertility – you can prevent or plan a pregnancy.
- It is very effective if the method is taught by a practitioner trained in NFP and you keep to the instructions.
- It is acceptable to all faiths and cultures.

## Bad Points about Natural Family Planning

- It offers no protection against STDs.
- You can't have sex during your fertile time unless you use another form of contraception.
- It takes time to learn (three to six cycles).
- You need to keep records.
- Changes in circumstances such as illness or stress may effect your ability to interpret fertility indicators.
- Both partners need to be involved and committed if the method is to be effective.

## Other Points about Natural Family Planning

NFP puts you completely in charge of your own fertility and increases your awareness of your body and how it functions.

If you have good instruction and your partner is committed this method can be most effective.

> *Connor and Aisling are Roman Catholics who sought expert advice and teaching for natural family planning. They have found this method works well for them, and are relieved because it fits within their belief system, making it an acceptable way to prevent unwanted pregnancy.*

All the above methods of contraception are widely available and free under the NHS. Do be sure to speak to your doctor or family planning specialist before deciding on which type of contraception to use, so you can find the best method for you. Some methods need a full medical history and regular blood pressure check-ups. With the right help and advice you can make an informed choice tailored to your lifestyle and circumstances.

## Emergency Contraception

Emergency contraception is exactly that – for emergencies only. For continuous, effective cover, use any of the methods outlined above. If you use contraception responsibly you are unlikely to need emergency methods; but, having said that, accidents do happen, and knowing what to do in the event takes the stress out of the situation and helps sort things out as speedily as possible. So what can you do if you find yourself staring at a split condom, or go to take your pill only to find you've missed three?

There are two methods of emergency contraception: the 'morning-after pill' and the IUD (intrauterine device).

### The 'Morning-After' Pill

The morning-after pill must be taken within 72 hours of unprotected sex, but the sooner the better (ideally within 24 hours). It comes in packs of two. The first pill should be taken immediately, and the second between 12 and 16 hours later. They work by stopping or delaying ovulation (egg release), or by preventing a fertilized egg implanting itself in the womb. They are extremely effective provided you don't have unprotected sex again afterwards. You will need to consult your doctor if you are on any sort of medication, and ideally you should consult your doctor before using this method.

After taking the morning-after pill you may feel sick and have tender breasts, stomach pain, or headaches. Most women don't suffer any other long- or short-term side effects. After using the morning-after pill most women find that their period arrives when it was due. However, it may be slightly early or up to a week late, and you may experience bleeding in between taking the pills and your next period. This is nothing to worry about.

The morning-after pill will not work if you take your first pill more than 72 hours after unprotected sex, or if you are sick within three hours of taking it. Nor will it work if you forget to take the second pill within the time-frame specified, or forget to take it at all.

The morning-after pill is available from a variety of sources and outlets free of charge. These include most family doctors, family planning clinics, sexual health clinics, GUM (genito-urinary medicine) clinics, and some hospital A&E (Accident and Emergency) departments (you should phone and check first). Also, some pharmacies offer a free service, although many will charge, as do some privately run clinics.

*Ben was shocked to discover his condom had split. He and his girlfriend concluded that this had happened because they had changed position frequently, which might have caused a strain on the condom. Hannah felt sick with anxiety. She had finished her period a week ago and so considered it highly likely that she was in her fertile stage. Ben and Hannah went to the night pharmacy and told the sympathetic pharmacist what had happened. The pharmacist was able to offer the morning-after pill and Hannah felt very relieved once she had taken the first tablet.*

## *The IUD as Emergency Contraception*

The copper IUD can be fitted up to 5 days after unprotected sex, whereas after 72 hours the morning-after pill cannot be used. Fitting a coil at this point can help prevent an egg becoming fertilized or implanting in the womb. It is most suitable for those women who do not want to take progestogen or cannot tolerate it. It is also ideal for those who think it would be suitable for continuous use as a permanent form of contraception. As soon as you are sure you are not pregnant, the IUD can be removed. But remember, sperm can live for up to 7 days, so do make sure you use additional contraception a week before you have the IUD taken out.

(For more detailed information on the general use of IUDs see pages 69–70.)

Using contraception responsibly not only protects against unwanted pregnancy, but in many cases also protects against sexually transmitted diseases – the downside of the sexual experience. The next chapter is intended as a cautionary tale.

# 4

# *Sexually Transmitted Diseases: A Cautionary Tale*

Sexually transmitted diseases, sometimes called genito-urinary infections, are on the increase. The fact that larger numbers of people are attending GUM clinics and sexual health clinics is not simply down to increased levels of awareness and/or sexual responsibility; it's also because more people are sexually active. More and more teenagers are having sex earlier, and more older people are having sex well into retirement. And the more partners you have, the greater the risk of infection. This should not put you off sex altogether. Using condoms or another barrier method of contraception can greatly reduce the risk of unwanted disease. Nonetheless, sexual diseases are spreading; and they do need to be treated as they can cause serious and permanent health problems, including infertility in women.

## How Are STDs Caught?

It only takes sex once with an infected partner to become infected yourself. A common assumption is that it is only people who sleep around who catch STDs. This is not true. Everyone is at risk if they have unprotected sex. You can be infected without knowing it, and so may pass infections on to new sexual partners. Even if you and your partner have been faithful it is still possible to become infected. This is because some infections lie dormant (asleep) in the body for long periods of time, only to reappear at a later date. You could also pass on an

STDs: A Cautionary Tale

infection without experiencing any symptoms, only for symptoms to appear in your partner. For all the above reasons it is important not to jump to the conclusion that your partner has been unfaithful just because one of you discovers an infection.

## Warning Signs and What To Do

If you suspect you could have an STD and have any of the symptoms listed below you will need to see your doctor as soon as possible, or visit your local GUM clinic (usually attached to the hospital).

Symptoms may include, for both men and women:

- discharge or leakage from the penis or vagina;
- a sore or blister near the vagina, penis or anus;
- a rash or irritation in any of the above areas;
- pain or a burning feeling when urinating;
- passing urine more often than usual;
- pain during intercourse.

It is normal for women to have a discharge to keep the genital area clean and healthy; you needn't be concerned unless your normal discharge changes colour, becomes thicker, smells different or unpleasant, and/or causes irritation. However, if you notice any of these happening, the sooner you see your doctor or a clinic the better.

It is possible to have an infection without any perceptible symptoms: so, even if you have no symptoms but suspect or are worried that you may have caught an infection, you should go for a check-up. Sexual health clinics are there to help you. No one will think badly of you or think you are wasting their time. These clinics are free and confidential, and the staff are trained to offer help and support. If you feel embarrassed, they will soon put you at ease. Most clinics offer appointments, so always telephone first. You will be asked questions about your sex life as the doctor will need to assess the kind of sex you have been having in order to find out which infection you may have. It is important that if you are pregnant you tell the doctor or nurse, as this will influence the type of treatment you receive. An examination of the genital area usually follows, and you will need to provide blood and urine samples. For women, a swab is usually taken from the vagina and the cervix. You may find this a bit uncomfortable, but it should not be painful. Sometimes the doctor will know what is wrong and give you treatment immediately. However, you may need to wait a few days for the results of any tests.

If you do find that you have an infection it is important that your partner is told, as well as any other partners you may have had in the previous few months, as they will also need to be seen and checked for infection. Staff at the clinic should be able to help you decide how to contact any previous partners, and how to tell your current partner. Couples often attend together. This is really helpful because you can give each other emotional support as well as establishing whether either of you has an infection and what needs to be done about it – and, in due course, that you are both free from infection. There are good reasons to be honest with your partner and tell him or her if you have an infection. While this is not easy, remember that you may in fact have caught the infection from them in the first place, and so be at risk of being reinfected after treatment if they are not also seen and checked.

## How to Protect Yourself from STDs

The best way to protect yourself from unwanted infections is to be aware of the following points:

- Although it only takes one sexual encounter to pass on any infection, you are at greater risk the more partners you have. A condom will help protect you from most infections if used properly. A diaphragm or cap can offer protection of the cervix from infection.
- If you have any inflammation, sore, or unusual discharge it is best not to have sex at all. Oral sex must also be avoided

if you or your partner have a cold sore on your mouth as these too can be passed on. Wait for them to heal fully.

• As soon as you can after sex, empty your bladder and wash the genital area. This might not always be possible, but it can help prevent infections such as cystitis (inflammation of the bladder) and urethritis (inflammation of the urethra).

Clearly, prevention is better than cure. By attending to the points above, you may avoid the hassle of dealing with an unwanted infection, enabling you to enjoy your sex life without worry.

## So What Are All These Infections . . .?

### *Chlamydia*

This disease is worthy of mention first because it is currently spreading so rapidly among younger people, although anyone who is sexually active can get it. The scary thing about chlamydia is that it is a silent disease, often showing no symptoms at all. It is found in both men and women and is passed on during sex. The bacteria can live inside the cells of the cervix (neck of the womb), the urethra (the tube through which you urinate), the rectum (back passage), and sometimes the eyes and throat. If you have vaginal, anal or oral sex, or share sex toys, you can pass on or receive the infection. Using a condom (male or female) helps prevent you getting or passing on chlamydia. Apart from genital-to-genital contact, the infection can be passed from the genital area to the eyes and from a pregnant woman to her baby. The exact process of how chlamydia spreads is not yet fully understood, and it is not yet known whether it is possible to pass the infection on to a partner through fingers being in contact with vaginal or seminal fluid. Research is still being carried out. However, you can't catch chlamydia from hugging and kissing, having a bath after someone else, or using the same towels. Nor will you be infected from toilet seats, swimming pools, or ordinary household items such as plates, cups, knives and forks.

If you have contracted chlamydia, symptoms may appear after about 3 weeks, many months later, only when the infection spreads to other parts of your body, or not at all.

Symptoms in women include:

- unusual discharge;
- pain on passing water;
- bleeding between periods (including women on the pill);
- bleeding after sex;
- pain and/or bleeding when you have sex;
- lower abdominal pain.

Symptoms in men include:

- a white/cloudy and watery discharge from the end of the penis;
- pain on passing water;
- painful swelling of the testicles.

Men and women rarely notice symptoms from infection of the rectum. However, some people experience discomfort and possibly a discharge from the area. Infection in the throat usually has no symptoms. Should your eyes become infected you may experience pain, swelling and irritation, and discharge (conjunctivitis).

Treatment is very effective providing you follow the course of antibiotics given. Couples should avoid vaginal, anal, and oral sex until the treatment is completed or you may risk reinfecting each other. If you are on the pill you should tell the doctor, as it may well affect which medication you can take. Being pregnant or breastfeeding will also influence the type of antibiotic that you can be given.

If chlamydia isn't treated it can spread throughout the body. This is especially serious in women if it reaches the reproductive organs. This can cause pelvic inflammatory disease (PID) and can lead to infertility. It can also lead to blocked fallopian tubes or an ectopic pregnancy (pregnancy that occurs outside the womb). In men, untreated chlamydia can lead to a painful infection in the testicles and the possibility of reduced fertility.

The message is clear: chlamydia is unlikely to go away without treatment, and if it goes untreated it may have serious effects. Also, while you remain infected you may pass the infection on to someone else.

## Genital Warts

Genital warts are caused by a similar virus to that which causes skin warts. There are 100 different types of human papillomavirus (HPV) that can cause these warts to appear at various places on the body: here we are concerned with the one that affects the genital and anal area. A few types of the virus are linked to changes in cervical cells that can lead to cervical cancer. (All sexually active women should ensure that they have regular cervical smear tests to detect any early warning signs of possible cancerous cells, regardless of whether they have had genital warts.)

Some warts are not visible, so you may be unaware that you have the virus, especially if they are inside the vagina or anus. Wart virus spreads in the same way as chlamydia (see page 83) and through the same sort of sexual contact. It can lie dormant for some time before any symptoms appear. It is unusual for genital warts to be transferred to the mouth during oral sex, but not impossible. Using a male condom or a latex square (dental dam) during oral sex can help prevent the spread of genital warts. As with all STDs, you won't necessarily know you have it until you actually see evidence that the infection is present and/or you and your partner get checked out.

Visible signs are small fleshy growths, bumps, or skin changes anywhere around the genital or anal area. They can be small, smooth, flat bumps that are hard to see, or large, pink, cauliflower-type bumps. The warts can appear in groups or on their own. Fortunately they are usually painless, but some can be itchy or cause inflammation, and sometimes bleeding can be experienced from the anus or the urethra.

There are various types of treatment, some of which can be applied at home while others need to be carried out in the clinic. As the infection is caused by a virus, antibiotics won't work.

The usual methods of treatment for genital warts are:

- painting a liquid chemical on to them (this is the most common form of treatment);
- using a liquid or cream at home;
- freezing them (cryotherapy);
- using heat (electrocutery);
- removal by surgery;
- laser treatment;
- less commonly, injecting a drug directly into the wart.

Treatments may be uncomfortable, but should not be painful.

### Gonorrhoea

Otherwise known as 'the clap', gonorrhoea has made a comeback in recent years after being on the decline. It is caused by a bacterium that thrives in warm, moist areas of the body. It affects both men and women, but often in women there are no symptoms. This can be dangerous if it means the disease goes untreated, because there is a risk of infertility if gonorrhoea attacks the ovaries and fallopian tubes, or causes chronic inflammation of the pelvic region. Approximately 1 in 10 men do not get any symptoms on contracting gonorrhoea. Symptoms differ for men and women but will usually appear between 2 and 10 days after becoming infected, though they may not show up until later. If a woman does exhibit symptoms they usually consist of the following:

- unusual discharge from the vagina or urethra;
- pain on urinating or blood in the urine;

- pain in the area just below the stomach (abdomen);
- some irritation or discharge from the anus (back passage);
- soreness and inflammation of the throat, if passed on through oral sex.

In men, the usual symptoms are:

- yellow discharge from the penis;
- pain or burning sensation on urinating;
- discharge from or irritation of the anus;
- sore throat (as for women).

Treatment is by a course of antibiotics. This usually cures the disease providing you follow the instructions and complete the course of medication prescribed. Follow-up appointments need to be attended to ensure that you are completely well again and free from infection.

## Syphilis

Syphilis has also begun to loom larger again in recent years. This infection is caused by a bacterium – *Treponema pallidum* – which resides in the blood and body fluids of an infected person, and is passed on through sexual contact. Syphilis can have very serious long-term effects on health if left untreated.

Syphilis acts in three stages, the first two being very infectious.

- Symptoms of stage 1 include a painless sore that appears on or near the vagina or penis, occasionally in the mouth or anus. This sore may appear any time between one and twelve weeks after sexual contact with an infected person. It lasts for 2 to 3 weeks before disappearing naturally.
- In stage 2, between 2 and 6 months after sexual contact, a rash appears on the body, accompanied by flu-like symptoms: headache, temperature and sore throat. Symptoms at this stage usually last between 2 and 6 weeks and may not be noticed as anything out of the ordinary.

87

- At stage 3, although there are no longer any perceptible symptoms, if the two earlier stages of the disease have not been treated the disease is still present and active in the body. Many years after the original infection irreversible damage can be caused to the heart, brain, and other vital organs.

Fortunately, the grave damage of stage 3 is not common today as early treatment by a course of antibiotics is completely effective as long as you follow instructions carefully, complete the course, and attend a follow-up appointment to ensure you are entirely cured.

## Genital Herpes

Genital herpes is caused by the virus herpes simplex II. It is very similar to herpes simplex I, which is responsible for the common cold sore appearing on the mouth. The downside of herpes is that it is incurable: once the virus is present in the body, it is there for life. However, treatment today can reduce the number of attacks and alleviate symptoms, or help to keep them at bay.

Symptoms include:

- a tingling sensation or itchy feeling on the shaft of the penis, or in the vagina;
- small painful blisters appearing on or around the genital area, which form over a day or two then burst and heal within a week or two;
- pain or a burning sensation on passing urine;
- flu-like symptoms: headache, high temperature, and backache.

The symptoms often appear 4 or 5 days after infection and can recur at intervals of several months, or even years. These symptoms can cause a lot of distress for the sufferer, but subsequent outbreaks are often not as severe as the initial one, and you do learn to manage the symptoms over time. Those of you who have cold sores will know that attacks can be avoided or made less severe by recognizing the signs early, i.e. tingling on the mouth, and treating the area before a sore develops. It is the same for genital herpes: recognizing the onset symptoms and applying treatment immediately can abort the outbreak completely. There are a number of treatments available in the form of ointment, tablets and creams, which help to get rid of the blisters and ease the pain. It is known that overwork, tiredness, and stress can bring on attacks, so learning to relax can help. (For advice on relaxation techniques and help in adjusting your lifestyle, see Part Two of this book, especially Chapter 7.)

## Vaginal Infections

Vaginal infections are remarkably common. Most women will experience them at least once in their lives, and some women experience them often. They are annoying and frustrating when they recur, and can have an impact on sexual behavior and activity. The two main ones are thrush and bacterial vaginosis (BV).

### Thrush

Thrush is a condition that is caused by a fungal or yeast-like organism called candida. This organism occurs naturally the body, and most of the time causes no problem. However, occasionally the yeast multiplies, causing pain and itching in the vagina and vulval area in women. In men, it may affect the penis, causing similar inflammation and discomfort.

For women, the usual symptoms are:

- a thick, white discharge from the vagina (similar to cottage cheese);
- possible redness and swelling of the vulva (area around the vagina);
- itching in and around the genital or anal area;
- soreness when passing urine.

For men, the main symptom is inflammation of the penis.

Treatment is simple. For women, it consists of a pessary inserted high into the vagina, and a cream to stop the itching. Men need only use the cream. Both can be bought over the counter at a pharmacy.

## Bacterial Vaginosis (BV)

BV is often confused with thrush. As a result, women often self-treat the condition and are surprised when this doesn't work. BV is a condition where the natural balance of bacteria found in the vagina is changed. If you have BV you have a higher number of undesirable bacteria, and relatively fewer of the 'good', protective bacteria. This is the reason why it is important to get checked out by your doctor or sexual health practitioner, as a test will identify the difference between thrush and BV.

Symptoms of BV include a thin, milky-grey or white discharge that has a rather unpleasant, 'fishy' smell. In some women (but not all) it can cause itching or burning.

The cause of BV is not fully understood and it can appear in women who are not sexually active. However, it occurs most often in women who have had a lot of sexual partners, or women with a long history of sexual experiences. An attack is sometimes associated with a change of sexual partner. While the majority of women have heard of thrush, BV is much less well known, and yet it is now the much more common of the two.

BV is treated with antibacterial agents in tablet, cream, or gel form. As they cannot be bought over the counter, you will need to see your doctor, who can decide what form of treatment is best for you. If BV isn't treated it can store up problems for the future, as it causes inflammation of the womb and fallopian tubes which may in turn lead to infertility. BV can also have detrimental effects in pregnancy. Such complications are not associated with untreated thrush, and so it is very important to make sure symptoms of BV are correctly diagnosed.

To minimize the chances of getting thrush or BV, it is advisable to wear loose clothing around the vulval area because it is well known that tight trousers or underwear can bring on both conditions. Choose natural fibres for underwear, and also wash and wipe from front to back after using the toilet. This will avoid spreading bacteria from the bowels to the vagina. Vaginal sprays, douches and some soap/bubble baths can also upset the natural bacterial balance of the vagina, so again it is best to stick to natural products.

## *Trichomoniasis*

Trichomoniasis ('trich' or 'TV') is caused by a small parasite that infects the vagina and urethra. The organism can live in the vagina, cervix, urethra, and bladder of women, and in the urethra and prostate of men.

In women, symptoms include:

- a yellow or white discharge with a very unpleasant smell;
- soreness/irritation around the vulval area;
- pain or burning on urination with symptoms similar to those of cystitis, i.e. increased urgency and frequency of using the toilet, and pain and discomfort while urinating.

Men usually have few or no symptoms but may experience discharge from the penis and pain on urinating. It is possible for men to carry the organism without knowing.

Treatment with a course of tablets prescribed by your doctor will cure the condition completely. You should let your doctor know if you are pregnant before starting any treatment program.

## *Pubic Lice ('Crabs')*

Pubic lice live in pubic hair and are spread by close bodily contact, often through sexual activity. Bedding, clothing and towels can also spread the infection. More disconcerting than dangerous, they can easily be treated and dealt with.

Symptoms include:

- severe itching of the genital area, especially at night when it is possible to see the tiny adult lice between the hair roots;
- small nits (eggs) appearing on pubic hair and underwear.

Treatment is straightforward, by a lotion that can be bought over the counter, although some products are more effective than others. Advice can be sought from your doctor or clinic as to the best product available. A comb similar to the one used for head lice can be used to remove any dead eggs after treatment. Take care to clean all personal clothing and bedding to prevent reinfection. Make sure that your partner and any recent partners are aware of the problem so that they can seek treatment if necessary.

## Scabies

Scabies is another condition that is easily passed on through sexual activity or close bodily contact. Tiny parasitic mites burrow into the skin and lay eggs in the genital area, underneath the arms, on the buttocks, on breasts and nipples, and in other places such as hands, feet, and stomach. It can take up to 6 weeks after contact with scabies for any signs of infection to become visible; indeed, you can have scabies without noticing any symptoms at all.

Symptoms include:

- an itchy rash, or tiny spots on the body;
- intense irritation and scratching, especially at night or after a shower or hot bath, which can lead to sore, inflamed skin.

Treatment is straightforward, requiring a special cream or lotion that can be obtained over the counter at the pharmacy. However, before you self-treat you need to be very sure that what you have is scabies. Also, scabies may not be the only infection with which you have come into contact. Therefore, it is a good idea to have a health check at your local GUM clinic or doctor. As with pubic lice, you need to ensure that all clothing, towels, and bedding are washed thoroughly (usually on the washing machine's 'hot' cycle, at a temperature above 50°C ). Again, it is essential that you inform recent partners to enable them to receive treatment and also help to avoid passing on the infection further.

## Hepatitis B

Hepatitis literally means 'inflammation of the liver'. There are different types: the one that can be spread through sexual contact (as well as through contact with other body fluids, such as saliva, urine, and blood) is hepatitis B. It can cause long-term liver damage in some people.

Symptoms occur in three stages, but, as with so many of these infections, you can have hepatitis B without symptoms and so unknowingly pass it on.

In the first stage, symptoms may appear between one and six months after infection. These include:

- flu-like symptoms, e.g. coughing and sore throat;
- tiredness;
- loss of appetite;
- pain in the joints.

Next follows a jaundice stage. This becomes apparent as your skin and the whites of your eyes turn yellowish. Urine changes from clear to darkish brown, and stools become light and clay-coloured. The infection also causes soreness in the lower abdomen. This stage can last anywhere between two and eight weeks. A further side effect is weight loss: some people report losses of up to 4.5 kg (10 lb) during a hepatitis outbreak.

Recovery is slow, but in this third stage the yellowish colouring of the skin and eyes will begin to fade and urine and stools will gradually return to normal. As it is a virus, hepatitis B cannot be treated by antibiotics and full recovery can take many months. There is no treatment apart from bed rest, eating well and looking after yourself.

There is now a vaccine available, but usually it is given only to partners of people suffering from the disease or people at high risk. If you think you may be at risk from hepatitis B, check with your local clinic or doctor to see if you could have the vaccine.

## HIV and AIDS

AIDS (acquired immune deficiency syndrome) is caused by a virus called HIV (human immunodeficiency virus). Once the virus has entered the body it begins to damage the body's natural defence system, causing the body to lose its immunity to disease. As yet, no cure to AIDS has been found, but people are living longer with the condition, supported by a variety of new drugs that are now available to help alleviate some of the life-threatening conditions commonly experienced by those carrying the virus. People rarely die of AIDS itself, but rather of one of a number of associated illnesses that would not necessarily be fatal to a healthy person: certain types of cancer, serious lung infections, and infections of the digestive system, the central nervous system, and the skin can all have catastrophic consequences for HIV/AIDS sufferers. The virus survives in certain body fluids, namely blood, semen, and vaginal and cervical fluid. So far there is no evidence to suggest that the virus is present in either saliva or tears.

You can become infected with the virus through sexual intercourse (vaginal or anal), or if infected blood gets into your bloodstream through sharing needles, syringes, or other drug-using apparatus. HIV can also be passed on to an unborn child if the mother is HIV positive, through the wall of the uterus (womb), or during childbirth and breastfeeding. Progress has been made in reducing the probability of unborn children contracting HIV.

People with HIV can look and feel perfectly well and may not know that they have the disease. This is a time when others are most at risk, as HIV is highly infectious. Unfortunately, most people diagnosed with HIV will eventually contract AIDS, half of them within 8 to 10 years of becoming infected.

As there is no cure, prevention is the message to focus on here. There are many ways to help reduce the risk to yourself and your partner.

- First and foremost: use a condom when you have sex. This will significantly reduce your risk of getting or passing on the disease. Both semen and a woman's genital fluid can carry the virus, so using a barrier method of contraception will protect both partners.
- Limit the number of sexual partners you have. It's obvious from the law of probability that the fewer people you have unprotected sex with, the less likely you are to meet someone with the virus.
- Think about the type of sex you are having, as some activities are more risky than others. Anal sex (where the penis enters the back passage) is slightly more risky than vaginal sex, as the anus was not really designed to have anything inserted into it and gets damaged more easily. Oral sex (mouth to genitals) also carries a risk if there are cuts or sores on the mouth that could become infected through contact with semen or vaginal fluid. Any activity that can break the skin or draw blood, particularly inside the anus or vagina, could increase your chance of contracting the virus.
- Remember, it isn't just sexual activity that can give you the virus. Any device used to pierce or puncture the skin can put you at risk. Avoid sharing hypodermic needles, syringes, ear-/body-piercing and tattooing equipment, or acupuncture needles. If you're having body-piercing done, always use a reputable practitioner.
- For those of you who use drugs, it is best not to inject. If you do, always stick to your own works and never share with others even if they seem perfectly well to you. You should

never need to share with anyone, as needle exchanges can be found in most towns and cities.
• Sadly, blood transfusions have also been identified in passing on HIV to haemophiliacs (people who lack blood clotting agents) and others. This is now less likely to occur as the blood transfusion services have improved testing procedures and the information required from those who want to donate blood.

Fortunately, HIV is not passed on through normal everyday activities. Therefore, people with HIV do not need to feel like social outcasts. Also, you needn't be worried about HIV testing as it is completely confidential at your clinic. It should be noted, however, that if you go to your doctor and ask for an HIV test, this will be noted on your medical records which others, for example insurance companies and employers, can ask to see. The test itself is a simple blood test to check for HIV antibodies. If these are present you are HIV positive. However, as the antibodies take time to appear after infection, you may need to wait for at least 3 months after contact to be sure. This is the reason why some people are asked to come back after a negative result. There is always a trained professional to talk to before and after the test. This person can give you all the help, advice, and support you need. You can find the number for the National AIDS Helpline in Appendix 1 under the Terrence Higgins Trust; the THT website can also guide you to other useful contacts, e.g. local sources of help. (See also the other AIDS organizations listed in Appendix 1.)

## Dealing with STDs

There is far more to sexually transmitted diseases than the physical symptoms. Discovering you have one can be horrific and lead to feelings of shame, embarrassment, guilt, and fear. Other emotions, such as blame, anger, and disbelief, can seriously affect any current relationships. It is especially difficult if you find you have an infection such as genital herpes that cannot be cured, only 'managed'.

The best way of working through these feelings is to talk to your partner and check things out before jumping to any conclusions. This is not easy. The best way to approach it may be to find a time and place that suits you both; when you can sit down together and will not be interrupted. Acknowledge that the situation is a difficult one, and try to stay as calm as possible. What you both need are the facts. Once you have these, you can help your partner to go for tests and, if necessary, get the right treatment. Try to avoid getting into a blaming situation by being positive about treatment and about how your relationship can be enhanced by a deeper knowledge and understanding of each other. This might also be a time for recommitting yourselves to your relationship in terms of trust, loyalty, and closeness.

If all this proves too difficult on your own, you may benefit from speaking to a relationship counsellor. Talking to your doctor or sexual health practitioner at your local clinic, whether on your own or with your partner, can also be very reassuring.

It can be very hard for someone who is looking for a new relationship to find they have an STD. When do you tell your new partner? How do you explain what having an STD means? Again, for those of you who are not in a relationship as well as those who are, counselling may be helpful.

In most cases, STDs can be successfully dealt with and you can then get on with your life. The only way STDs need affect your future sexual behavior is in making sure you practise safe sex and take care to avoid risky activities.

*Gwen (41) and Steve (47) had both been married and enjoyed single lives with several other partners before they met. Once they decided to move in together they felt the time was right for them to go for a medical checkup. They were using condoms, but as they were committed to each other they looked forward to being able to stop using them. They visited their local clinic together and* discussed their sexual histories with the nurse. Tests were carried out on both to check that they were both healthy. They also underwent an AIDS test. The nurse asked them to return for a further AIDS test in 3 months, advising them to continue with condoms until the second test results were through. Eventually all the tests came back clear, and Gwen and Steve were able to enjoy a very satisfactory sex life, confident that neither could infect the other as a consequence of their previous sexual relationships and behaviors.

# 5

# Sex and the Internet: Another Cautionary Tale

The Internet, once the domain of academics, scientists, and industrial companies, has become the World Wide Web, one of the largest consumer-based enterprises in the world. Computers offering access to it now sit in your front room or office, in Internet cafés, and in various other public places. Hotels and even public libraries offer Internet services to ordinary people. You can even surf the Web on the new generation of cellphones.

In fact, sometimes it seems that you no longer need to leave home at all. Everything you could ever want is obtainable 'on the net', from home shopping (groceries, clothing, furniture), to mortgages and cars. You can book a theatre seat or a table in a restaurant, find a mechanic or a dentist. Many businesses have websites through which they sell their goods, from insurance or cheap flights. In many ways the Internet is the best thing since sliced bread. So why include it in a book on overcoming sexual problems? Because sex is also available on the Internet.

On the positive side, you can find all sorts of information on the Internet to help improve your knowledge and understanding of sex. Information is available in huge detail on any questions that you have ever wanted to ask – though there's no guarantee, of course, that it's all reliable: websites vary just like any other published sources (which is why I have recommended some that I am confident are reliable in Appendix 1). You can even have therapy online. This is excellent news for people who have little time but need some advice or help with a particular issue. The Internet is there 24/7, 12 months a year: you can access information on whatever you need to know, whenever you go looking for it. Also, because you remain anonymous, you don't need to feel embarrassed or inhibited. In the privacy of your own home you can do whatever you like. Chat rooms can be great places to meet other people. Good relationships have reportedly been made over the net via email, and the potential exists for the friendless to find like-minded people and feel less isolated and alone. This is the good news.

The bad news is that there are a lot of people out there who want to exploit vulnerable people. The Internet is the perfect place to do this because it is so readily available, because anonymity can be maintained, and because it is immediate. Furthermore, the Internet can be compulsive. It can hold people prisoner for hours on end. This may not be a problem if you live by yourself, but is likely to become a huge one if you live with others. It can disrupt and interfere in relationships and family life.

> *When George became unemployed he started playing computer games and surfing the net for jobs. But what began as a positive occupation, fully supported and actively encouraged by his wife Zoe, became a nightmare. George started spending more and more time checking out links between websites, purely out of curiosity. Initially he found himself chatting to people about being unemployed. This quickly developed into more personal information being shared. Zoe was devastated to discover that George had formed a relationship with another woman that included very intimate conversations. She felt betrayed and angry. Despite George insisting that he had never met the other woman, Zoe felt as if he had been having an affair.*

The above scenario is quite mild in relation to some situations that can arise through Internet use – and this is not to belittle Zoe's experience, which was real and very painful.

## Sex and the Internet

'Cyber-sex' is a term used to describe sexual behavior connected with the Internet. This can be anything from downloading pornographic material to watching others in sexually explicit situations through a webcam. Most of you will be concerned by the recent media coverage of how paedophiles use the Internet to 'groom' young children. As children and young people become increasingly proficient in computer use, so it becomes ever more difficult to protect them from the dangers of the Internet. However, it is every parent's responsibility not to allow children access to websites without their prior knowledge and consent.

Research shows that Internet use is not gender-specific: men and women access the Internet equally. What they are looking for and why varies from one individual to another, but generally a big issue is the amount of time spent away from other family pursuits.

*Lloyd was really fed up as Tina was always on the computer emailing friends and family. It was the first thing she did when she came home and often the last thing she did at night. Sometimes they didn't even eat together. Tina saw nothing wrong in keeping in touch with her vast circle of friends. She did not see that in doing so she was neglecting her very best friend – Lloyd.*

For some, the problem can be dealt with fairly straightforwardly by talking through the problem and coming up with a sensible compromise. However, for others it can become a very serious issue, especially if the behavior is damaging or illegal.

What you do on the Internet is in one sense your own business. However, it can be very upsetting for others when compulsive behavior becomes abusive.

*Fiona was horrified at the amount of porn that Craig was looking at, especially as she was aware that their young children were often about while he did it. They had endless rows about it until Fiona ended up in the spare bedroom. She no longer felt like sex with Craig. She felt she couldn't live up to the 'perfect' women Craig was looking at on the Internet. Also, she didn't like some of the images she had seen Craig downloading. It was all very disturbing.*

When a relationship becomes this unhappy, it is time to take action and seek help. Like any addiction, compulsive attachment to the Internet is a very hard habit to break once established. If you suspect that your Internet use could put you or others at risk, professional help may be the only way forward.

## PART TWO

# Managing Sexual Problems – A Self-Help Guide

This is the part where *you* take control and start to feel good about your sexual self. The exercises contained within this part of the book have been tried and tested over many years by sex therapists and others working in the field of sexual health. Many people have benefited from the help given by professionals in the form of a sex therapy program tailor-made to their individual needs. The exercises here have been adapted for you to follow in the privacy of your own home. These exercises require time and patience. You don't get firm muscles from going to the gym only once! It takes weeks of practice to get things right. This is not intended to put you off, just to make you aware that change is not easy and does not occur overnight; so don't be disheartened if you don't find your sex life instantly transformed. If you follow the carefully graded tasks, you will gradually build up positive behaviors and reduce and finally extinguish unhelpful ones in relation to your sexual problem.

# PART TWO

# Managing Social Problems
## A Self-Help Guide

# 6

# *Setting Your Goals*

The first step in addressing your sexual problem is to set your own goals. This means asking yourself some questions. For a start, will you be doing this by yourself? This could be your choice even if you are in a relationship. Then think as closely as you can about what you are hoping to achieve. Setting yourself a goal or a target is very helpful as it makes you focus on your needs, and those of your partner if you are working on the problem together. For example, if you have premature ejaculation your goal will probably be 'to overcome the problem of PE'. This is a good goal because it is specific: goals that are vague are not helpful because it's not easy to know when you have reached them. For example, you might initially have as your goal 'to have a better sex life'. This statement may sound positive, but what does it really mean? In what way would you like better sex, and what would a better sex life look like to you? How would you know when you had attained your goal?

---

### Exercise

- Think about your sex life as it happens now. What are the good aspects about it and the not-so-good aspects? Make a list of each.
- What would you like to be different? It may be that you find it hard to talk to your sexual partner, or that you are in the wrong relationship and need a change.

---

Defining the problem here will help you towards setting your goal.

- Write a list of goals relating to the problem. Try to be as open as possible: write down anything that comes to mind, in any order. It doesn't matter at this stage if the goals are realistic or not.
- Look through your goals and start to critically assess what each of them means to you and how specific and practical they are. Dismiss the unrealistic ones until you are left with the goal or goals you really want to work on.

To help you with this exercise, consider the following scenario.

*Darren has been going out with Helen for 10 months. He loves her sense of humour and finds her very attractive. Sexually things have not been going well as Darren has PE. Helen tries to compensate for this by using her sense of humour to ease the tension the PE is causing in the relationship. Darren has not been able to tell Helen how bad this makes him feel. He would like Helen to take the problem seriously and help him to find a solution. So far he hasn't been able to find the right time or opportunity to talk to Helen about this. He is also embarrassed. After speaking to a friend Darren decides to work out a way of tackling the problem.*

Darren's list of possible goals looks like this:

- Sort out PE (essential).
- Write Helen a letter (so as not to face her).
- End the relationship (avoiding the issue).
- Pretend it's OK and try to forget about it (avoiding the issue again).
- Get Helen on her own to talk, but not in the bedroom (neutral space).

On looking at his list, Darren decides that working on the problem of PE is his top priority. Second, he thinks about Helen and what she means to him. He definitely doesn't want to end the relationship, but knows he can't go on pretending their sex life is OK. Writing a letter might work, but Darren isn't confident he will be able to say what he really feels, as letter-writing is not his style. Talking to Helen in a neutral space seems the best way forward, as Darren hopes he would be able to explain his feelings better face to face.

Darren's goals are:

- to speak to Helen as soon as he can arrange a suitable time and place; and
- to seek help for his PE no matter what the outcome of his talk with Helen.

Darren has found a way forward that not only offers the possibility of improving his relationship but has clarified for him how important it is to get some help for his PE. It will depend on the outcome of his discussion with Helen whether they work on the problem together or not.

## Self-Help for Singles

Certain of the exercises set out in the following chapters are for all to use, irrespective of whether you are single or in a relationship, or whether you are working on your problem independently or as a couple. Others are designed specifically either for those working alone or for couples. If you are going to work on the problem yourself, start by setting a goal or goals, as described in the previous section. If you're unsure how motivated you are, or whether you have negative thinking patterns that might inhibit your commitment to pursuing these goals, you might want to do the negative thinking exercise provided later in this chapter. Once you are happy with your goal(s), you can start to work through the exercises designed for singles and relevant to your particular problem. Relaxation exercises (described in Chapter 7) will help put you in a receptive condition. Exercises in body awareness, using the pelvic floor muscles, and fantasy (described in Chapter 8) will help set the scene and put you in the right frame of mind before starting the program of exercises specific to your particular problem (set out in Chapters 9 and 10).

A typical program of self-help might look like this:

*Brenda has vaginismus. She has been unable to have intercourse since her first attempts resulted in her boyfriend not being able to get his penis inside her. He subsequently dumped her. Other relationships ended as Brenda was reluctant to put herself into this embarrassing position again. She bravely went to see her doctor but was so upset that he was unable to give her an internal examination. The doctor explained to her what vaginismus was and that she needed to learn to relax. Armed with this diagnosis, Brenda looked for information on the subject to increase her understanding of what was happening to her body.*

*Brenda decided to work on this problem herself before risking any more relationships. Goal-setting was her first task. What did she want to achieve? Resolving her vaginismus and understanding the problem better became her two main goals. Understanding the problem was interesting. On looking back at her first sexual experience, she realized that her boyfriend at that time was also sexually inexperienced. His constant 'stabbing' at her vagina with his penis had caused her consider-able discomfort and pain. Brenda resolved to get to know her own body better. First, the body awareness program helped Brenda to relax. She learned to use the pelvic floor muscle exercises to take control of her vagina. She used fantasy to help ease her anxiety, and found to her delight that she was orgasmic through self-stimulation. Once Brenda felt more comfortable with her body she was able to move on to the more specific exercises designed to overcome vaginismus. Brenda also used the negative thinking exercise to help her recognize any barriers she might be putting up to prevent her reaching her goal. As Brenda's confidence increased, she found that she was able to respond positively to male attention in a way she had not been able to before.*

Maybe there is more than one sexual problem to be addressed – a situation known as 'dual dysfunction'. The program can be adapted to accommodate this, by focusing first on one problem and then on another.

*Emlyn had had PE and as a consequence had lost his erection. He worked through the erectile dysfunction program, and then, having regained his erection, proceeded to the program for PE.*

## Self-Help for Couples

The process is essentially the same if you are working as a couple. First, both of you will need to work *separately* through the goal-setting exercise. Once each of you has worked out the problem from your own point of view, and thought of some goals, you will need to share your findings with your partner. You can then negotiate a shared plan in which both your needs are met and acknowledged. This is a time to really go for being honest and proactive with each other. Acknowledging a problem can often be painful. Hearing your partner say something you were unaware of can arouse feelings of hurt, rejection, and disbelief. However, rather than letting this interfere with solving the problem, it is perfectly possible to look at it from a more positive angle. Your relationship now has the chance to develop into something more open and honest.

*Rachel and Nathan had been together for many years and had always had an active sex life. More recently, however, problems at work had affected Nathan badly. He had become depressed and lost not only his erection, but his zest for life. This enthusiasm and energy for life were aspects of Nathan that Rachel had found very attractive. His doctor suggested a change in direction away from the high-powered, frantic world of finance into something different. Rachel and Nathan looked at the options and decided to sell up and move to the country. Although this did seem to be an improvement, Nathan was still unable to keep his erection. However, as he had regained his interest in sex, they decided to work on the problem.*

*The goals that they set themselves were more foreplay and fun as well as working on the erection. Shared relaxation exercises and sensate focus helped take the pressure off Nathan's erection. Nathan used the fantasy exercise to help him stay focused. Rachel also wanted more leisurely orgasms during foreplay, which she had missed as sex had become non-existent. They worked through the erectile dysfunction program and, to the delight of both, Nathan was soon experiencing erections again.*

Again, couples may experience 'dual dysfunctions', where there is more than one sexual problem in the relationship. For example, a woman with vaginismus may be in a relationship with a man who has erectile dysfunction, and as a result both may be suffering from a loss of desire or interest in sex. This may appear a bit complicated, but dual dysfunctions can be tackled through self-help techniques. All the exercises and tasks set out in the following chapters can be adjusted to individual needs within a dual dysfunction scenario. You just need to be a bit more creative in how you organize your program. Using the body awareness program in Chapter 8 (alongside the more specific exercises for couples) can be helpful in raising individual awareness that can then be shared within the relationship.

## Motivation for Change

You may already have experienced the buzz of making plans to do something new in your life: get a new job, take up a new hobby, lose a few pounds, or stop smoking. But none of these things will actually happen if the motivation to change is not there. The classic time for attempts at change is New Year. How many of you have made New Year's resolutions, only for them to be forgotten or abandoned by 2 January? What starts with hope and determination often ends in disappointment and a sense of failure – but not always. Look at the times when you *did* carry something through to its conclusion. Finishing a course at work, completing a degree or other qualification, getting that decorating job done at last, building that extension . . .

The following exercise will help you explore your own motivation and help you to see what makes change possible.

---

### Exercise

- What was the last job, task, or plan that you saw through to the end?
- What made it possible?
- What resources did you need in order to fulfil your goal?
- How did you feel when you had achieved what you set out to do?
- Would you be able to use this information to make other goals successful?

---

It is essential to consider these questions if you are to understand what gets in the way and stops your progress in things you want to change. I was struck by the very convincing arguments a friend had for stopping smoking, and the strength of feeling she was putting into her plan to stop. She had covered all eventualities, for example, how she would cope in social situations like parties, how she would avoid smoking after meals and while drinking. At the end of our discussion it seemed as easy as blinking for her to stop. However, I asked her a final question: 'Do you want to stop?' – at which point she fell silent, looked at her plan, and said: 'No!' My friend is still smoking. You can make all the plans in the world to do something, but if it really isn't what you want then you won't succeed.

Here is another exercise that can help in working out motivation: a simple piece of brainstorming.

---

### Exercise

Find a large blank sheet of paper. Write at the top what it is that you want to do: your goal. Now divide the sheet down the middle, and write at the top of the two halves the following two headings: 'What helps me doing what I want to do?' and 'What hinders me doing what I want to do?' Write down everything and anything that comes into your head. This technique will also help with goal-setting.

---

Once you have decided that you *do* want change, you will need to keep your enthusiasm and your motivation high, and here you may need some help. Careful consideration of what you have written down in the exercise above will help you to identify what you need, not only from yourself but from others too. Having people around to support you can really make a difference. Having a sexual problem can feel very isolating, but sharing it with someone else can help to break down barriers of embarrassment, and in some cases shame. Often it is a relief to talk about your problem and know that you are not alone. A good friend who you feel confident will keep offering encouragement, or a partner or family member who is aware of the problem, can give much-needed positive support.

At the same time, you can do an awful lot to support yourself. Giving yourself encouragement by way of rewards can help keep you motivated.

*During her self-help program to tackle her vaginismus, Brenda used to buy herself treats such as massage oil or body lotions. After one particularly big breakthrough she went to the best hair salon in town and had a completely new style and colour to reflect her growing confidence.*

*Rachel and Nathan promised themselves a second honeymoon as soon as their sex life was back on track.*

## Anxiety and Negative Thinking

Anxiety is a major contributor to loss of motivation, sending negative messages through the body that in turn cause unpleasant sensations. Messages such as 'I am bound to let her down' or 'It's not going to work' affect your ability to respond sexually. Physical and emotional responses to anxiety can be extremely uncomfortable, including racing heartbeat, sweating, dry mouth, and dizziness, to name just a few. It is best not to try any of the exercises while feeling this way. Talking to a partner or friend about what is making you anxious can help get to the cause of the anxiety and allow you to focus on alleviating the symptoms.

> *Paddy was convinced that he was a sexual failure when his erection failed. He was also convinced his new wife would be disappointed in him and ultimately leave him. In fact, Elisabeth had no intention of leaving Paddy. Learning this helped him overcome his anxiety, leaving them free to work on the sexual problem together.*

Anxiety is often the result of persistent and repeated negative thoughts. The following section is designed to help you to evaluate for yourself whether or not you think negatively, and to show how this type of thinking pattern can affect your sex life. There then follows an exercise to help you identify and overcome negative thoughts.

---

### Exercise

Ask yourself the following questions:

- Do I see my glass as half full or half empty?
- Do all my silver linings have big black clouds?
- Do I always think the worst in any given situation?
- Am I an optimist or a pessimist?
- Am I easily discouraged?
- Do I use universal language, such as 'nothing', 'always', 'never', 'everyone', 'everything'?

---

Florence always fears the worst. Her friends describe her outlook as predominantly gloomy. A typical scenario for Florence would look like this.

*Being invited to apply for promotion at work, Florence immediately thinks that perhaps she isn't doing her current job well enough and so her boss wants to get rid of her. She frets and fumes over her application and as a result doesn't put in a very good piece of work. At the interview she is nervous and appears ill at ease, despite lots of encouragement from the panel of interviewers, which includes her boss. The panel do their best to support Florence but are left disappointed that she is unable to rise to the challenge. After the interview they conclude that she must not want the job and decide not to offer it to her. Her boss is puzzled as he believes she deserves promotion, being very good at what she does. On hearing she is unsuccessful Florence is aware of feeling relieved. Subconsciously, the whole event has confirmed to Florence that she isn't good enough or clever enough to be considered for promotion. The panel's decision was therefore right.*

Unless confronted with her negative thinking pattern, Florence will never rise to anything more than she already is. For some, this may be OK; we are not all necessarily ambitious. However, in this case Florence is clearly not fulfilling her potential. It may take considerable time for Florence to realize this – or she may never realize it at all, because she 'always' feels that 'everything' goes wrong for her and that 'nothing' goes right. 'Everyone' is better than her.

If you look at these statements carefully you will see that Florence is using universal language to put herself down. These statements cannot really be true. How can 'everyone' be better than her? Florence doesn't and couldn't possibly know 'everybody'. Also, things *do* go right, even for Florence. So 'always', 'nothing', and 'everything' are tools that contribute to her negative thinking about herself.

Occasionally, feeling negative is justified. Sometimes things do go wrong, and life can be hard. However, you can usually talk yourself out of a negative situation if your outlook is generally optimistic.

> *Theo applies for promotion and is turned down. Theo is disappointed but makes an appointment with his line manager to discuss his application and interview. Theo listens carefully to the feedback given and decides to take another qualification to fill some gaps in his experience. He is also encouraged to work on his presentation and interview style. Theo is happy to do this and determined to succeed next time round.*

Let's look now at how negative thinking can affect your sex life.

> *Irene really likes Scott. She has fancied him for ages but is convinced he wouldn't be interested in her. Her thoughts usually run along the lines of 'Why would a gorgeous guy like him be interested in me?' As a consequence, when Scott does look in her direction she always looks away or pretends not to notice. Scott concludes that Irene isn't in the slightest bit interested in him.*

> *Henry's negative attitude has just lost him another relationship. Girlfriends just cannot cope with his constant negativity. Life seems hard to Henry, who is quite unaware of what he is doing. He is often heard to say, 'Relationships always go wrong for me.'*

What Henry is failing to see is that it is his behavior that is undermining his relationships. It's very tempting to blame others when things don't go the way you want them to – and it's also a convenient way of avoiding looking at your own behavior. Remember, you can't change other people; you can only change yourself.

What can Florence, Irene and Henry do about this? Recognizing that there is a problem is always the best place to start. The following three-stage exercise, adapted from B. Zilbergeld's *The New Male Sexuality*, is designed here to help you identify and change negative thinking patterns.

115

# Negative Thinking: A Three-Stage Exercise

## *Stage 1*

To get maximum benefit from this exercise, you will need to allow a couple of weeks for this first stage. Buy a small notepad or book to carry around with you to take notes. Every time you are aware of a negative feeling, making a negative statement, or thinking a negative thought, write it down. If it is not convenient to write something down because of the environment you are in (e.g. driving a car, in a meeting at work), then try to hold on to the thought, feeling, or statement until such time as you can write it down.

At the end of the fortnight go over your findings and see what instances of negative thinking you have gathered. Sometimes you may be undecided whether or not a statement, thought, or feeling is negative. To help you decide, ask yourself the following questions :

- Does this make me feel better?
- Does this help me to act as I would like?
- Does this help me to think in a constructive way about my situation?
- Does this reinforce positive images I have about myself?
- Does this improve my relationships?

If the answers are mostly 'no', it's a negative thought!

You now have all the knowledge you need for you to consider change. This is the basis for the next stage of the exercise.

## *Stage 2*

Having increased your awareness of your negative thoughts, feelings, and statements, you will need to continue to monitor them. However, this time, instead of just writing them down, you will need to look at them, reassess them, then turn them into something positive. This is often referred to as 'reframing'.

116

For example, if a thought comes into your head that says, 'That person is looking at me, she obviously thinks my hair looks dreadful', try to rephrase that thought and turn it into something more positive, for example, 'That person is looking at me, I wonder if she knows me', or 'Perhaps my hair is looking good today'. Again, write down each thought as it first occurs to you, and the reframed thought, as soon as you can, so that you don't forget.

It is important that in your reframed statements and thoughts you use words and ideas that are acceptable and mean something to you. You will not be able to sustain change if what you tell yourself is not believable to you.

This stage can take time and considerable effort, but it is well worth it if it results in a positive change to your attitude, and as a consequence to your life. It can take months to build up a positive response mechanism, but with practice you will succeed. You don't have to wait until you've worked right through stage 2 before you begin on the sexual self-help exercises described in the following chapters, either: the two sets of exercises can very usefully be run alongside each other.

## Stage 3

The previous two stages were about identifying and modifying unhelpful negative thoughts, feelings, and statements about yourself. This stage is about creating a more positive self-image, rather than simply responding to and adjusting negative thinking. It can be done alongside the first two stages.

During the day take some time, a few minutes, to say something good about yourself. It is helpful if you find regular time spots, for example, when looking in the bathroom mirror while shaving or putting on make-up, during your tea/coffee break, at lunchtime, in the afternoon break and/or before your evening meal. You are far more likely to remember to do this exercise if you develop a regular pattern. What you choose to say is up to you, but it could include positive thoughts along the lines of 'I feel good today' or 'I did that really well'. People who use positive statements, or mantras, like this often feel good about themselves, and also tend to be popular with others.

Once you have assessed your general attitude to life and taken steps to make it more positive, you can apply the same exercise to your sex life. Alternatively, you may find that your general attitude is already positive, and it is only in your sex life that this kind of negative thinking happens. If this is the case, you will only need to use the techniques described in this exercise in conjunction with your sex life.

Eradicating negative thinking from your day-to-day life can have a positive 'knock-on' effect either way, sexually or generally. It is difficult to be positive in the one area and for this not to cross over into the other areas of your life. Positive thoughts are contagious. You probably know people who always manage to see the positive in any given situation and have perhaps wondered how they do it. In fact, what you are learning to do by following the three-stage exercise is what positive people do naturally and all the time. You can learn from observing positive people in action, as well as practising on yourself. When you have made a start on positive thinking, you can use your new approach to life to help focus on your sexual problem.

# 7

# Relaxation, Stress Management, and Lifestyle Choices

## Relaxation

The first thing you need to learn to do before starting the exercises for your specific problem is to relax. Those of you who do any form of meditation, yoga or tai chi can use what you know from these disciplines to help you to relax. However, some of you might already be thinking, 'Where on earth will I find the time to do that on top of everything else I do?' This may be part of the problem. Making time for yourself is a very necessary part of any successful self-help program. You may have small children, or a job that requires a lot of driving away from home, or work antisocial shift cycles. Finding the time to relax in such circumstances may prove difficult, but careful planning and creative use of the time you do have can often work wonders. Also, the exercise suggested here can be done anywhere, more or less. One woman I know managed to do it while sitting in her dentist's waiting room. As long as you have a reasonable chair or place to sit you can do it. Ideally, lie on the floor using a comfy mat or cushions. Your bed or sofa could be even better.

### Relaxation Exercise

Trying to concentrate on carrying out exercises and reading a book at the same time is not very relaxing! So, if you are unfamiliar with any kind of relaxation exercise, it is probably best if you read right through the instructions first to get an idea of what you need to do. Once you have read the instructions through you could record them on to a tape, so that you can listen to your own voice (or someone else's) giving you the instructions.

First of all, find a quiet time and a suitable place to sit or lie down. The bed is often the best place. Make yourself as comfortable as you can. Adjust yourself and your clothing accordingly. Use cushions or pillows if extra support is needed. Once settled, pay attention to how you are breathing. Is it normal and regular? Are you breathing a little heavily or quickly? Breathing quickly can be a sign of anxiety, especially if you feel your heart is beating a little faster than usual. Concentrate fully and empty your mind of any distracting or irritating thoughts. Close your eyes and slowly take a deep breath in until your lungs are full, then breathe out slowly and evenly. Take a few minutes to practise breathing in this way until you have established a nice rhythm. You will need to use this deep breathing during the following muscle-tensing exercises.

- Take a deep breath in and tense the muscles in your feet by curling up your toes and squeezing them tightly. Hold your breath and your muscles for a few seconds before releasing your muscles and breathing out slowly.
- Next, concentrate on tensing your ankles by bending your feet upwards and pressing your heels down. Take a deep breath, holding the muscles tight for a few seconds, then slowly breathe out, letting your muscles relax.
- Tense the muscles in your calves next. Take a deep breath, again holding for a few seconds before releasing your muscles as you slowly breathe out.
- Take a deep breath as you tense your thigh muscles by pushing your legs together. Hold tight for a few seconds before letting your legs go and breathing out.
- Tighten the muscles in your buttocks, tensing up as you take a deep breath. Hold for a few seconds and release as you slowly breathe out.

- Tense the muscles in your tummy. Take a deep breath. Hold tight for a few seconds before letting go as you breathe out.
- The next muscle group includes your arms and your hands. Bend your elbows and make fists with your hands. Tense these muscles with a deep breath. Hold tight for a few seconds before slowly letting go and breathing out.
- Take a deep breath while you tense the muscles in your neck and shoulders. Hunch your shoulders up towards your ears and your spine. Press your head back against your chair or pillow. Hold the tension for a few seconds before slowly letting go and breathing out.
- Think about all the muscles in your face: clench your jaw, frown, and close your eyes tightly as you take a deep breath. Hold for a few seconds before relaxing and breathing out.
- Finally, tense all your muscles at once: feet, ankles, calves, thighs, buttocks, tummy, arms, shoulders and face. Taking a deep breath, hold tightly for a few seconds and then slowly relax all your muscles as you breathe out.

Practise the muscle-tensing exercises a few times until you really know what you are doing. Then try to extend the time that you are holding each group of muscles tight until you can manage about ten seconds. This will help you really feel the difference when you let go.

Once you have finished the sequence, continue to breathe slowly and deeply. It is often recommended that you now think of something pleasant at this stage, to maintain the deeply relaxed state that you should now be in. Imagine a scene or place that you like, or someone you would like to be with. If you like the beach, you might imagine a quiet seashore somewhere. You could picture the sea gently rolling up the beach. You could hear the waves lapping and the seabirds calling in the distance. Imagine it's a hot day and the sun is beating down on you. Feel the heat. A gentle breeze offers some relief from the sun's rays. It is a perfect situation. Feel the sand beneath the blanket that you are lying on. Feel how it moves with you as you settle into your place on the beach. Run your fingers over the sand. Feel the heat and allow the sand to run through your fingers, soft and warm. Doesn't it feel good? All is right with your world. You feel calm, serene, at peace. Stay with this image for as long as you feel comfortable. Of course, this is just one suggestion; there may be another situation that is more attractive to you – perhaps a country field, or a woodland glade. Use whatever appeals to you most.

Relaxation and good sex go hand in hand. Feeling worried, anxious, or tired will inhibit your natural response mechanisms. Learning to relax is part of taking control of your situation and allowing yourself to enjoy your sexual life. Once you have mastered this relaxation program, use it before you have sex either on your own or with your partner. This will reduce your anxiety and help you to focus on more positive thoughts and feelings.

> *Tim is working on his premature ejaculation (PE), helped by his girlfriend Shannon. He is going to cook her a meal this evening and she is planning to stay overnight. He is aware of feeling anxious about how the evening will go. Tim remembers his relaxation program and takes himself off to have a quick shower before lying down to go through the muscle-tensing exercises. Concentrating on relaxation takes Tim's mind off what might happen later, and he is able to focus on the pleasurable parts of his evening with Shannon. He imagines her arriving, the warm welcome he gives her, and her positive response. The meal is perfect and the atmosphere is just how he wants it. Low lights and candles, music they both like, and the whole night together to enjoy themselves. He pictures them after dinner, relaxing on the sofa, talking and laughing together until they kiss. Tim takes Shannon's hand and leads her to the bedroom . . . By the time Shannon arrives in reality, Tim is very relaxed and really looking forward to whatever happens next.*

## Relaxation for Couples

You can also practise relaxation together. Make sure you are both familiar with the format and have each practised a few times on your own first. Choose a nice place to relax. Take a duvet to your sitting room or lounge and use some cushions for extra comfort, or lie down on your bed. If the weather is nice you could try outside in the garden, or drive to the countryside: relaxation can be done anywhere, although you will need to be as comfortable as possible. You may like to go through the sequence together, closing your eyes and each working at your own pace; or, if you prefer, one of you can give instructions while the other relaxes, and then you can change places. You can share your ideal scenes together, or simply think about your own. Take time after relaxing to share what felt good and perhaps have a cuddle.

Learning to use the relaxation techniques *before* you start any of the self-help exercises for overcoming your sexual problem will help to create just the right climate for change. Being familiar with the instructions will reduce the time you spend before a session, but don't worry if you haven't always got the time: include the relaxation program when you can, or if you are feeling particularly stressed or anxious. Also, you don't need to be preparing for a particular exercise or session to enjoy relaxing. You may have had a very hard day, and find that a few minutes' relaxation helps you to switch off and enjoy the rest of your evening. Taking time for yourself doesn't have to involve long periods. You can do this exercise even if you only have 15 minutes to spare. Soon you will find it becomes no real effort at all to fit relaxation in.

## Relaxation and Sleep

Those of you who have trouble sleeping may find that relaxation before bedtime helps you get a better night's sleep.

*Work was getting Nadia down: she had so much to do. Even when she got into bed, her brain would not stop working. She thought about reports she had to write, people she had to contact. It was driving her mad. Having been given relaxation exercises as part of a sex therapy program, Nadia decided to try to use the same technique at bedtime. After the muscle-tensing sequence, Nadia took herself off into her favourite fantasy place. Staying focused on this pleasant and restful scene helped Nadia to fall asleep, her mind no longer racing with thoughts of work.*

Lack of sleep can be a real problem. It tends to take two forms: first, being unable to get off to sleep, and second, waking up after only a couple of hours. Waking is often accompanied by a need to go to the bathroom. This can sometimes be associated with age: as you get older, your body may no longer need the 8 hours' sleep a night that your brain thinks it does. However, once a situation like Nadia's has developed it can continue long after the initial cause (in this case, work stress) has been resolved. Sleeplessness can become a habit – your body gets used to waking up once, twice a night, sometimes even more often. Keeping your partner awake, or being kept awake by them, can also create difficulties, especially if you both need to get up early in the morning. There may be ways to manage this, for example, occasionally sleeping separately (if you have another room available) or using earplugs. The worst thing you can do is worry about it, as this is likely simply to exacerbate the problem.

As well as relaxing before bed, a milky drink can sometimes help to make you feel drowsy. Also, it is best to get to bed as soon as you start to feel tired and sleepy. If the clock says it is too early to go to bed, we often follow that instead of our own internal clock. This can mean you 'get over' feeling sleepy, so that when you do finally go to bed, you are wakeful again. If you go to bed at ten o'clock and wake at two, at least you will have had 4 hours' sleep. Then, rather than lie there wondering why you can't go back to sleep, do something else. Get up, or read until you feel sleepy again. This can often help you to get enough sleep to do whatever you need to do the next day. Also, drink the bulk of your liquid needs during the day, and limit what you have in the evening. This can help reduce the need to get up in the night to go to the bathroom.

Some people wake because it gets light. Why not use an eye-mask to keep you asleep longer? Your partner may think it strange going to bed with Zorro, but if it helps . . . Night workers can also experience sleep problems when they return to a normal daily routine. Again, getting to bed when your body tells you to can help you readjust. Being kept awake by young children or a new baby can also take its toll. For more information on getting a good night's sleep, see *The Good Sleep Guide* by Michael Van Straten (details are given in Appendix 1).

## Stress Management and Lifestyle

Nadia is not alone in feeling stressed at work. Many people are finding nowadays that work is encroaching more and more into their personal lives. In fact, for some people work *becomes* their life. Equally, not having work can be stressful, especially with the added strain of worries about money. Stress comes in many different forms. A certain amount is helpful: it can motivate us and get things done. Too much stress, on the other hand, can be harmful: emotionally, mentally, behaviorally, and physically. The stress response is widely recognized as a survival strategy linked to the need to prepare for 'flight or fight'. It is a necessary function to healthy living. It is when the levels of stress go beyond your ability to cope with them that trouble strikes.

### What Sort of Stress?

So what is unhealthy stress? One definition is an adverse reaction you might experience in response to excessive pressures or demands put on you. However, while it is often fairly easy to talk about feeling 'stressed' in a general way, it is much harder to identify yourself specifically as anxious, or frightened, or angry, or sad. When looking for a solution to stress you need to identify correctly which feeling or emotion you are dealing with.

---

### Exercise

Next time you feel 'stressed', try to focus on the actual emotion, and ask yourself what the feeling *really* is.
   'When I feel stressed I am really feeling . . .'

- anxious?
- guilty?
- angry?
- bored?
- a failure?
- frustrated?

---

The feelings listed in the exercise are just a small selection of feelings that often underlie sexual problems. There are others that may fit your situation or circumstances better. The important thing here is for you to begin to understand exactly *what* you are feeling when you are 'stressed'.

*Penny is feeling very stressed. She is caring for elderly parents, running a home and a job, and at the same time bringing up teenage children. Penny's husband is in the forces and is often away for long periods of time. She feels at the end of her tether, both emotionally and physically. Penny identifies her main emotion as guilt. She feels torn in so many different ways and feels under pressure. She feels guilty at not spending enough time with her parents or her children, on her home or on her job. No wonder she is so tired and lacking in energy when her husband comes home wanting to rekindle his sexual relationship with her. No wonder she feels guilty all the time, especially when taking any time to do anything for herself. Once Penny could recognize her underlying emotions and could describe how she felt, she was able to start rethinking her life and working on overcoming some of the problems facing her.*

Stress can be attributed to many different things. Identifying the source of your particular stress can help you to cope better. If your vaginismus is causing guilt or unhappiness and affecting your relationship, then dealing with the problem will take the stress out of the situation. Feeling bored or frustrated with your partner can lead to arguments and tension between you. However, sex is only one of many reasons for feeling stressed. Below is a list of events commonly used in assessing stress, with the most stressful at the top, working downwards towards the less stressful. In stress assessment exercises they usually have number values attached, so that you can 'count up' your stress points to see how stressed you are. The helpfulness of these scales is debatable: I am sure you already know how stressed you are feeling. You will see that sexual problems are located about a third of the way down; yet it is a fact that all of the other factors listed here can *contribute towards* sexual problems. Therefore, if you can tick one or several items from the top area of the list (the ones at the top are the most stressful), it's fair to assume that stress is playing a major part in your sexual problem.

## Stress Scale: Causes of Stress, from Most to Least Stressful

- Death of a partner;
- divorce;
- marital separation;
- prison term;
- death of close family member;
- personal injury or illness;
- moving house;
- marriage;
- being sacked from your job;
- marital reconciliation;
- retirement;
- illness or injury of family member;
- pregnancy;
- sexual problems;
- new baby;
- changes in financial circumstances;
- death of a close friend;
- change of career;

- increase in number of arguments with partner;
- large mortgage or loan;
- repossession in terms of mortgage or loan;
- child leaving home;
- in-law or family problems;
- partner starts a new job or stops working;
- child starting school or college;
- changes in living conditions;
- changes in personal habits;
- trouble at work;
- changes in conditions or hours of work;
- changes in social activities;
- changes in sleeping habits;
- changes in eating habits;
- holidays;
- religious festivals;
- minor violations of the law (e.g. speeding ticket).

*Bert was fired from his job at the same time as the interest rate on his mortgage was rising. He and his wife Nancy had large credit card debts, and two children were about to start new schools. Their house was repossessed and they ended up moving three times, as the rented accommodation they moved to originally was totally unsuitable. Bert's and Nancy's stress levels were sky-high as they tried to manage all the different areas of their lives that had gone wrong. Is it surprising that they had gone off sex? Seeking help via a reputable debt counselling agency was the first step to taking control of their lives again.*

Another way to ascertain whether you are suffering from stress is by recognizing some of the different ways in which stress might affect you. Remember, you can be affected physically, mentally, behaviorally and emotionally. Here are some examples of these four categories:

Physical symptoms include:

- muscle tension, leading to backache, aching shoulders, headaches;

- dry mouth;
- sweating (especially in palms of hands);
- cold hands;
- erratic breathing;
- dizzy spells;
- chest pains;
- knot in stomach;
- sick feeling or nausea;
- restlessness (e.g. pacing);
- going to the bathroom more often than normal;
- diarrhoea.

Of course, many of these could be indicators of something else. Do not hesitate to visit your doctor if you are worried that some other health problem is affecting you.

Mental symptoms include:

- inability to concentrate;
- inability to make simple decisions;
- loss of confidence;
- being unusually tired;
- memory lapses;
- muddled thinking;
- making rash decisions or a tendency to lose perspective.

Here again it is important to recognize what is unusual and what is just part of your individual response to normal circumstances. Some people find it hard to make decisions and are naturally indecisive. For others, making rash decisions is part of their makeup. Forgetting things can be a regular habit. Lack of concentration can be due to boredom rather than stress. It is only wise not to take these lists too literally; but still, they may suggest warning signs.

Behavioral symptoms include:

- smoking or drinking alcohol to excess;
- over- or under-eating;

- lack of sleep or oversleeping;
- biting nails or hair-pulling;
- withdrawal from social life;
- not looking after yourself (in grooming and hygiene);
- talking too much;
- obsessive compulsive behaviors;
- reckless driving;
- becoming a workaholic;
- taking excessive amounts of time off work.

Some of these can be due to addiction rather than stress, and it is important to consider carefully what the underlying reasons for some of these behaviors might be.

Emotional symptoms include:

- anxiety;
- depression;
- panic attacks;
- angry outbursts or irritability;
- feelings of hopelessness;
- feelings of hostility, resentment, or animosity;
- feelings of guilt;
- increased cynicism;
- undue aggression;
- nightmares;
- increased moodiness;
- feelings of insecurity;
- crying;
- fear of criticism.

Again, assess carefully what some of these feelings or experiences might mean. If you have suffered a bereavement, it's not surprising that you may feel depressed or hopeless and prone to crying. In such circumstances these feelings are considered perfectly natural and to be expected. Equally, feelings of insecurity could be the result of losing a job or being burgled.

So, a word of warning: while lists such as these can be helpful when trying to identify the types of stress in your life, they can also seem a bit prescriptive – tending to tell you what you feel rather than helping you to find out for yourself. I know someone who regularly thinks he is dying when reading a medical book. He is convinced he has all of the symptoms and that he is really ill. Needless to say, he is still alive and well!

The physical environment can also impact on you in ways that cause stress. This includes factors like noise, temperature, and climate, as well as the neighbourhood and type of housing you live in. Public transport or lack of it can affect your ability to get to work on time. The place where you work as well as your hours of work can also be sources of stress, as can changes in routine, accidents, hospital appointments, and bad news phone calls. I am sure you can think of many more examples.

Once you know where you are in terms of stress, the next step is learning how to manage it. Take a look at the three stages of stress outlined below.

## The Three Stages of Stress

- *Stage One:* You feel alert, energized, able to laugh and put things into perspective. You feel motivated and can act quickly. During this stage stress can be useful. For example, your boss comes in with an urgent job for you to do. Stress kicks in (sudden panic) as the adrenaline starts pumping around your body. You get your act together and get the job done.
- *Stage Two:* You start to feel under the weather and niggling little ailments plague you. You feel edgy, helpless, and tired. Unable to sleep properly, you feel tearful, below par, and generally unwell. This can be OK for a little while, but if allowed to continue this stage will gradually wear you down and lead you into stage three.
- *Stage Three:* You are overtaken by a sense of not being in touch with reality and feel frightened. This is often associated with chronic behavior patterns that others notice, but

131

that you are unable to see for yourself: things like rocking yourself, fidgeting, hand-clenching, and so on. You may experience serious depression, and other ailments such as tension headaches or migraine.

At stage three you fail to function effectively. Therefore, it is crucial to recognize when stage one has slipped into stage two. You need to take charge before your stress takes you into stage three, as this stage is much harder to deal with.

## Managing Stress

One way to manage stress is to take a practical approach, confronting the causes head-on and problem-solving how to respond. On page 133 is a 'Managing Stress' form. Try filling it in with the details of a recent stressful episode. You may find it a useful means of identifying and understanding how stress has affected you, and minimizing its effects on you in the future.

## Diet, Exercise, Relaxation, and Positive Thinking

Most women (and many men) are reported as being constantly on weight-loss diets. Generally, diets don't work. They can be demoralizing and make you feel a failure when you don't stick to them; and, arguably, they themselves can make you fat. Certainly, anything that makes you feel deprived is not likely to last long. However, eating well and at regular times helps you to feel better and more able to deal with potentially stressful situations.

Try to eat a range of healthy foods that fit more or less into your lifestyle. If you need to lose weight, reduce portion sizes. Avoid fatty foods, and cut down on salt, sugar and processed foods. Try to stick to the recommended intake of five portions of fresh vegetables and fruit a day. Avoiding carbohydrates in the evening has proved effective for some people as this is the time you will be least likely to work off the food you are eating. In essence, eating healthily is about eating real food in a sensible

## Managing Stress

*Description of what happened to cause the stress*
*(Who was involved? Where did it happen?)*




*What did you do?*




*What was the stress experienced?*




*How would you do it differently?*
*(What will you say/think/feel next time this happens?)*




*What support mechanisms do you need?*

routine. Most of you will already know what to do: in fact, many of us are now dietary experts, at least in theory, as a result of reading all the information presented in well-researched publications and on the media.

We also all know by now that exercise is good for us. It need not be too burdensome to be beneficial. Going for a brisk walk, or taking up dancing, swimming or a yoga class, may be all it takes to achieve a more positive outlook on life. Just taking the dog and/or the children to the park can increase your energy levels. Exercise need not be a chore if you choose something that you enjoy; and it will markedly reduce stress levels.

As explained at the beginning of this chapter, relaxation can help calm you down. If you start to feel stressed out, remember to breathe slowly and deeply. Simply taking a few deep breaths can spell the difference between coping and not coping.

Using positive thinking as a way of lessening stress is also extremely helpful. Try changing messages to yourself that reinforce feelings of inadequacy, such as 'It's all piling up, I'll never get finished, I can't cope,' into positive, helpful messages, such as: 'OK, things are really piling up, how shall I approach this? Let me take one step at a time, prioritize what I can do today and leave the rest until tomorrow.' You are only human after all, not a machine. Talking to yourself calmly and positively can reduce stress and give you back control by making sense of what is happening to you. Setting clear and manageable goals for yourself and being more assertive – that is, accepting your limitations and learning to say no – will also help keep you on the right path towards greater well-being.

## Other Ways of Coping with Stress

Another way of helping stress is to give yourself treats or rewards. This may be as simple as giving yourself some praise, e.g. saying to yourself: 'Didn't I do well?' Or treat someone else. Invite your partner or a friend out for dinner or a trip to the cinema. Do something or plan something you really want to do. Give your partner a sensuous massage or ask him/her to give you one. Ask for support. Friends and colleagues can help. You may feel this to be a sign of weakness, reluctant to be seen as 'not coping'. But a trouble shared really is a trouble halved, and most people love to be needed. Choose the right person to support you, though: it won't help if the person you confide in adds to your stress rather than reduces it.

Here are some emergency coping strategies that you may already recognize:

- *Humour*: Always a good one for reducing stress. Laugh it off or see the funny side.
- *Calming*: Tell yourself to calm down. Repeat this while you relax your facial, shoulder, and neck muscles.
- *Reason*: Acknowledge that this is not as big a problem as you think it is now. From experience you know that in a year, a month, a week, it will just be a memory.
- *Distancing*: Make a space for the problem and the people involved. Walk away from the space, leaving the problem and the people behind. Look back to see your role in events.
- *Move it*: Give yourself time by moving the problem to later in the day. Suggest another time to discuss it. Plan your approach and what you want to say before the newly agreed time.
- *Worry session*: Allow yourself a certain amount of time to work through all your worries in one go. Put a time limit on the session and do not exceed it.

## A Good Word for Stress!

Remember, stress is not all bad. Stress can be a great motivator and source for action. So it's also worth knowing how to thrive on a certain amount of stress. Here are some strategies for surviving and thriving under stress:
*Emotional strategies:*

- releasing emotions (letting them out appropriately);
- emotional distance (being able to separate yourself from unhelpful emotions);

135

- emotional support (being able to give support or ask for support yourself);
- emotional control (being able to hold on or let go appropriately).

*Physical strategies:*

- proper diet, rest and exercise;
- maintaining a balanced body, without strains and tensions;
- relaxation.

*Mental–spiritual strategies:*

- cultivating a positive stance on life;
- maintaining realistic expectations;
- self-management: taking responsibility for what happens to both your inner and outer selves.

Finally, give yourself permission *not* to be perfect. Like yourself and others will like you too. Acknowledge and accept your imperfections, but most of all value yourself for the wonderful and unique human being that you are. For more information on coping with stress, see Appendix 1.

## *Lifestyle*

This is a very important area to consider, as the way you are living your life may very well be the cause of your current sexual difficulties and indeed lie at the heart of why you are stressed. In Chapter 2 we saw how the demands of Laura's and Ed's jobs were seriously affecting the quality of their lives. Without a major change nothing was going to improve, and certainly a baby was out of the question. However, it is not always easy to change a job or a situation, especially if you have a mortgage to pay and children to support. Choices have to be made and priorities set.

---

### Exercise

Ask yourself the following questions:

- Am I happy with my current lifestyle?
- What gives me quality of life?
- Am I happy with my relationship?
- Am I happy with my job?

---

Knowing what you can change and what you cannot is important in overcoming lifestyle problems. Remember Phil, whose case we looked at in Chapter 2? Phil's drinking after work was seriously harming his relationship with his wife Tricia. They sought help through counselling, where they were able not only to work on their relationship but also to identify the reasons behind Phil's drinking.

*Phil was feeling pressure as a result of overwork and long hours. He didn't feel able to leave his job as he was not confident of finding employment elsewhere in his field. Phil's company and other companies like his were reducing staff, and this had created a fear of redundancy. Phil knew that while Tricia was not happy with the state of their marriage, she liked their current lifestyle. On the positive side, she had plenty of money and a big house, and the children were in private schools. Phil felt trapped and unable to cope: hence the drinking, and the devastating effect on their sex life. Tricia was shocked and upset to belatedly learn how Phil really felt. Discussing what their options might be was part of their road to recovery.*

Lots of elements of lifestyle can affect your sexual responses and sexual relationships. Burning the candle at both ends or overindulging occasionally need not be a problem. However, if this happens regularly then it could quickly become one. Smoking, drinking, overeating, while all enjoyable at the time, can have long-term effects that can harm your sex life. Feeling bloated after a huge meal is not conducive to active sex: you're

want to go to sleep. Drinking too much can have
ications, as we have seen; and heavy drinking can
exacerbate, erectile problems. Smoking is a longer-
te...    ...lem that affects the circulation. Remember, it's blood
flow that creates the male erection; and arousal in women is
also dependent on blood flow. Recreational drugs are often
credited with enhancing sexual arousal. However, the long-
term effects are not good if used excessively.

If you want your body to work for you and give you pleasure,
then it is common sense not to abuse it. Health is everything.
All the money in the world will not help you if your health
fails. Take all things in moderation. This includes a sensible
diet and regular exercise. Get high on life rather than using
substitutes to avoid or deny the problems in your life. Tackle
problems head-on and you will end up feeling happier, healthier, and better able to enjoy your lifestyle.

Another area of lifestyle worth considering in relation to a
good sex life is hobbies and interests. Allowing an interest,
however satisfying, to take over your life can be bad news for a
relationship.

*Barbara really likes Noel, and they have been going out together
for a couple of years – but Barbara is not sure the relationship can
go any further, because Noel, lives, breathes and sleeps football.
If he isn't watching he is playing. He also has a whole social life
built around football. Barbara isn't prepared to commit herself to
someone whose love of football is stronger than his feelings for her.
Sadly for Barbara, she doesn't even like football, even though she
has tried to get involved just to be with Noel.*

With luck, Barbara will fall for someone else who has interests
in common with her. Noel may even find a girlfriend who is as
mad on the game as himself. This would be a better situation
for them both. Sadly, you can't always choose the people you
fall in love with; so it can take time to get over a relationship
that feels right in every other sense, except for the football, job,
drinking, or whatever the issue is.

Becoming so caught up with work that you have no time to focus on what really matters outside it is another area of concern. Some people don't have time to meet people or form relationships because of the job they do. This can be fine while you are excited and caught up in what you do, but it has a downside if weekends or evenings spread out in front of you with nothing to do and no one to see. People who live for their jobs often neglect relationships – with family and friends as well as potential partners. Again, finding a healthy balance between what you do and what you want is important. It is nice to have it all – money, lifestyle, interests, property – but it can come at a tremendous personal cost.

---

### Exercise

Ask yourself the following questions:

- What options for change do I have?
- How can I actively improve my quality of life?
- Is there anyone who could help me explore my options?

---

If your lifestyle is affecting your sex life, it makes good sense to give some thought to what you might do about it before you find yourself in a very difficult position (like Phil and Tricia). Take action and do something now, before your lifestyle does serious damage to your life and relationships.

# The Self-Help Program: First Stages

The two previous chapters have been about helping you to prepare for what is coming next. Whether you are working on your problem alone or with a partner, by now you will have looked at your motivation for change, explored and possibly worked on the negative thinking exercises, learned to relax, and assessed your stress levels and lifestyle. You are now in a good position to start actively working on overcoming your sexual problem.

The exercises in this chapter are designed to set the scene and create a comfortable climate in which to work on achieving the specific goals you have set. When sex goes wrong it often leads to long periods of sexual avoidance, so it may feel tempting to 'get on with it' and leave this section out. However, rushing straight on to the next chapters (dealing with specific dysfunctions) and avoiding this one is strictly not recommended. Overcoming sexual problems isn't just about getting to the goal. It is about enjoying the journey as well. The general rule is not to move to the next step until you feel completely at ease with the current one. Far better to take a little bit longer than to move on when you are not ready.

## Body Awareness

Why should we cultivate 'body awareness'? What does that mean? Sex is not only about intercourse, orgasms, and ejaculation.

It is about many other things, including how you feel about your appearance, your attitude towards sex, your experiences of sex to date, and how much you really know about sex. Family background also plays a part. Remember Paula, who was actively discouraged from touching her genitals as a child and was quite shocked to learn that people do? Her experience is not an uncommon one. Many people are uncomfortable with their genitalia, for a variety of reasons. The body awareness exercises given here are designed to help overcome that discomfort, whether it be the result of dissatisfaction with your appearance, or of some earlier trauma, or of negative ideas and beliefs about sex rooted in family attitudes and values. You may like to remind yourself of your answers to the questions posed in Chapter 1 under 'Psychological Factors'.

Body awareness is helpful to everyone, whether you are single or in a relationship. This section will help increase your awareness and confidence in your own body. Getting to know yourself better and feeling comfortable and confident is part of the way to having good sex or a successful sexual relationship. If you don't really understand how you tick or what turns you on, how can you expect someone else to know?

Separate instructions follow for men and women to take you through the exercise in easy steps.

## Body Awareness for Women

### Step I

Find a time when you can be on your own with no distractions. Switch off the phone. Make sure you will not be disturbed for about 30–45 minutes. Run a bath that is not too hot and use your favourite bubble bath or oil to relax in. Make sure the bathroom is comfortably warm. Place some soft towels within easy reach, step into the bath, and relax. Recreate the scene from your relaxation sessions to help you settle down. Remember to breathe in a very relaxed way, allowing all bodily tension to slip away.

When you feel completely relaxed, switch your focus to your body. How does it feel in the water? What sensations are you aware of? Get a sense of your skin and other parts of your body – your arms, hands, legs, feet, bottom, back, and tummy: move them gently in the water. Be aware of your breasts and nipples and your genital area. Think positively about what you are experiencing and feeling in the bath. When you are ready, remove the plug and allow the water to drain away, taking all your stresses and strains with it and leaving you with all the good feelings you have been focusing on.

Wrap yourself in a large, warm towel and concentrate for a moment on how you usually dry yourself. Do you rush, using rapid motions to get yourself dry as quickly as possible? This time, remove the towel slowly and focus on different parts of your body. Dry your arms first. Try rubbing slowly and gently, then apply a bit more pressure or just pat yourself dry. How does this feel? Try the same movements on your chest, shoulders, legs, and tummy. Run the towel across your back, again applying different techniques such as rubbing slowly, pulling it tight, or letting it fall to your buttocks. Concentrate next on your feet, and dry your toes carefully. Then dry your hands and fingers. Put a robe on and reflect on your experience. What have you learned about yourself? How did it feel?

*Note:* If you do not have a bath or cannot use one for some reason, for example a disability, then have a shower instead, following the same sequence.

## Step II

If you felt comfortable with step I, continue with step II. Otherwise, repeat step I on one or more occasions until you are completely at ease before moving on to step II.

Step II is all about touching and becoming more familiar with your body. Before starting, repeat step I – have a bath or shower and dry yourself. Then, using your favourite oil, lotion, talc, or cream, begin to apply it in the following way. Starting with your face and neck, gently work the cream into your skin, taking care around the eyes. How does that feel? What part of your face or neck do you like being touched? Run your hands through your hair and feel the shape of your head and the back of your neck. Use different strokes to see what you like best.

Move on next to your shoulders and arms. Apply the oil or lotion in as many ways as you can: gently, firmly, slowly. Rub down the arm from the shoulder to your hands, rub your hands together, apply cream to each finger, look at the nails. Take note of what feels best.

Do the same with your chest, breasts and tummy. Take your time. Enjoy the sensation of your own touch. Move down to your thighs, legs and feet. Feet can be very pleasurable to touch. If you are ticklish, apply a firm grip to help accustom yourself to touching them. Massage some cream or lotion into your toes. How does it feel? Apply some to your buttocks and rub it in. Again, think about what feels good. Try as many different ways of touching yourself as you can. What do you like best, fast or slow movement, kneading or squeezing? It may be difficult to do much with your back. Try applying some cream/lotion to the back of your hand and rub as far as you can go.

When you have finished applying cream, lotion, oil, or talc all over your body, focus next on particular parts. Touch your breasts: how do they feel? Heavy, soft? Pay attention to the different parts. Note how warm your skin feels underneath your breasts, between your legs, under your arms, and between your buttocks. Run your fingers through your pubic hair. How does it feel? Be aware of your shape and size. Which bits do you like touching most?

You may feel a bit odd or strange the first time you do the touching exercise, but with practice it will become easier and more familiar. Repeat the exercise until you are comfortable. Always take it slowly and think about what you are learning about how your body likes to be touched. When you feel ready, spend a little more time on your breasts. Massage them gently and see if you can note any changes in your breasts or nipples. Do they feel a little firmer? Have your nipples become erect? These changes are a normal response to touch. Next explore your genital area: what does it feel like? Note the shape, texture, and temperature.

When you have finished step II, lie down for a little while and relax. Think about what you have just done. Go over each step in turn. How did you feel when touching your body, especially your breasts and genitals? Try to think about what new information you have gained.

As before, do not move on to step III until you are completely comfortable with the first two steps.

## *Step III*

You will be aware of feelings you have about how you look. Some things you may like, others you may dislike. These feelings can affect how you feel sexually. This step is designed to help overcome any negative thoughts and feelings you may have about your body.

For step III you will need a full-length mirror, or, failing that, one in which you can at least see most of you. Repeat step I to relax. After your bath apply some cream, oil or lotion, but this time as you touch yourself look at yourself in the mirror. Pay attention to the part you are rubbing or touching. What do you like about this part of your body? Work down your body as you did in step II, watching yourself as you go. When you have finished, stand in front of the mirror and focus on what you see.

Start at the top and focus on your hair, your face, your eyes, your nose and your skin. What is good about each part of what you see? Next, focus on your shoulders, arms, hands, fingers, breasts, stomach, hips and pubic hair. Take each in turn and think about shape and size. What do you like about these different parts of your body? Finally, look at your legs, feet and toes, and apply the same question.

You may need a hand mirror to look at your back and your bottom. Again, focus on what is good.

After you have finished lie down and relax. Ask yourself what this experience was like for you. Go over again in your mind what you have seen and how you experienced the exercise.

144

Repeat the exercise at least twice more. With practice it will become much easier.

## Step IV: Genital Touching

You can do this exercise on its own, but initially you will probably feel more relaxed if you repeat steps I and II first. You will need a small mirror for this exercise, preferably one that can stand up on its own. Lie on the bed and relax. Breathe in to a count of 5 seconds, hold your breath for 5 seconds and breathe out to a count of 10 seconds. Repeat this until you feel completely relaxed.

Lean against the headboard and use extra pillows if you need more support. Open your legs and place the mirror where you can comfortably see your genital area. Those of you unfamiliar with how you look may only get this far. If you feel unable to continue, stop now and try again another day. Don't worry: the more you look at your genital area the less strange this will seem. Think about a time when you were unhappy with a particular haircut or style. Didn't it take only a couple of days for it to seem quite established and normal?

Check out first your pubic hair. What colour is it? Is it straight or curly, long or short, where does it start and finish? Some women complain that they have too much pubic hair. Others lament that it is getting thinner and greyer. Run your fingers through and see what you feel about yours.

Next look at your vaginal lips (labia). These comprise inner and outer lips. The outer lips vary in shape and size, as do the inner lips. Mostly, the inner lips are smaller, but not in everyone. Sometimes the lips are larger on one side than the other, or the inner lips hang down between the outer lips. Hold the outer lips and gently part them to reveal the inner lips more clearly. Note the colour and texture.

The inner lips usually meet at the top of the clitoral hood, but not always. Look for your clitoral shaft and above it you will see the clitoral hood and the clitoris itself. The clitoral hood is a fold of skin that protects the clitoris. Hold this back to reveal the clitoris itself. The clitoris is highly sensitive to touch. Although the vagina and indeed the whole body is involved in sexual stimulation, it is the clitoris that holds the key to sexual feelings in women.

Now move down to the vagina itself. If you look carefully you will spot the urethra at the top. This is the small opening through which urine passes. Below this, note the size and shape of the vaginal opening, its colour and texture. Moving still further back you will find the anus (back passage). The area between the vagina and the anus is called the perineum.

Feel each part carefully. Which parts are most sensitive to your touch? You may find yourself becoming aroused (turned on). If so, you may notice your labia becoming larger and changing colour. Your clitoris will become hard and erect and disappear under the clitoral hood. Feel the inside of your vagina and how it has become moist.

Stop now and relax. Allow yourself to become aware of any feelings you might have about doing this exercise. Go back over the experience. What did you feel when looking at your genitals? What did you like or dislike? Have you discovered anything you were not previously aware of? If so, what did you learn?

Many women, like Paula in our previous example, are unfamiliar with what they look like 'down there'. In such cases it is hardly surprising if you feel uncomfortable with or embarrassed by what you see for the first time. The more familiar you become with this part of your body, the better you will feel. Do not worry if you felt unable to carry the exercise through to the end. It can take a few sessions to feel comfortable with what you are doing. Repeat the exercise and go as far as you can. Try to go a little bit further each time until you have completed every step.

Positive thinking and regular repetition of the exercises will soon enable you to move on to the more specific exercises for your sexual problem. If you are in a relationship you should be able to share your new knowledge with your partner and move onto the sensate focus section.

## Body Awareness for Me

The steps set out below are designed to hel̶
ease with your body, to understand better ho̶
identify new knowledge about how you lik̶
Allow yourself between 30 and 45 minutes for ̶̶̶̶̶̶̶̶̶̶̶̶̶̶̶̶̶̶̶̶ ̶̶̶̶̶̶̶̶
a time when you are on your own and sure of not being disturbed. Switch off the phone. You may like to do some deep breathing and relaxation before you start to clear your mind and help you concentrate.

### *Step I*

To start with, run a bath or shower. This exercise is not only about washing, but about increasing your awareness of yourself in relation to your body. If you have a bath, try adding something to the water – some oil or relaxing cream bath. It isn't just women who like to feel pampered! If you've chosen to have a bath, step into the water, lie down, and relax. Empty your mind for a few minutes before you allow yourself to become aware of how you are feeling. Are you comfortable? Focus on different parts of your body and how they feel in the water. Allow your hands to run through the water: feel its warmth. Feel the effect of the water on your arms, legs, back, shoulders and bottom. How do your penis and scrotum feel? Note any pleasurable sensations you are aware of.

If you prefer to shower, allow the water to run warm first before stepping in. Once you're under the shower, move round so you are completely wet, then slowly allow each part of your body to connect with the rush of water. Take each part in turn: your head, your shoulders, chest, back, buttocks, arms, legs. Notice how each part feels when the water hits. Use your hands or a sponge to soap yourself all over. Be aware of how your body responds to the different textures of the sponge and hands. Use different strokes, rubbing, rotating: what feels really good?

When you have finished, dry yourself carefully with a warm towel. To discover what your skin prefers, try different ways of

ℒ yourself – rubbing, patting, faster, slower – or just wrap
· towel around you completely to soak up the moisture on
your skin. What did you learn? What did you like? Take some
time to relax and think about this experience.

## Step II

Repeat step I before you begin on step II. This exercise is all
about touch: how you like to be touched and how it feels. After
your bath or shower, use some oil or other product to massage
your skin. Begin with your shoulders, arms, and hands. Rub the
oil over your shoulders, using whatever stroke or pressure feels
good to you. Move down your arms, rubbing and stroking until
you reach your hands. Oil the tops of your hands and fingers
and rub your hands together. What feels best? Firm strokes or
more leisurely, gentle strokes?

Next, rub oil into your chest, exploring your nipples and
breast area. Note any changes. Do the nipples feel soft or hard?
If you have a lot of chest hair you may find talc easier to use
than oil. Experiment to see what feels best. Move down to your
stomach. Continue to rub and stroke, and try different ways to
massage yourself.

Run your hands over your pubic hair. Feel its texture, thick-
ness: is it soft or wiry? Feel your penis, feel its weight in your
hand, note its colour and size. If you start to feel aroused, that's
fine, just continue. If you feel uncomfortable, explore the
feeling. What is happening? Men are used to holding their
penises to go to the bathroom or to wash, but touching yourself
in this way may feel somewhat strange. That's OK: this is your
body and you are free to touch it any way you like.

Note the skin of the scrotum, how its texture is different from
your penis. The top of the penis is smooth and soft, as is the
foreskin. Feel the difference by going back to your scrotum.
Feel the testicles gently, how they move under your touch.
The exercise is not about becoming aroused or erect, but if you
do, notice how the penis lengthens and becomes heavier to
hold. Use a small mirror to see your perineum, the area between

your anus and scrotum. This area can be extremely sensitive to touch.

Move on to your buttocks and do your best to touch some of your back. Feel the skin and note any differences in texture. Explore the rest of your body, hips, thighs, legs, and finally your feet and toes.

Take some time after this touching exercise to relax and think about what you have just done and how it felt. What did you notice during the exercise? Certain parts of the body change in temperature in response to touch. Were you aware of this? What did you learn that was new? Repeat this exercise several times until you feel comfortable and confident with touching yourself in this way.

## Step III

By now you will be feeling familiar with the exercises and the new things you have learned about your body and how you like to be touched. Step III is about observation. You may be aware of feelings you have about how you look. Some things you may like, others you may not like as much. These feelings can affect how you feel sexually. The next step is designed to help overcome any negative thoughts and feelings you may have about your body.

For step III you will need a full-length mirror, or, failing that, one in which you can at least see most of you. Repeat step I by way of preparation and relaxation. After your bath/shower, stand in front of the mirror with some oil or massage lotion (whatever you like) and watch yourself as you rub your skin with the cream, oil, or lotion. Begin with your shoulders and work down, as in step II. What are you aware of? What do you like about what you see? When you have finished, stand in front of the mirror and look at yourself. Starting from the top, look at your head and face. What are your best features, your hair, eyes, nose, mouth? Look at the shape of your face, your head, ears. What about your skin. Is it smooth, dark, or light? What features do you like best?

Next look at your shoulders, chest, stomach, arms, hands and fingers. Note each part in turn. What is good about them, the shapes, size, skin colour and/or texture? Is your chest smooth and hairless, or hairy? What about your muscles? Tense your arms to see how firm they are. Move down to your pubic hair, penis and scrotum. What do you like about what you see? Carry on your observations by looking at your legs and feet. Move in front of the mirror so you can see more. Turn round to see your back and buttocks, or use a small hand mirror to help you see better.

When you have finished, sit or lie down and think about the exercise. What did you discover for yourself? What was new? Focus on all the good points. Repeat this exercise several times until you feel completely comfortable and accepting of yourself. This is you, warts and all – and it's fine.

## Step IV: Genital Touching

You can do step IV on its own, but you may feel more comfortable if you have a bath or shower and relax first. Most men are very familiar with their penises and will have masturbated from a young age. However, masturbation is almost exclusively geared towards getting an erection and ejaculating. This exercise is designed to help you experience the whole of your body as sexually responsive.

Lie down on the bed, or somewhere else quiet and comfortable. The exercise requires you to think not only about *how* you are touching yourself, using your hands (fingers and palms), but also to think about the *part* that you are touching. Use all the knowledge gained from the previous steps about what feels good.

You may like to close your eyes to really focus as you begin to explore your body: shoulders, chest, stomach, arms and hands. Be aware of different sensations and feelings as you use different forms of touch, including light stroking, heavier kneading or squeezing, and rubbing.

Next, move down to your genital area. Touch the area around your lower abdomen and inner thighs. Be aware of temperature, texture and colour. Hold your penis in your hands. Note the colour and shape. If you are uncircumcised, gently ease the foreskin back to reveal the glans (top of the penis). Note its smoothness and sensitivity. Run your hands over the scrotum. Gently feel each testicle. Note its size and shape. Then move down to feel the perineum, the skin between the scrotum and the anus. Switch your focus back to your penis and vary your touch. Which parts are most sensitive? You may like to touch other parts of your body at the same time. If you become aroused, use the opportunity to note the changes between your flaccid state and your aroused state. The skin of the scrotum will become tougher and more leathery-looking. The testicles will rise up into the scrotal sac. The penis will lengthen and thicken. Note that the veins may become more obvious and the penis will darken, although you may not notice this unless you are light-skinned. Think about the kinds of touch that produced your erection, and what you do to keep your penis erect.

If you feel uncomfortable at any stage, simply stop and return to the exercise another day. Repeat the whole exercise again until you can complete it comfortably. Ask yourself how you felt about touching yourself generally. What did you feel when touching your genitals? What did you learn that was new? Armed with your new knowledge about yourself, you are now ready to proceed to the next stage. If you are in a relationship, share your experience with your partner and move on to sensate focus.

## Masturbation

It's worth pausing here to give some consideration to the topic of masturbation, because when you completed the body awareness exercises you may have found that you quite naturally moved on to ejaculation or orgasm at the end of step IV. Others may have experienced different feelings and not felt comfortable with stimulating to orgasm.

Masturbation is not something that is openly discussed. When it is, it is often spoken of in a derogatory sense. 'What a wanker!'

(especially in the UK) is now a fairly common expletive used to deride someone or put them down – not a nice term at all.

There are lots of myths about masturbation. Some religious groups told children they would go blind or become mentally ill if they masturbated: a very frightening thought. One girl I spoke to at a youth group said girls couldn't masturbate because they didn't have penises! Women who indulged in this activity were considered immature and were supposed to give up the practice once involved in 'adult' sexual behavior, i.e. intercourse. It is perhaps not surprising that some of these ideas have infiltrated the social psyche and had some influence on sexual behavior. Paula's mother gave her a very clear message that she should not touch her genitals. Parents actively encourage children to learn about themselves, to feed themselves, to move from crawling to walking: yet children are encouraged *not* to touch their genitals – especially girls, perhaps because boys need to hold their penises to urinate. However, this activity apart, the same message applies to boys. Possibly because of the dual role of the genitals (for sex and waste disposal), it has been historically regarded as 'dirty' to touch 'down there'. Yet if you are clean you are in no more – indeed, perhaps less – danger of infection from your genitals than you are from your mouth, nose, or hands. At any rate, far from stopping masturbation, these messages only serve to send the behavior underground, with the inevitable result of associating it with guilt, anxiety, and shame. Obviously, it wouldn't be appropriate for us all to start masturbating in public! But private experimentation shouldn't be discouraged.

What counts here, however, is what *you* feel about masturbation. If you regard the practice as a normal, healthy outlet for sexual feelings, then that is fine. But if you find it difficult or it makes you anxious, then it may be time to think about where those feelings come from. Have you genuinely decided that it's not for you, or are you influenced by other messages? If so, where do those messages come from? The important thing is that you make up your own mind about what is right for you. For some the practice can be a lonely experience, while for others is can be completely satisfying. If you have

difficulty achieving orgasm, help is provided i|
Chapter 9.

There are many positive aspects to mast|
be very pleasurable and you don't have to rel|
to release sexual tension. Also, you can please yourself and
not have to worry about pleasing someone else. No one will
ever be able to do it as well as you: you are your own expert.
Also, most men and women experience much more intense
feelings through masturbation than through intercourse. This
is not to say that intercourse isn't as good; it's just different.

Masturbation can also be an activity to be enjoyed when
intercourse requires too much energy or one of you is not in the
mood. Having said that, if you are in a relationship, masturbation should not be a constant substitute for intercourse, or used
to avoid problems in the relationship. If this is the case, you
need to look at what is going wrong and work on resolving the
issues involved.

## Pelvic Floor Exercises

These exercises have long been recommended for women
after childbirth who need to strengthen muscle tone and
tackle any bladder problems that have occurred after delivery. However, they are now also used more widely, as it is
recognized that the effects are beneficial in many more
ways. Women report greater pleasure and sexual responsive-
ness after doing the exercises, which strengthen the pelvic
floor muscles and increase blood flow to the genitals – vital
in the process of arousal. Also, these exercises have proved
especially useful to women who lack sensation in this area,
or who have experienced difficulty with tampons or sexual
penetration. Men who have done the exercises have reported
better ejaculatory control, and better and stronger erections. The exercises strengthen the muscles surrounding the
penis and increase blood flow. As blood flow into the penis
is essential for erection to occur, this is indeed a valuable
discovery.

## Pelvic Floor Exercises for Women

You will only need a few minutes twice a day for the exercise. Choose a time you will remember, such as when you clean your teeth. First, you need to identify the right muscles. The easiest way is to stop the flow of urine next time you go to the toilet. Try a few times to make sure you know exactly which muscle it is you are going to exercise (but don't make a habit of stopping your urine as this can cause problems). Lie down. If you feel able to put your finger gently inside the entrance to your vagina and tense the muscle, then do so. Don't worry if you can't feel anything at this stage. It may be that your muscles are not strong enough yet. If you can feel the contraction, this is the muscle you are working on. If you feel unable to put a finger in at the moment, just follow the instructions as set out below.

There are four stages to the exercise:

1  Tighten the muscle and let go.
2  Repeat (1) between 10 and 15 times.
3  Tighten the muscle and hold for 3 seconds, then let go.
4  Repeat (3) between 10 and 15 times.

Practice stages 1 and 2, the first exercise of tightening and letting go, until you can do 15 twice a day. Build up slowly: as with all exercise, overdoing it can lead to soreness. Be careful that you are not tightening your stomach or thigh muscles, because these are not the muscles you are working on. Once you are comfortable with this, move on to stages 3 and 4, tightening and holding the muscle for 3 seconds before letting go. When you can do 10–15 repetitions twice a day, begin to work on increasing the number of repetitions – up to 40 or 50, more if you can.

Once you have established a good routine you can do a combination of these exercises whenever you think of them – waiting for a bus, watching television, preparing a meal, whenever you have few minutes to spare. The benefits will begin to show after a month or two. Try the finger test again if you are able. You should now be able to notice a considerable difference. Starting pelvic floor exercises at the beginning of your program of self-help means you will be ready to put them to good use when you start the more specific exercises designed for your particular sexual problem.

## *Pelvic Floor Exercises for Men*

This exercise has been found to be as good for men as for women. To identify the correct muscle, you can either contract your buttocks or stop the flow of urine mid-stream. The muscles used to stop the flow of urine are the ones you will be working on.

The exercise has four stages:

1 Tighten the muscle and let go.
2 Repeat (1) between 10 and 15 times.
3 Tighten the muscle and hold for three seconds, then let go.
4 Repeat (3) between 10 and 15 times.

Take care that you are not squeezing your stomach or thigh muscles at the same time. Build up the repetitions gradually to prevent the muscle becoming sore. With practice it will become easier. Do stages 1 and 2 twice a day until you are comfortable, and then move on to stages 3 and 4. When you have established a routine and you can comfortably do 15 of each exercise twice a day, begin to increase the number of repetitions of each to around 40–50, or more. Also, do the exercise more frequently, whenever you can: while driving, during a work break, or waiting for an appointment. As the exercises can't be seen, you can do them anywhere.

These exercises take a couple of months to show results. Therefore, starting them at the beginning of your self-help program will mean that you will be ready to put them to practical use during the more specific exercises set out for your particular sexual problem.

## Sensate Focus

This exercise is designed for couples. While you are working through the exercise, you need to agree with each other not to have sex, or to masturbate, outside these sessions (although it is ok to be affectionate). This may seem harsh for some of you, but if your sexual relationship is no longer working or you are not enjoying sex for some reason, you will need to put your previous sexual behavior behind you. Sensate focus is about learning new ways to be intimate together. This restriction on sexual activity outside the exercise can also reduce anxiety if it is some time since you had sex and you do not know how to start again. It is valuable, too, for many people later in life. Many older couples enjoy the closeness and tenderness that can be shared through this exercise at a time when energy levels, illness, or disability inhibit full sexual activity.

One couple told me that if they did nothing else sexually together they would still do sensate focus as they found it so relaxing and intimate. It also gave them a closeness that they didn't always feel when they had quick, routine sex. Sensate focus is part of the whole ethos of relaxing, making time for yourself, and taking pleasure when so much else in your life may be very difficult.

How does it work? The whole exercise is planned to take five weeks, though it may take longer if you need to allow more time for particular stages. In the first week, you need to plan and find time for three sessions. Each session will take approximately one and a half to two hours, including preparation time.

### Preparation

Have a simple light meal (or a takeaway if you don't want to be bothered with the washing-up). Turn off the telephone. Decide where you are going to do the exercise and prepare the room. Time of year can often help you decide. If it is cold and wintry you may decide to bring a duvet downstairs and lie in front of the

156

fire. Alternatively, the bedroom may be warmer with the heating turned up. In summer you may choose to open the windows to let in some air to cool you down. Those of you with a private garden or balcony may like to do the exercise outside. Choosing the right place will add to your comfort and relaxation.

Taking it in turns to prepare the room will help you both feel involved. It also allows you to introduce subtle changes. If it is a daytime session, you may like to close the curtains to create a cosy, intimate space, especially if it is a dull day. If it is evening and dark, you may choose to do something more romantic, for instance, light some candles (ensuring that they are safe!) or burn some scented oil. Use your imagination – what would you like? While one of you prepares the room the other should go and have a bath or shower. Baths are more relaxing, but not everybody likes them. Whichever you choose, try to use this time not only to get clean but to relax and anticipate the time ahead . . . time which you will spend with your partner enjoying each other without external pressures. The person who prepared the room now has their bath, and again uses the time to relax and think positive thoughts about your time together. Try to avoid using any skin lotions or creams after your bath/shower unless you feel it necessary. If you have bathed first, while waiting for your partner to have their bath or shower you can run through the relaxation exercise provided in Chapter 7. This will help you to stay focused. You don't want to start thinking about work or everything you have to do the next day. Relaxation will help to keep distracting thoughts, feelings, and emotions away.

## Week One

Decide who is going to be the 'active partner' first. As with preparing the room, take it in turns. This helps create a feeling of sharing and equality. When you are both ready, take off your towels or dressing gowns. If you are the passive partner this time around, lie tummy down on the bed or on a comfortable rug/duvet on the floor. Make yourself as comfortable and relaxed as possible. Stay focused on what the active partner is doing and remain still. This exercise is to be done in silence. Do not comment unless something your partner is doing is uncomfortable or painful in any way. Not only will remaining quiet help you both to concentrate, it will help contain any possible feelings of embarrassment or anxiety. Now you are ready to start.

If you are the active partner, imagine yourself on a journey – but not the type of journey where you can't wait to reach the other end. This journey is going via the scenic route. It will take at least half an hour. You are going to take pleasure from touching your partner's body during this exercise. In this respect, sensate focus is slightly different from the normal type of massage, which is given for the benefit of the person receiving it. Sensate focus uses a lighter touch and provides as much pleasure for the person who is giving the massage as the one receiving it.

Use your five senses (the three 's's – sight, sound and smell – and the two 't's: taste and touch), your hands, and any other parts of your body you like. Start by touching the top of your partner's head. Feel the shape and size, smell the head and hair, run your fingers through the hair, use soft massage strokes all around the head and neck. Move down to the shoulders, kneading, squeezing, using whatever strokes you like. Massage the back, run your fingers down the spine, kiss, taste, pummel the skin, for women use your hair if it's long enough, or your breasts: whatever feels good. You may like to leave the arms and hands until your partner turns over. Next move over the buttocks, again using whatever feels good. Work down the tops of the legs over the calves and down towards the feet. If your partner is ticklish, use firm hand movements and avoid the soft, fluttery ones. Feel the toes and do whatever you like with them. All of this should take about 15 minutes. Then give your partner's big toe a gentle tweak to indicate that he/she should turn over.

With your partner now lying on his or her back, start again from the top, exploring the face, the nose, the lips; circle the eyes, kissing, licking, tasting, and touching. Move on to the chest, but avoid breasts and nipples as these are off limits for now. Massage the chest and tummy, be creative in your touch, doesn't that feel good? Massage the arms and hands. Note the different textures of skin: the inner arm is often soft, while the elbow can be much firmer. Explore each finger, the shape and size, lick, bite gently, suck, feel the palms and the difference from the top of the hand. Do not touch the vaginal area or the penis. Go around the penis, whatever it is doing, whether it is erect, partly erect or flaccid. Do not part the legs or touch the vulval area. Massage the tops of the legs, work down over the knees and shins to the top of the feet. This should take about another 15 minutes, so that the whole session has lasted roughly half an hour. This exercise is about *you* taking pleasure from your partner; doing what pleases *you*. At this stage you do not need to worry about what your partner wants, and neither do they need to be thinking about what you want.

When you have finished, swap places and let your partner begin their journey down your body while you relax and think about your own experience. When your partner has followed the same sequence of instructions, put on your robes/towel. Cuddle up and talk about the experience and your feelings together.

---

### Sensate Focus: Questions to Ask Each Other

- What felt good?
- What did you enjoy?
- Were there any difficult parts?
- What have you learned for yourself?
- Which role felt more comfortable?
- Did you feel any pressure in either role?
- Did you feel anxious at all? If so, did the anxiety lessen or increase as the exercise progressed?

---

It is important to be honest with your partner and yourself as this will help build up the good communication needed to improve your sex life. Some people like to start a diary at this stage, in which each of you records how the session went for you. This does not need to be done straight after you have finished; it can be written up afterwards at a time convenient to you. It helps you to build up a record of what you have done and how it felt, including your successes and the things that felt less helpful. If you do this regularly you will have created your own sex therapy guide. You can use this if ever a problem arises again, or if for some reason sex stops for a while.

For some of you this exercise will feel very straightforward and pose no particular problems. For others it may evoke some anxiety. This will depend on your sexual history and background. For instance, some of you may have felt uncomfortable taking all your clothes off, especially if you haven't appeared naked in front of each other for a while, have put on weight, or have had an operation that has left a scar. In these circumstances don't be put off, just adapt. You can wear some underwear at first, or use a towel. As the sexual areas are temporarily no-go areas, it does no harm to cover them up at this stage. The important thing is that you feel comfortable. The underwear or towel can be removed as you start to feel more confident. You can repeat the body awareness exercises described earlier in this chapter to help you overcome any negative feelings you may have about your body.

The exercise will need repeating twice more so that you have completed three sessions in the first week. Try to allow a day in between sessions: this is much better than doing them one day after another. Also be flexible. Provided you do three exercises before moving on, it doesn't matter if it takes a week and a half. And if you still don't feel quite comfortable after three sessions, it's fine to do another one or two before moving on to the next stage. The important thing is to plan in advance when you are going to do the exercises. If you don't stick to this plan there is a possibility that the program will run into the sand as other things get in the way.

## Week Two

In week two you repeat *all* of the above, with some added extras. You can also give feedback during the session this week, but keep talk to a minimum. This is the week I call 'fun week'. As well as using your five senses and various parts of your body, you can use whatever else you like during the massage. This may include lotions, talc, creams, aromatherapy massage oils, food or drink: whatever you fancy. Think about smell. What smells do you like? What feels good? What looks good? It is important that when you are the active partner you use the products you like rather than what your partner likes. OK, so she might not like smelling of beer, but *you* might think it tastes good and enjoy licking it off. Equally, he might not like smelling of roses, but so what? It is your choice. Besides, you can always wash again afterwards. The point here is to have some fun and be imaginative. Use feathers, silky material, chocolate. A word of caution, though: if you have a skin complaint or any allergies make sure you use what is safe. One couple had to use a water-based cream as the guy had psoriasis (a skin complaint). Also, be careful what you use on your face and especially round the eyes. The sexual areas are still off limits during this exercise.

Again, attempt to complete three sessions over the week, taking care to talk over and record your findings after each one; and again, if you need to, take time for one or two additional sessions so that you are completely comfortable before moving on.

## Week Three

The following week, repeat again everything you have already done, but now include the breasts and genitals. Do not pay any particular attention to the sexual areas, but as you make your journey over your partner's body give them as much attention as you would any other part of the body. The focus is on building trust and confidence. By now you are familiar and comfortable with touching each other and giving and receiving pleasure. Build on this during the three sessions you do this week. Talk about each session afterwards in the same way. If you still feel uncomfortable in any way, do not move on to the next stage yet; instead, go back to where you did feel comfortable and work your way through the instructions again.

## *Week Four*

Week four is about learning what each of you likes. Having completed the massage as before, focus on the sexual areas. Take a look at your partner's penis/vagina. Note the colour and texture of the skin, feel the warmth, feel her breasts and his nipples, note the size and colour. Do no more than look and gently touch. Should you start to feel any anxiety, stop and talk to each other about what is making you feel uncomfortable. As with any of the stages described above, it is really important not to move on to the next stage until you feel OK. Once the exercise is complete, discuss together how it felt in the usual way.

## *Week Five*

Week five is about giving and receiving pleasure for mutual enjoyment. Repeat all of the above, but now tell each other what feels good as it happens.

A word about kissing: couples often lose the art of good kissing once a relationship is established. Kissing is vitally important as a way of 'oiling the works' or getting things going. Practice kissing standing up, or develop your technique during sensate focus. Always discuss what works for you and enjoy.

By the time you have followed this sequence through to the end of week five – and of course, this may have taken longer than five weeks if you have returned to earlier stages to make sure you are comfortable before progressing – you are now ready to move on to the training program designed to overcome your particular sexual problem. The exercises to do this are set out for you in the next two chapters.

First, though, some thoughts about fantasy.

## Fantasy

What is a fantasy? Is it a thought or a daydream, a wild imagining or a wish? It can be all of these. Essentially, a fantasy is a mental image, a way of using your imagination to enhance or cope with part of your life. You may have a fantasy about winning the lottery, in which you imagine how you could spend all that money. Or you may dream of becoming famous one day: imagine all that adulation. Your fantasy may be unobtainable: 'I want to live for ever.' Or quite simply you may just fancy the girl next door and imagine what it would be like to go out with her. Everybody fantasizes to some extent. Anybody who has ever said 'I wish . . .' has the capacity to think about something they would like and imagine how it might be. Wishes, hopes, and dreams are translated into fantasies to help us cope with disappointment. We may know we will never win the lottery; but sometimes it doesn't hurt to dream. The important thing is to be able to separate fantasy from reality. Fantasies hurt no one as long as they remain just that – fantasies.

For those experiencing sexual problems, the use of fantasy or imagination can be a very useful tool in helping to overcome negative thinking and distancing yourself from unhelpful behavior. Remember Rachel and Nathan in Chapter 6? During treatment of Nathan's erectile dysfunction, he used fantasy to help take his mind off thoughts about not getting an erection.

For some, the use of fantasy can seem like a betrayal (remember Esther and Rubin in Chapter 2?). Disloyalty towards the other person is often given as a reason not to use fantasy within a relationship. However, while fantasy can include erotic imagery involving other people, it can also be about sharing and loving the person you are with. Fantasy can mean imagining anything from you and your partner in bed together in a romantic setting to an orgy! What is important is that you find an acceptable level for you, either on your own or with a partner.

You may think of questions to ask yourself at this point. These may be helpful in establishing whether you feel happy about fantasy or not. The fact is that sex is more about what happens between the ears than what happens between the legs. You can be pleasuring yourself or being pleasured by a partner, but it is what goes on in the mind that invariably takes you to that point of exquisite release into orgasm or ejaculation. Ask

---

**Questions to Ask Yourself**

Do I use fantasy often/sometimes/never?
If never, why might that be?
Am I happy with this situation?
Do my fantasies involve other people? Are these people
I know or are they strangers?
Are my fantasies sexually explicit or more romantic in
content?
Do I feel comfortable with my fantasies?
Can I share my fantasies with others or do I prefer to
keep them to myself?

---

anyone what is it that triggers orgasm/ejaculation and they will
more times than not say it was something they were thinking
about at the time, even if that thought was just 'Oh my good-
ness, this is so wonderful'. What is going on in your head can
be the difference between orgasm and no orgasm. Thinking
about tomorrow's shopping, picking the kids up, or a deadline
to be met at work doesn't usually result in orgasm, although
these may be helpful tools in delaying ejaculation for a man
suffering from PE!

Unfortunately, fantasies can be associated with very mixed
feelings. Many people experience guilt, embarrassment, and
shame at the thought of what turns them on. Again, it is important to stress that as long as a fantasy remains a fantasy, then it
can do no harm, either to you or to others. Also, it is up to you
where you go in your own mind. There are many books that can
help on this subject, a few of which are listed in Appendix 1.

In order to help you to feel more comfortable around fantasy,
you can explore ways to develop and increase your capacity to
fantasize. The subjects for fantasy can include anything that
you feel good about. You might want to remember a sexual
encounter that was particularly special or arousing; or a certain
place you went to that holds special meaning or significance,
maybe associated with more erotic images or scenes. Stick with

what feels OK to you. You may like to lie down, close your eyes, and do your relaxation techniques first. Remember the scene or story you created as part of your relaxation program before following the instructions below.

---

### Exercise: Fantasy

1 Establish a pattern of relaxed breathing.
2 Imagine a scene that you are familiar with: your home, maybe the bedroom, a place you went on holiday, a beach or somewhere else.
3 Now see yourself. What are you doing? what are you wearing?
4 Imagine yourself as part of the scene you thought of in step 2.
5 What are you doing in the scene? Are you alone or with someone else?
6 Take that thought a step further.
7 Build on the picture you have created for yourself.

---

This exercise can help you during self-pleasuring (masturbation) or when having sex with a partner. Some couples like to share fantasies or tell each other different ones while taking it in turns to stimulate each other. Find out for yourself what feels best for you. Some people do not like to share their fantasies. This might be because they don't work, or they don't have the desired effect when shared, or possibly because the content makes them feel uncomfortable. That's fine: just do what works for you.

Fantasy is part of the treatment program for the various sexual problems outlined in the next chapter. Becoming familiar and comfortable with fantasy will enhance the next stage of your journey towards overcoming your sexual problem.

# Specific Problems: Self-Help for Singles

These exercises are designed specifically for those of you not currently in a relationship, or who prefer to work on your sexual problem alone. The first section addresses male problems; the second section addresses female problems; and a final section deals with the loss of desire that can affect both men and women equally.

As suggested earlier, preparing the ground and making sure that you are in the best frame of mind will serve you well. If you have worked through Chapters 6 and 7 so that you are clear about the goal you want to achieve, relaxed, and sure of your motivation, you are already primed for success.

A general point before you start: make sure you have completed all the exercises set out in previous chapters that are *relevant* to you. Pelvic floor muscle exercises are especially important for those of you suffering from vaginismus, premature ejaculation, or erectile dysfunction. If you have already been doing these exercises for a while, you may well have noticed a strengthening and an increase in sensation in the genital area, especially if you have been practising them regularly. Instructions on how to incorporate these exercises into the following programs will be explained along the way.

# Male Problems

To make the most of the following treatment strategies it is important to recognize both the advantages and disadvantages of working on your own. On the plus side, you don't have to consider anyone else in terms of time (you arrange a convenient time and take as long as you need beyond the minimum time specified), energy (you can stop or postpone an exercise if you feel too tired), or manageability (you need only focus on what you can do). Nor do you have to consider anyone else's feelings, just your own. The possible downside is that you may lose confidence when you are with a partner and feel under pressure to perform with them, thereby forgetting all the good things you have learned on your own. In order to overcome these potential problems, some general help will be given at the end of this section on specific male problems.

## *Erectile Dysfunction*

One of the main issues here is that once you lose faith in your ability to achieve or keep an erection, it is easy to feel that you will never feel good about yourself again. Well, take heart: this program is all about helping you to regain your confidence, not only in your ability to achieve an erection but in your ability to keep it for as long as you need it. Also, the program will help you to believe that if your erection does go down (and erections usually do go down a little, as it is quite hard to maintain *high* levels of sexual arousal over a period of time), you can get it back again. For those of you who have become 'spectators', watching your own performance, emphasis will be placed on getting you back in touch with how you *feel*, rather than what you *expect* from yourself in a sexual situation. The body awareness exercise set out in Chapter 8 will have helped you feel more confident and better about yourself. This is the point where all the hard work you have put in earlier in the book starts to pay off.

The instructions below follow on from the body awareness exercise, so have a bath or shower and use the relaxation technique set out in Chapter 7 before you start. Make sure your bedroom or the room you are using is nice and warm, or airy if it's a hot day. Make sure you will not be disturbed. Switch off the phone and try to avoid visitors: don't answer the door. After your bath and general preparation, lie down on the bed or in a suitable place that is comfy. Close your eyes and touch your body in the ways that you have learned, and pay attention to your breathing. Keep it slow and deep, as during your relaxation sessions. You may have already experienced an erection during your body awareness sessions. If you have not, don't worry. You will soon find yourself responding as you apply what you have learned. Remember, sex happens between the ears as much as between the legs. Positive mental attitude is what is needed here. If you are in the older age bracket try to remember that more tactile stimulation is needed alongside positive thoughts. Your penis needs a firm hand. Using your hand, start with stroking and generally feeling around your penis and scrotum. Explore between your legs and inner thighs. Remember what feels good.

## Stage 1

- As you begin to feel your erection grow, focus on what it feels like, the specific sensations. Use different strokes to stimulate yourself until you are sure you are fully erect.
- Then allow your erection to go away. Distract yourself in any way that works until you are soft and pliable again.
- Repeat as above twice more: achieve a good, firm erection and then let it go again.
- On the fourth time stimulate to a full erection and continue to ejaculation and release.

What did you learn about your erection?

If you experienced any difficulty with the exercise, think back to the start. Where did it seem not to work? Did you have trouble getting an erection at all? Think about what was going on inside your head. Did you *think* it wouldn't work? If so, were you half-hearted in your attempt? Did you feel anxious? Anxiety will seriously affect your ability to become erect. Once your body has gone into 'flight or fight' mode you will not be getting an erection. What has caused your anxiety? Answering these questions honestly will enable you to assess what happened and try again. If you were thinking negatively, try to reframe your thoughts. For example: 'OK, so it didn't work this time; I guess I am feeling a bit tired. Perhaps it wasn't the right time. I will try again tomorrow.'

If you managed an erection once or twice, and then lost it or ejaculated before the fourth time, again ask yourself what you learned from the experience. Try to identify what you were feeling when you lost the erection. If you have been practising pelvic floor muscle exercises, they will help you now by increasing blood flow into the penis while you stimulate yourself. What happened to make you ejaculate when you were not ready to? Did you just get carried away, or were you worried you might lose your erection before you had the chance to come? Were you distracted by negative thoughts? Think carefully about what happened.

Fantasy is a helpful way to stop yourself thinking negative thoughts. If you feel comfortable doing so, use a magazine or book to get you into the right frame of mind while doing the exercises. The important thing is not to get carried away and go for orgasm before you have achieved a strong enough erection. Armed with this information, go back and repeat the exercise above. Stimulate yourself to a good erection three times, letting it go in between. You can ejaculate on the fourth occasion. Erections are achieved in two stages, becoming stronger and firmer as arousal levels increase. Make sure you don't stop stimulating your penis too soon or you won't reach the higher arousal level and accompanying hard erection.

Repeat stage 1 three or four times (or more) until you are regularly getting an erection. As you gain in confidence, keep your erection for a little while before letting it go. By this means you take control of your erection, rather than it being in control of you.

## Stage 2

When you are satisfied with stage 1, move on to stage 2 (how many sessions you have at the first stage is up to you, as long as you have a minimum of three or four successful sessions before moving on). Ensure all the right conditions apply: room, temperature, bath/shower, and/or relaxation.

- Begin the exercise in the same way as before, only this time use a suitable lubricant. Rub your hands together with the lubricant and stimulate your penis to a full erection in the way you know how.
- Allow the erection to go away again. After a short break, use more lubricant to restimulate yourself another two times, letting the erection go in between.
- On the fourth occasion stimulate to full erection, and ejaculate.

This exercise will help you feel a little bit more like you would if inside a woman. Use your full hand to grasp your penis. Try to imagine what it would be like inside a woman. You may like to think of someone you already know or are seeing. You may like to fantasize about what turns you on. Either way, enjoy the feel of a wet, hard penis. Repeat this exercise as many times as you like but for a minimum of three to four sessions.

By now you will be feeling much more confident about your erection, and your ability to keep it and to enjoy your orgasm. This may be as far as you need to go. However, if your aim is to overcome your erectile problem in order to start looking for someone to share your newfound confidence with, then take a look at the section on page 197 and the exercise on 'Wants and Needs for Good Sex', which will help you stay in control.

### Premature Ejaculation

Premature ejaculation is a problem that many men experience during their sexual lives. The reasons for it are many, including faulty learning, difficult relationships, situational circumstances, and psychological issues, to name just a few.

The exercises described here are designed to overcome the problem by helping you to recognize your 'point of inevitability': that is, the physical moment after which you will have an orgasm no matter what you do or don't do. This involves becoming more aware of the sensations experienced prior to ejaculation. Together with the body awareness and pelvic floor exercises, and relaxation, the following exercises will help to lessen your anxiety and enable you to gain control, thereby increasing your confidence. These instructions are for you to carry out on your own. Should your circumstances change, in that you find a partner or decide to work with an existing partner, then you may decide to move on to the instructions for working in couples provided in Chapter 10.

Before you start on these exercises, make sure you have done the preparation work outlined in Chapters 7 and 8. The exercises follow on from body awareness, so you will need to have become familiar and comfortable with that process. Also, pelvic floor exercises are extremely beneficial when working with PE; if you have already been doing them for a few weeks you will probably be starting to feel the results by now. Taking time to relax will also help the exercises to flow better and reduce anxiety. If you feel anxious or tense at any time, just stop and think about those feelings and their origins, then try to relax to help towards overcoming them.

It is best not to masturbate or have sex while working on the program. You should aim for three sessions a week at each stage, depending on your health, age and usual sexual practice. It isn't helpful to do more than this, as more frequent sessions put you in danger of going into overload, where sex becomes the main focus of your life instead of being just a part of it. Try to space the sessions out and do other things in between. It may seem logical that the more you do the quicker the problem will be solved. However, this isn't about speed. It's about learning to slow down and enjoy the ride, rather than getting there in a heated rush.

Switch off the phone and take a bath or shower in the usual way. Find a comfy place to relax and be by yourself without being disturbed. The first part of the exercise is to help you to become aware of your genital sensations.

## Stage 1

- Lie or sit down and begin to stroke or touch your penis in the way you do usually.
- Enjoy your erection as it starts to grow. Use different types of touch until you feel really excited and turned on.
- As your pleasure increases, slow down a little and focus on what you are feeling in your genitals.
- Once you are in touch with what is happening at the base of your penis, increase your stimulation until you can feel your orgasm coming. Continue to ejaculation. It is important that you just let go and enjoy the experience.

What did you learn about your body during this exercise? You may feel that you came too quickly, but that is not the important issue here. Were you able to connect with your bodily sensations? You may need to repeat this exercise several times until you are familiar with what is happening inside you.

Once you feel confident that you recognize the sensations prior to ejaculation, move on to the next exercise. This time you are going to learn to take control of your bodily sensations. Repeat the preparations for the session as before, that is, take a bath or shower and relax.

## Stage 2

- Stimulate yourself with your hand, concentrating on what you are feeling inside.
- Continue stimulating until you feel yourself to be very close to orgasm, and then stop.

- Stop long enough for your excitement levels to drop slightly (probably a few seconds or a bit longer), but without allowing your erection to go down.
- When you feel ready, start stimulating yourself again until the arousal levels build up, and then stop again.
- Repeat this stopping and starting again (three times in all); then on the fourth time continue until you can let go and enjoy your orgasm.

What have you learned from this exercise? Were you able to complete the full three start/stops, or did you ejaculate after the first, second, or third time? If you did, don't worry. Think about what happened inside you when you came. This is how you will learn control. Did you fail to stop stimulating yourself on time? You will know for next time to stop a little earlier than you did this time. With practice you will get it right. Repeat the process three or four times so as to really get to grips with your feelings/sensations and when you need to stop to delay your orgasm.

It is hard to say how many sessions you will need in order to feel fully confident that you are in control. It will depend on how severe the problem is. Some of you may gain control after a few sessions, for others it will take longer. Don't let this put you off. You will gain control. You just need practice.

Once you feel you have mastered the first two stages, you can move on to the next stage, which is all about becoming used to staying aroused using a wet hand. This is a helpful exercise as the wet hand is more similar to the feel of being inside a women's vagina, and it is often this that triggers ejaculation. As before, prepare by taking a bath or shower and making sure you are relaxed.

## Stage 3

- Begin your self-stimulation. Once you feel aroused, put some lubricant on your hands, rub them together, and then stimulate your penis with your 'wet' hand.

- Do the stop/start exercise in the same way as in stage 2, applying more lubricant as you go.
- Repeat this three times, and on the fourth occasion allow yourself to let go and enjoy your orgasm.
- Another way to enjoy the sensation of a 'wet' hand is to do the exercise in the bath or shower, using soap or shower gel to stimulate your penis. Again, repeat three times, and let go and enjoy your orgasm on the fourth time.

What was this experience like? Were you able to complete the exercise successfully, or did you come on the first, second or third attempt? If you did come too soon, what made you lose your focus on your sensations? Repeat the whole exercise as many times as you need to in order to gain control under these conditions.

The next stage helps you move on to being able to continue stimulating yourself without stopping and without ejaculating. Again, prepare in the usual way, making sure you are completely relaxed and free of tension before you start.

## Stage 4

- Begin stimulating yourself in the usual way. Enjoy seeing your erection grow.
- Continue to a high level of arousal and then this time, instead of stopping completely, slow down. Continue slowly to stimulate yourself.
- Allow your arousal levels to increase again, and then slow the pace right down again.
- Repeat twice (three times in all) and ejaculate on the fourth occasion.
- Try the same exercise in the bath or shower as before, slowing down instead of stopping when you feel close to orgasm.

If you found that you were ejaculating after the first, second or third attempt, ask yourself what was different from before.

Did you lose concentration? With practice you will find that you are able to control your ejaculation without actually stopping.

The next and final stage will help you not only to stop ejaculating by slowing things down, but also to remain in a highly aroused state for as long as you want to remain there.

### Stage 5

By now you will be very aware of your sensations and able to keep in control of your ejaculation. To increase the length of time between getting turned on and coming, imagine the time between feeling no sexual sensations and ejaculating as a scale from 0 to 10. Nought is no sexual feeling, and 10 is ejaculation. Imagine the stop/start exercise (stage 2) in relation to the scale. When stimulating yourself you may be stopping at around 8 and dropping back to 3 or 4 before starting again. If you stop at 9 you may just be too late to hold on. If you stop at 4 or 5 you may be stopping too soon. The point is not just to be able to control ejaculation, but to enjoy what you are doing as well. By staying in a range from about 6 to 8 you will not only remain in control but be able to take maximum pleasure from the experience.

- Start your session in the usual way, but this time imagine the scale in your head as your excitement rises.
- Take your arousal up to about level 6 or 7, then slow things down until you are back at 5. Increase your stimulation until you are back at 7. Don't hold back, just go with the feelings and enjoy this level of pleasure and arousal.
- Continue in this way for a couple of minutes, then go on to enjoy your orgasm.
- With practice you will find that you can control your level of arousal just by increasing or decreasing the level of stimulation and the pressure you use. Aim to go only as far as 8; avoid 9, as this is too close to orgasm. Try to increase the time to five minutes of high arousal.

Most men are happy to remain at a level of between 5 and 7 during sexual intercourse, occasionally moving up to 8 for a short period before they increase stimulation to orgasm. There are not many men who can, or want to, remain as high as 9, as by then they will want to ejaculate.

This technique can be used when with a partner. Once you are inside the vagina, instead of stopping (which might be frustrating for your partner as well as you) just slow the pace down slightly. Your partner is likely to find this quite sensual. She may be unaware that you are practising a technique designed to help stop you coming too quickly. If you follow all the instructions above, and only move on to the next stage when you are completely confident you have mastered the stage before it, then you can regard your PE as a thing of the past.

A word of caution: it is always useful to go on practising stop/start from time to time even after you have conquered your PE. This is because certain situations can increase the likelihood of PE returning, for example a period of time without masturbation or sexual intercourse, or if you have been ill or unwell and not felt like sex for a time. It could also recur because of stress, either at home or at work. Whatever the reason, repeat the self-help exercises after any period of abstinence to avoid worry and frustration later on. You may also find it helpful to read the section on page 197 about what you want and need from sex.

## Male Orgasmic Dysfunction

Many of you reading this may well have experienced orgasmic dysfunction while with a partner. If you are still with a partner you may like to move on to self-help for couples (Chapter 10). However, if your problem relates to masturbation by yourself, or you are currently not in a relationship because of this problem, then these instructions are for you.

The program is aimed to help you identify pleasurable sensations by increasing physical stimulation and reducing fear and worry. This problem is often linked to 'spectating', that is, watching your own performance. As with erectile dysfunction, this sends the wrong messages through your central nervous system and so inhibits your natural responses. Anxiety is no friend of sexual pleasure. Guilt or shame connected with masturbation can also play a part in inhibiting your natural response mechanism. Whatever the reason for the problem, the fact that you are reading this indicates a desire to solve the problem. By following the instructions below you can start to have positive experiences that will culminate in saying goodbye to the problem.

You will first need to go through the body awareness program carefully, as this will help you overcome some of the negative feelings you may have about your body. Also practise the exercises on relaxation, strengthening the pelvic floor muscles, and fantasy if you haven't done so already. Once you have completed those exercises you will be ready to try the following.

Find a time when you can be relaxed on your own for about 30–45 minutes. Make sure the phone is switched off and that the room is warm and comfy. Take a bath or shower as described in the body awareness exercise. Lie down on the bed or your own chosen place and use the techniques described earlier in order to relax. Allow your imagination to take you to a nice place where you feel good about yourself. When you are fully relaxed, move on to the instructions given below.

## Stage 1

- Move your hands over your body in the way that you have learned to do before. Use different strokes, rubbing, kneading, squeezing. How much pressure do you like, firm or soft? Remember what feels good.
- Stroke around your penis, touching your inner thighs, lower abdomen, and perineum (the area between your legs). Think about what you are doing and how good it feels.
- Next stroke your penis, using different techniques as above. What feels good? Do you like firm, hard pressure or a gentle touch? Tease yourself to erection. Note how your penis feels and what it looks like.
- Continue to stimulate yourself using whatever strokes feel best. As your excitement rises, focus on these feelings in order to reach maximum arousal.

177

- If you feel your orgasm coming, do not hold back. Just let go and enjoy the sense of release and the pleasure you feel.

What did you learn about yourself during this exercise? Were you able to let go or did something get in the way? If you were able to reach a high level of arousal but not ejaculate, then think about what happened. Did negative thoughts play a part? Did you start to feel anxious or tense? Remember: sex is not just between the legs; it is very much between the ears too, and what goes on in your head can make all the difference between success and failure. Repeat the exercise again twice. Take your new understanding into the exercise and use it to help free you.

## Stage 2

- Repeat stage 1 to stimulation of your penis.
- Now, instead of focusing on your bodily sensations, use a fantasy to increase your physical pleasure. If you haven't used fantasy or have ambivalent feelings about using it, reread the section on fantasy in Chapter 8.
- Give yourself permission to enjoy what you are doing. The image or fantasy will help you to maximize your sexual feelings and help you let go and enjoy your orgasm.

Were you able to use fantasy to help you get rid of your inhibitions? How did it feel? Repeat the process described above twice more until you feel comfortable and confident about what you are doing. To add to your pleasure, use a lubricant on your hands as you stimulate yourself.

If you are finding it hard to fantasize and you have still not ejaculated, concentrate again on your bodily sensations and follow stage 3.

## Stage 3

- Repeat stage 1, only this time use an oil or lotion or similar product to create pleasurable sensations all over your body.

- Concentrate fully on what you are doing and how it feels.
- Use a suitable lubricant on your penis and touch yourself in the way you like best. Use your whole hand to stimulate your penis. Experience the sensations your 'wet' hand is giving you. Increase your stimulation when you feel ready. Tease your penis. Allow yourself to reach a high level of enjoyment and then slow down.
- Play around and enjoy yourself until you reach maximum arousal and then focus completely on your orgasm. Let it go, ejaculate, enjoy!

Repeat this exercise twice more to consolidate what you have learned about yourself.

Did that work better for you? Were you able to let go freely and without anxiety? Or do you still need to practise some more? Precisely how long it will take to overcome the problem will depend on a variety of factors, including how old you are, your usual level of sexual activity, and your attitude towards sex.

Further strategies that can help towards overcoming this problem include the negative thinking exercise (Chapter 6) and pelvic floor muscle exercises (Chapter 8). These will respectively increase your awareness of negative thought patterns and focus your attention on the sensations in your genital area. Practise the pelvic floor exercises during self-stimulation as described in the above stages. If you continue to practise regularly and use positive thinking, you will find that as your confidence grows your ability to ejaculate will come naturally and freely.

If you are hoping to use your new awareness to find a partner, it is important to recognize what your needs are so you are able to share those with him or her. This should help ensure that you get the best from your sexual activity.

## Identifying Wants and Needs from Sex

The following exercise is designed to help you identify what you want and need from sex. Men are often not as good as women at sharing feelings in this way. Also, there are lots of sexual myths around about what being 'a real man' is. One such myth is that men are always ready for sex. This is not always the case. Men need nurturing and caring about just as much as women. Foreplay is not just for women. Men, too, need time to get into the mood. Remember Sam in Chapter 1? He lost his erection because of the kind of sex he was having. He wasn't interested in many of the girls he took to bed and as a consequence lost his erection.

---

### Exercise: Wants and Needs for Good Sex

- Think of a time when you had a good sexual experience. What made it good? Identify the key factors and write them down.
- Now think of a time when sex was not so good. What happened? How did it make you feel? Identify the key factors and write them down.
- Compare these two lists. Can you see the difference between what made sex a good experience and what made it a not so good one?

---

You need to think about what you want from sex in order to make sure that you don't allow yourself to get into situations where you know you will fail. One-night stands can work against you if you are sensitive to losing your erection or coming too quickly, or if you have anxieties about whether you will be able to ejaculate at all. This type of situation can put you under great pressure to perform. If you need time to unwind from a busy day, or if work problems are getting you down, then relaxation techniques or just a sensual massage (see body awareness) can help get you relaxed and settled. Obviously, if you do have a partner it is important to consider her needs as well, but not at any cost to you. Finding a caring partner who will accept how you feel and not put you under pressure can make all the difference. Perhaps you can do the same for them when they don't feel well or in the mood for sex.

## Female Problems

To make the most of the following treatment strategies it is important to recognize both the advantages and disadvantages of working on your own. On the plus side, you don't have to consider anyone else in terms of time (you arrange a convenient time and take as long as you need beyond the minimum time specified), energy (you can stop or postpone an exercise if you feel too tired), or manageability (you need only focus on what you can do). Nor do you have to consider anyone else's feelings, just your own. The possible downside is that you may lose confidence when you are with a partner and feel under pressure to perform with them, thereby forgetting all the good things you have learned on your own. In order to overcome these potential problems, some general help will be given at the end of this section on specific female problems.

### *Vaginismus*

The program is designed to help you overcome the involuntary spasm of the muscles surrounding the vagina. You will need to work through the body awareness program first, and also to practise pelvic floor muscle exercises (both set out in Chapter 8). Relaxation is also highly recommended, although you may not need to follow the exercise in Chapter 7 if you are already familiar with a similar technique or regularly practising some other form of relaxation. However, if relaxation is new to you then try out the relaxation instructions a few times first. This will ensure you get the maximum benefit from the following exercise.

You will need about 30–45 minutes to yourself. Ensure you will not be disturbed or interrupted by the phone. Complete all the body awareness exercises until you are completely comfortable with looking at your own genitals. If you have started pelvic floor muscle exercises, you may have already noticed some changes in how the muscles in this area work. Decide where you are going to carry out the exercises. This may be your bedroom, or another room where you can lie down comfortably. Depending on the time of day, you might do various things to create a nice environment, for example using candles or calming music at night, or shutting the curtains or blinds if it's a sunny day. Make sure you have some comfy cushions or pillows to support you.

*Stage 1*

- Take a nice relaxing bath before you start, following body awareness step 1, and taking care to dry yourself in the way you like. Go through to the room of your choice and lie down.
- Begin by relaxing and thinking positive thoughts. After going through the sequence of muscle tensing and releasing, you may like to think of your favourite place and just stay there quietly for a few moments. This should help dispel any tension or anxiety you may be feeling.
- When you are ready, start to touch yourself, your tummy, arms, breasts, legs, inner thighs. Remember what feels good.
- Allow your hand to go down and touch your genital area. Let your fingers find your clitoris and your vaginal lips. You should feel familiar and comfortable about touching this area since completing the body awareness exercise.
- Touch your clitoris in a way that you enjoy, allow yourself to experience all the pleasurable sensations that you are able to create.
- As you start to feel aroused, allow your fingers to feel your vaginal lips. Notice how they have become fuller and puffy. Explore a bit further. Allow your fingers to touch the entrance to your vagina. Does it feel slightly wet? If you are feeling at all anxious at this stage, then stop and think about what you are doing in a constructive and positive way.
- If you are feeling comfortable, allow your little finger (make sure that your fingernail is cut short to avoid any scratching or discomfort) to enter into your vagina as far as the first joint. If this starts to make you feel tense, use the pelvic floor muscle exercise to help to relax the area. When you feel

more in control, try to insert your little finger again. If you manage less than the first joint, that is fine. You have still done really well. Stop now and think about what you have achieved.

Repeat the process two or three times until you feel comfortable with the exercise. If the problem is a longstanding one it may take a few more repetitions of this stage to become completely comfortable. If the problem of vaginismus has arisen after a previously satisfactory sex life you may find that your body responds more quickly, as it remembers what felt good before the incident that caused the problem. Either way, move on to stage 2 only when you are entirely happy with the first stage.

For Stage 2 it is important to recognize that your vagina is not an *actual* space, but a *potential* one. The insides of the vagina lie close together, and the skin is not smooth and flat, but ridgy and bumpy. During sexual arousal the vagina opens and lengthens. In fact, it becomes penis-shaped. Moisture is released from the sides of the vagina to lubricate it and make penetration easier. If you are not fully aroused this will not happen; so it is not surprising that penetration can be difficult or even painful. Many women do not believe that they are big enough inside to accommodate a tampon, let alone a penis! The reality is that you *are* big enough, but under the right circumstances.

## Stage 2

- Repeat all of stage 1.
- This time, think of a fantasy that you are comfortable with and let your mind focus on the story.
- At the same time, arouse yourself as before, allowing your vagina to moisten and your vaginal lips to open.
- Concentrate on your fantasy as you put the tip of your little finger inside the entrance to your vagina. Let your finger explore the space for a few seconds. Then push your finger

183

gently inside your vagina, negotiating any 'bumps' by moving your finger up and down or slightly to the side.

- With your finger inside, practise your pelvic floor exercise. Feel your muscles tighten around your finger and notice the difference as you relax the muscles. Continue to tighten and relax your muscles around your finger for a minute or so or until you are ready to stop.

- Next, see how far you can put your finger inside. Tense your pelvic floor muscles and, on relaxing, move your finger further into your vagina. If you manage the second joint, that is excellent. If you can only manage the first one, withdraw your finger then work on becoming more aroused and try one more time.

- Repeat the whole exercise at least two or three times (more if you need to) until you feel really comfortable with the whole process.

- A variation on this exercise can be carried out while you are having your bath. Relax in the water and then touch yourself in the way you have before. The water will help your vagina to open. Place the palm of your hand on your pubic bone (the hard area just above the vulval area) and let your first finger just touch the outside of the vagina. Think positive thoughts as you let your finger slide gently inside your vagina to the first joint (you should only attempt using your first or index finger if you have been able to insert your little finger before).

- Repeat this exercise as many times as is necessary for you to be able to insert the whole of your index finger.

After you have completed stage 2, think about what you have achieved. If you have found yourself getting anxious during the exercises, then check out what is happening to you. Are you thinking negative thoughts? Make sure you are completely relaxed, and use fantasy to help distract you. Perhaps you were not able to feel any improvement when squeezing your pelvic floor muscles? This could be because you haven't been doing the exercises for very long. Increase the amount of times a day you practise from two to three, or four. Remember, when you are used to pelvic floor muscle exercises you can do them any time, anywhere.

## Stage 3
Stage 3 is about being able to get two fingers inside your vagina. This may seem quite daunting, but if you are completely relaxed, aroused, and moist you will have created the right climate for it to be possible for you to insert two fingers.

- Repeat stages 1 and 2.
- Really concentrate on how good touching yourself feels, and ensure that your body is responding by using the pelvic floor exercises to increase sensation.
- When you feel your vagina is ready, introduce one finger first. If you feel yourself tensing up, use the pelvic floor muscle exercise to relax and then arouse yourself again.
- When you're ready, introduce the tops of your two fingers into your vagina up to the first joint. How does that feel? Practise pelvic floor muscle exercises while your fingers are inserted. Can you feel the difference in tightness between tensing and letting go?
- If you are feeling OK you can continue by putting your fingers in as far as feels comfortable. When you feel you have gone far enough, stop and think about what you have achieved.

How did that feel? If you were able to complete the exercise fully then that is great. If you had to stop, that's OK; you have still done really well. Repeat the exercise again a few more times until you feel completely comfortable with it.

## Stage 4
This stage is about introducing something more penis-like inside you. There are several options, and maybe you can think of some more. Vaginal trainers are probably the best, as they are designed for the purpose of aiding vaginismic women with penetration.

They come in four different sizes, graded for comfort. However, they are not available free of charge. Two suppliers are listed in Appendix 1 for those of you who may want to order them.

A cheaper way is to use candles. This may sound a bit strange, but with a condom fitted over them they can do the same job as the trainers. Use different sizes and thicknesses to help you get used to feeling something bigger inside you. An even cheaper and just as satisfactory option is a suitably shaped vegetable – a courgette (zucchini), for example. Courgettes vary a lot in size and can easily be used in the same way as trainers and candles. Cut off the end to get a better shape; again, always use a condom, and make sure you use a lubricant on the condom to help with penetration. You may be able to think of other things that could help. Some small vibrators are excellent for the purpose, and again these come in various sizes. Once you can comfortably put two fingers inside yourself you will be ready to use graded trainers, a vibrator, or candles. This will increase your confidence that you can put something penis-like inside your vagina.

- Repeat stage 1 by having a bath, relaxing, and pleasuring yourself in the way you like best. If you are using trainers, have the first one ready (they come with instructions for use), or prepare an alternative.

- When you are properly aroused, slowly introduce the end of the trainer into your vaginal opening. Gently push the trainer in (about an inch, or 2 centimetres, will do) and practice your pelvic floor muscle exercise. Can you feel the pressure of your vagina around the trainer? Do a few more pelvic floor exercises and then relax your vagina and gently push the trainer inside. *Only go as far as you feel comfortable on the first attempt.*

- Remove the trainer and think about how that felt. If you started to feel tense or uncomfortable, then consider why. Do you need more stimulation beforehand? Did you use fantasy to help you? If not, remember to use fantasy next time. Also, did you experience any negative thoughts? If so, consider how you might replace them with positive ones.

Repeat this exercise as many times as you need until you can comfortably put the trainer inside you to its full length.

## Stage 5

- Repeat all of stage 4, remembering all you have learned about yourself and your body.
- When you are ready, insert the next size up of whatever item you are using, starting with the tip as before and practising your pelvic floor exercises before trying to go further inside.
- Once you can comfortably take the next size, apply the same conditions and instructions for the remaining two sizes.

If you experience any problems while working through this exercise, simply return to the previous stage. Start to rebuild your confidence by putting a smaller size in first and then progressing to the bigger sizes. Once you can insert the largest size you can really start to believe that penetration with a penis is possible.

Something that often helps is to remember that many women all over the world have babies without problems, and to date no man has ever had a penis as big as a full-term baby. If you can give birth, you can have sex. Even if you don't ever want a baby, the fact is that your body is designed to make one, and accommodate its delivery.

A word here about tampons. A lot of vaginismic women find using tampons impossible or very difficult. One of the main reasons for this is that they seem to come up against a block. This is why I have emphasized above that the inside of the vagina is ridgy and bumpy. The tampon needs to be *negotiated* inside. Remember, the vagina is a potential space, not an actual one. Another reason can be that they are not inserted high enough into the vagina. The tampon needs to go beyond the outer third, so that you cannot feel it. (If it is placed in the outer third it will be extremely uncomfortable, even painful.) Pelvic floor exercises can help considerably with tampon insertion. The key is relaxation of the pelvic floor muscles and confidence that you know where the tampon is going. Using the right size is also very important. When experimenting with tampons, always use the very smallest one first.

## Dyspareunia

Dyspareunia, or painful sex, can occur for a lot of reasons. This program is designed to help you to overcome the causes and consequences of pain, and enable you to experience comfortable sex again. If you are in a relationship and would like to work on the problem with your partner, move on to Chapter 10, where instructions are given on how to tackle this problem as a couple.

Perhaps you have chosen to work on the problem alone because you are avoiding sex and/or feeling pretty bad about it. Dyspareunia is a distressing problem that could be affecting an existing relationship or preventing you from seeking out new ones. If your sex life has come to a halt because of this problem you may just need to rebuild confidence in your ability to experience pain-free sex. Whatever your circumstances, if it suits you to work on the problem on your own first of all, then this section is for you.

A word of caution. If the pain is severe, or if you are still having treatment for an illness or other condition, then now may not be the time to start self-help. Make sure your doctor has given you the all-clear in terms of being physically ready to have sex again first.

Before starting, make sure you have learned to relax (Chapter 7), completed the body awareness program, and practised the pelvic floor muscle exercises (both in Chapter 8). These will all help you overcome any anxiety or apprehension you may feel about starting the self-help exercises. The exercises on motivation for change and negative thinking (Chapter 6) may also be helpful.

Allow yourself around 30–45 minutes for each session. Make sure you will not be disturbed by anyone or interrupted by the telephone. Have a bath before you start, relax, and follow the instructions in the body awareness exercise.

*Stage 1*

- Carry out all the steps of body awareness to genital touching.
- Use fantasy to enhance your sexual feelings while stroking, rubbing or touching yourself. Use a lubricant to increase sensitivity and help your natural lubrication to flow.
- When your vagina is open, puffy, and wet, use your little finger to probe inside gently. Practise your pelvic floor muscle exercises on your finger a few times. Note how your vagina relaxes after tensing the muscle. If you feel any discomfort at all, withdraw your finger and think about what you have achieved.
- How did your finger feel inside you? Did it feel strange? Did you feel awkward or worried? Most importantly, did you experience any pain? If so, what caused this? Were you sufficiently aroused? Did you make sure your fingernail was cut short and sanded smooth?

Repeat this exercise at least two or three times (more if you wish) until you really understand how your body responds to touch, and what it feels like to have a finger inside you. When you are happy with the results of stage 1, move on to stage 2.

*Stage 2*
This exercise is designed to help you become more aware of the inside of your vagina and how it can give you pleasure.

- Repeat all of stage 1.
- When you are suitably aroused, slowly put your finger inside you (you can use extra lubricant on your finger if you wish) and gently feel your way around the inside of your vagina.
- What does it feel like? Soft, warm, moist? Use your imagination to think what it might look like. See it as a positive space.
- Move the pad of your finger to the top of your vaginal wall (tummy side up) and feel around until you locate your G-spot.

This is an area of sensitive nerve endings that can give very pleasurable sensations if rubbed or stimulated.

- Gently explore this area to see how it feels to you. When you are ready, stop and think about what you have done.
- Did that feel good to you? What does your vagina feel like? Did you feel any pain?

Repeat this exercise two or three times (more if you wish) until you can comfortably allow your finger to explore and enjoy your vagina without pain or discomfort.

When you feel ready, try to put two fingers inside, taking it slowly and carefully. See how that feels. If you feel no pain at all, then you are ready to move on to vaginal trainers. For this next step you can follow the program outlined above for vaginismus, beginning with stage 4.

When you have completed all the exercises, you will be ready to try penetrative sex again. If you have any problems, just go back to the stage where you felt comfortable and work your way forward again. Continue to challenge any negative thinking until you have reached your goal.

*Note*: If you experience any pain during these exercises it is advisable to stop immediately and consult your doctor.

## Orgasmic Dysfunction

Not being able to have an orgasm can be one of the most frustrating experiences a woman can have. Being on the brink, knowing yourself to be very aroused and excited, and just not being able to 'get there' can be maddening. Not to experience that release, climax, orgasm, or whatever you want to call it, can also make you feel less sexually attractive. As more than one woman has told me, 'I just want to be normal'.

There are many reasons why you might not be able to climax. It may be due to a negative body image or low self-esteem. It could be an effect of guilt or shame, in turn the result of messages received in childhood about sex being 'dirty'. Remember Paula, in Chapter 1? It could also be the result of a poor relationship or bad sexual experiences, including pressure from a partner, that is stopping you from letting go. Anxiety about any of these can prevent you from fully enjoying yourself sexually. Sometimes you might find yourself 'spectating' or watching yourself, and not liking what you think you see. Whatever the reason for the problem, this program can help you to learn what your body needs to enjoy sexual feelings that can end in orgasm.

In order to get in touch with the sensations that can arise in your genital area it is important first of all to do the pelvic floor muscle exercises. These will not only enhance sensitivity but also increase blood flow to the area – essential for sexual arousal. If you have already been working on these exercises you will probably have noticed an improvement in muscle tone. The instructions below will explain how to fully incorporate these exercises into the program. Body awareness (Chapter 8) and relaxation (Chapter 7) are two more areas that you will need to be completely familiar with (especially if your problem is linked to poor body image) before you start the exercises here. If your problem is linked to 'spectating' (watching yourself, instead of concentrating on feeling), or negative thinking, then work through the negative thinking exercise (Chapter 6). The fantasy exercise (Chapter 8) can also contribute towards overcoming spectating behavior. Armed with all this information and experience, you will be ready to begin the specific exercises.

Allow yourself plenty of time for the exercises (around 30–45 minutes for each session), and make sure you will not disturbed by anyone or interrupted by the telephone. Have a bath before you start and relax according to the body awareness instructions.

## Stage 1

- This exercise is about experiencing intense physical sensations through manual stimulation. Follow body awareness to the genital touching stage.

- In your relaxed state, allow yourself to think of a fantasy that appeals to you. Follow the thought through to create a scene that you can build on.
- At the same time, begin to pleasure your body. Touch your lower abdomen, your inner thighs, your pubic hair, and finally your vagina and clitoris. Allow your hands to move freely and luxuriously until you are aware of pleasurable sensations.
- Touch and feel your vagina. Is it open? Is it moist and puffy? Allow your fingers to explore its wetness. Use some of your natural lubrication to stimulate your clitoris.
- What type of touch do you prefer? Experiment with what feels good. Use a finger or several fingers to gently rub, stroke or caress your clitoris.
- Allow your fingers to increase the stimulation as you stay with your fantasy. You will notice your body tensing up as the stimulation increases. Go with the feelings for a while, then stop.

How did that feel to you? Did it feel good and were you sorry to stop? Or did you feel anxious and uncomfortable? Explore your feelings. It is crucial that you are honest with yourself. Did you feel silly? Embarrassed? What was preventing you from enjoying yourself? Did you feel unable to fantasize? Did you feel uncomfortable as you became aware of how your body was responding? Or did it feel as if nothing was happening? Learn from the experience and try to build on it. Repeat this exercise at least two or three times (more if you wish) until you are able to reach a highly aroused state. See if you can remain at this high level for a while and enjoy the good feelings that you have produced.

## Orgasmic Triggers

Before moving on to stage 2, it is helpful to have some techniques at your disposal that you can use during these exercises to help you achieve your goal. When having an orgasm, women naturally tense certain muscles, put their heads back and arch their backs, without consciously realizing what they are doing. If you practise these 'orgasmic triggers' so that you are more aware of them, you can use them to help overcome your difficulty in achieving orgasm. Don't worry if you feel a bit silly at first: nobody is going to see you.

First, arch your back, tense up your tummy and thigh muscles, and hold your head back (over the edge of the bed is a good position). Second, practise the pelvic floor muscle exercises while fantasizing. Third, *pretend* to have an orgasm: breathe rapidly, pant, make noises while stimulating yourself, feel your way into what an orgasm might be like. Put these all together in a way that suits you.

## The Phases of Orgasm

It is also helpful to understand the process of the female orgasm. There are four distinct phases. In stage 1 of this exercise, you have been working through the first phase, arousal. Here is the full sequence:

- *Arousal*: Within 10–20 seconds of starting to feel turned on, your vagina will start producing natural lubrication from the inner walls and blood will flow into the pelvic area (your pelvic floor muscle exercises will enhance this process). Your temperature will start to rise, creating a redness or flushing over your tummy, chest, and neck. The vulval area and your vaginal lips will become engorged (full) with blood, making them appear darker in colour. Inside your vagina lengthens and widens, extending beyond the cervix (in effect, becoming penis-shaped), while your uterus (womb) tilts backwards and upwards in readiness for intercourse.
- *Plateau*: During this phase your vagina expands further, and the clitoris stiffens, swells, increases in size, and moves under the clitoral hood. During stimulation the movement of the clitoral hood adds to the pleasurable sensations. Your body is working harder, so your blood pressure increases, as do your heart rate and breathing. At this point you will be longing for release and satisfaction through orgasm.

193

- *Orgasm*: At the very peak of stimulation your body will tense and stiffen as you experience orgasmic contractions at 0.8-second intervals. These will vary in length and intensity before they gradually fade away. Part of the final trigger into orgasm comes from a reflex in the brain, and if you are inhibited, nervous, or anxious the normal orgasmic response can be blocked. Under these conditions you will not achieve an orgasm.
- *Resolution*: When all your contractions have faded away, the blood will drain away from the genital area and the feelings of 'puffiness' will go. The 'sex flush' will fade and your heart rate, breathing and blood pressure will return to normal levels.

Having reached a high state of arousal and the plateau stage during stage 1, you can now move on to stage 2.

*Stage 2*

- Repeat all of stage 1.
- This time combine your fantasy with stimulation, but don't stop when you begin to feel your body prepare for orgasm. Keep whatever image you have focused on in your mind as you increase the pressure, speed, and intensity of your touch.
- Allow yourself to let go fully at peak stimulation.

Were you able to experience an orgasm? If so, what helped you get there? Was it your fantasy, your touch, or a combination of both? Think about how it happened in order to learn from the experience and be able to recreate your success again.

If you have still not experienced orgasm despite following the instructions, it may well be that you need to think some more about what you are doing. Is fantasy not working for you? Are you worried about how you look, or scared by the intensity of your feelings? Do you feel bad or embarrassed about what you are doing? Is it physically difficult for you to stimulate yourself enough?

Not everyone can achieve the kind of physical stimulation sufficient for orgasm. This may be due to the time it takes to get you going. Some women report their hand getting tired after a certain amount of stimulation so that they have to stop before they have reached orgasm. If this applies to you, then a vibrator may well be the answer. For some women a vibrator is the only way they can achieve orgasm on their own. You can obtain a vibrator through the websites listed under 'Sex Aids' in Apendix 1. (All these sites are recommended as they are reliable, confidential and trustworthy.) Stage 3 takes you through the process of learning to use it.

If you have achieved orgasm through manual stimulation, you can skip stage 3 and go straight to stage 4.

## Stage 3: Using a Vibrator

Vibrators come in different shapes and sizes. Make sure you buy one that suits you. Some women are put off by the sound. If this applies to you, make sure the one you choose is silent, or at least quiet. Details, pictures and relevant information are available when browsing through the site.

Make sure the vibrations are adjusted to the intensity that is comfortable to you. Try on your hand first. When you are fully relaxed and mentally in tune, gently apply the vibrator over your body before moving to your clitoral area. Experiment first of all and don't expect too much, especially if this is a new experience for you.

- Follow the instructions given under stages 1 and 2, but instead of using your hand allow the vibrator to stimulate you in a way that feels good.
- Do not become distracted. Concentrate fully on what is happening to your body.
- Apply the vibrator directly to the clitoral area until you are at the peak of pleasure. Gently hold it there and allow yourself to experience your orgasm fully.

Repeat this exercise two or three times (more if you wish) until you understand fully what your body likes best. Think about how you felt using the vibrator. Did you have an orgasm? Once you know how an orgasm feels using a vibrator, you can go back to manual stimulation and try to achieve one by hand. Just follow the instructions at stage 2. If you are still experiencing blocks to orgasm, ask yourself the following questions:

- Am I really prepared to let myself go?
- If not, then what is stopping me?
- Do I feel anxious, worried, or stupid while stimulating myself?
- Am I using fantasy wholeheartedly?

Remember, the psychological reasons for not having an orgasm are often the hardest to work through. Finding out what they are may require a bit more time. Go back over some of the earlier examples and exercises to try to pinpoint what is getting in the way for you. Once you know what is getting in the way you can begin the program again from stage 1. As long as you remain motivated and don't lose heart you will win through in the end.

## Stage 4

This stage is about experiencing something like having a penis inside you. For this you can follow the program set out under 'Vaginismus' from stage 4. While the main issue for vaginismic women is actual penetration, for you it is to learn to experience vaginal contractions. You need only follow the instructions as far as putting a trainer or vibrator inside your vagina.

- Place the vibrator (or alternative) inside your vagina when you are completely aroused. Use additional lubrication if needed.
- Enjoy the sensations this produces. Use fantasy to enhance the experience and create warm, glowing feelings.
- Move the vibrator in such a way as to raise your arousal levels. Seek out the G-spot (this area of sensitive nerve endings is located on the tummy side of your vagina). Experiment with

different strokes, thrusting gently in and out, or rotating the vibrator. See what feels good and enjoy the sensations.

Repeat this exercise as often as feels good. Practice makes perfect, and you can have lots of pleasure along the way. Also, this experience will help to prepare you for partner sex again if that is what you want. Take at look at the next section for further encouragement.

## Identifying Wants and Needs from Sex

Now you have overcome your sexual problem, you may be thinking about starting to go out to meet people with a view to forming a new relationship. One of the most important things about sex is to ensure that you feel completely comfortable with the situation/circumstances that lead to sex. Sometimes you can find yourself in a situation that is not to your liking. Being able to say no, and for this to be accepted, is essential to building up a good and trusting relationship. Having gone to so much trouble and effort to sort out the sexual problem from your side, it would be dreadful to find all your hard work undermined because you have a bad experience or get into an unwanted situation. To help you guard yourself against this possibility, the following exercise is to help you think about what you want and need from sex.

---

### Exercise: Wants and Needs for Good Sex

- Think of a time when you had a good sexual experience. What made it good? Identify the key factors and write them down.
- Now think of a time when sex was not so good. What happened? How did it make you feel? Identify the key factors and write them down.
- Compare these two lists. Can you see the difference between what made sex a good experience and a not so good one?

---

You will need to build on what you know is good for you and try to avoid situations of the kind that might lead to a negative experience. Unless you feel really confident that everything is going to work, try to avoid sexual encounters that do not give you the time or space to relax, and to concentrate on how your body feels. If someone sweeps you off your feet and it feels right, then by all means go for it. Sex is to be enjoyed, after all, otherwise why bother? Once you have got the basics right, you can then move on to experiment with all sorts of fun activities. Sex can be such a hugely rewarding experience. Make sure it is for you!

## Loss of Desire/Interest

Why do people go off sex? This is quite a complex subject. Loss of sexual desire/interest in sex can apply equally to both men and women. There may be deep psychological reasons why you lose interest; or the reason could be as simple as not fancying your partner any more. Also, whether you act on sexual desire is a matter of choice. Sometimes you may feel turned on and yet 'can't be bothered' to do anything about it, or you are in the wrong place at the wrong time. If you ignore your sexual feelings often enough you can learn to literally switch yourself off so that you are rarely aware of them. If you are happy with this situation you will have no need for this book. Alternatively, if it is a concern then help is at hand. 'Use it or lose it' as the old saying goes.

So, as a single person, what can you do about recreating your interest in sex if it has gone away?

First, you should ask yourself: 'Is this what I want?' Your particular situation is clearly going to play a big part in deciding whether or not you want to do anything about your lack of interest in sex. You may have lost your desire because you haven't had a partner for a while and don't see the point of working on loss of desire while you're not in a relationship. You may believe that meeting the right person would spontaneously reignite your interest in sex – and you may be right. Whatever the reason, remember the section on motivation in Chapter 6: you need to want to rekindle your interest in sex if you're going to be successful.

Second, think about the possible factors that might be contributing to the situation. Some common causes of going off sex are:

- feeling bad about yourself or your body (feeling unattractive), or feeling depressed;
- a family history or background that identified sex as 'dirty' or unacceptable;
- a history of sexual abuse;
- stress caused by events at work or at home, relationships or lifestyle;
- hormonal changes, and/or a response to medication;
- substance abuse e.g. drugs, alcohol;
- fear of success or failure; fears to do with rejection and performance.

Do any of these relate to you? Can you recognize yourself in any of them? If so, you may benefit from some of the earlier exercises designed to help identify and overcome negative thinking, stress, and motivation problems. Look back at Chapters 6 and 7 and work through the exercises given here. Once you have thought about and completed the tasks and exercises recommended, you may like to work on the following self-help strategy aimed at rekindling your sexual interest and desire.

## Step 1

For the first step you need to find a quiet place where you can sit for about 30 minutes and think about the following questions (you may like to write your answers down to keep and refer to again).

- Think about when you last had a sexual thought, feeling, or image. How did you respond? Did you ignore it? Did it worry you? Did you have a vague sense that you could act on it and didn't?

- Next, think about your life. Is there anything in your current situation that prevents you from thinking sexual thoughts (daydreams, fantasies) or acting on sexual urges (masturbation)?

Is there any connection between these two areas? If so, think about how you can change things (see Chapter 6 on setting goals). How long it is before you start to feel sexual again will depend on how long you have been 'off sex' and your motivation for change. You may feel quite anxious about disturbing the status quo, confronting things that you have been successfully avoiding. You will need to feel totally confident that this is what you want to be doing before you move on to step 2.

## Step 2

Again, allow yourself about 30 minutes of quiet, uninterrupted time.

- Lie down and follow the relaxation instructions in Chapter 7 (or use your own equivalent).
- When you feel suitably relaxed, create a fantasy, or use an old one that you remember used to turn you on (you need do no more than think at this stage).
- How did you feel thinking sexually again? Did your mind fight it? Did you find it hard to imagine something . . . or did you feel yourself slipping easily back into fantasizing?

If you felt uneasy at all, repeat this exercise two or three times (or more) until you feel comfortable with sexual thinking.

## Step 3

This stage is about allowing yourself to get in touch with your body again.

- Follow the (male or female, as appropriate) body awareness program as set out in Chapter 8, through to genital touching. Use pelvic floor muscle exercises to increase sensitivity to your penis/vagina. Take it slowly, moving forward only when you feel really comfortable with what you are doing.
- Use fantasy to create a mind–body connection. Carry on pleasuring yourself as you allow your fantasy to develop. Stay focused and concentrate on reaching a high level of arousal, then enjoy your orgasm.
- If you experienced any difficulties with this, leave it a couple of days and then try again, repeating the exercise until you feel comfortable with what is happening. Once you have succeeded you can begin to build up a pattern of positive sexual behavior.

If you have discovered that your loss of desire/interest is due to a particular sexual problem, for example PE or vaginismus, you may feel encouraged to continue with self-help. If so, then find the particular program for your sexual problem in this chapter and follow the instructions for working through it.

# 10

# Specific Problems: Self-Help for Couples

This chapter is designed for couples who have chosen to work together on their sexual problem. It is best for both of you to read the book so that you each fully understand what you need to do.

Goal-setting is very important in order to establish what you are hoping to achieve. Setting realistic goals that you are both agreed on should ensure positive results. Checking out your motivation and deciding whether or not you need to complete the negative thinking exercise could save a lot of time and possible frustration later on. Refer back to Chapter 6 for guidance in these areas. You may also find it useful to have practised pelvic floor muscle exercises, relaxation, and fantasy before you start the specific exercises in this chapter, and also, depending on the circumstances, body awareness for one or both of you. You might also need to consider stress and lifestyle when planning your program of self-help. Chapters 7 and 8 will give you helpful guidance here.

Discuss your strategies together and help each other to create the right kind of atmosphere for the exercises. If you have small children, then one of you could spend some time occupying them while the other completes some of the exercises. If you are older, you may prefer to do sessions in the morning when you feel more active, or during the afternoon after you have completed whatever else you need to do. If you are at work full-time and so need to do the exercises in the evening, begin with a simple light meal that doesn't take hours to prepare. Plan your time carefully in advance. Don't allow that pile of ironing, or the need to sort out that pile of bills, to distract you from your scheduled session. If you and your partner are not living together, work out where and when you will do the sessions. If you are a shift worker, again think about how you will fit in the time with your partner.

Aim to have three sessions a week, leaving a day or two in between sessions. If this feels too concentrated you can spread them out a little bit more, but be careful not to allow too much time to lapse between sessions as this could affect your progress and your motivation to keep going, especially if things don't quite run according to plan. Inevitably the rest of life will go on: deadlines have to be met, school open evenings have to be attended, work can take you away from home, and so on. Nevertheless, don't lose focus: try to minimize delays, gaps and other time-consuming activities.

You will also need to confine your sexual activity to these planned sessions. Although you can continue to be affectionate together, to kiss and cuddle, please try to avoid intercourse and/or masturbation. The reason for this is that your sex life has probably suffered as a result of the sexual problem and in order to put this right you will need to put past behavior behind you and start to learn new, more positive ways of being together.

If you are tense or anxious about starting the exercises, then talk to each other and share your concerns. Good communication is part of the program and will enable you to be more open and honest in your relationship. It is no good for either of you if something isn't working, but you are unable to say what it is. This will only lead to frustration and disappointment later on. Start as you mean to go on, positively, and with the confidence that the problem can and will be solved.

In the section on 'male problems' that follows, the instructions are addressed to the male partner; in the section on 'female problems', they are addressed to the female partner. This is assuming a heterosexual partnership; however, all the exercises can be successfully adapted for use by gay, lesbian and bisexual couples.

## Male problems

### *Erectile Dysfunction*

Erectile dysfunction is extremely distressing but also very common. There are many causes, including medical, physical, and, of course, psychological ones. If you have any reason to suspect your problem may be a medical one, please see your doctor.

This program is designed to help if you have no physical or medical reason for your erection failing. A good indicator of this is if you experience night or morning erections. You may or may not have problems getting and keeping an erection during masturbation. This program is designed to help you to regain your faith in your ability to achieve and keep an erection. It will also restore your confidence that once you have lost an erection you can get it back again; and it will help to reduce anxiety and minimize performance fears.

### *Getting Started*

Follow the instructions for sensate focus (Chapter 8) and incorporate the pelvic floor muscles exercises into the first week of that program. Enjoy 'fun week' and discuss together all the good things you are learning. When you have completed all the tasks over the five weeks and have created the right atmosphere, you will be ready to begin working on the erectile problem itself. However, it is essential for you to be relaxed if the program is to work. Relaxation techniques can be carried out while your partner is in the bath/shower. Allow an hour for the exercise and make sure you will not be disturbed or interrupted by the phone. After your bath/shower lie down together and massage in the usual way. By now you will know what you each like.

As your partner will be doing much of the actual work during these sessions, it is a good idea to think about her pleasure and when she has an orgasm (if she would like that). Some men prefer to give pleasure first, especially if their desire drops after they have had an orgasm so that they lose interest in further sex play, while for others it makes no difference. Discuss together how and when you will include this before you start. If you both know beforehand the order in which you are going to do things, this will keep to a minimum any interruptions in the flow of the session. It is also useful to have a box of tissues handy. Some people are uncomfortable with bodily fluids. Being able to mop up soon after ejaculation can avoid this becoming a problem.

## Stage 1

Lie down on the bed with your head at the foot end. Your partner needs to sit between your legs with her back supported by pillows against the bed-head. Put your legs over hers (you may need to bend them) in the kind of position you might adopt to 'row a boat'. You will need to move your bottom up the bed slightly so that your partner can comfortably sit and hold your penis. If your partner is unable to sit in this way you may need to experiment with other ways that are comfortable, yet give easy access to your penis.

- Your partner needs to stimulate your penis in a way that feels good to you. To start with, try stimulating yourself with your partner's hand on yours so that she can feel exactly how you like to be touched. Enjoy the sensations this produces.
- When she has got the right movement, swap over so that she holds your penis and you put your hand over hers until you feel she has got the pressure, rhythm, and speed just right.
- Your partner continues to stimulate you by herself. You may need to repeat this a few times in order to get it completely right. Use fantasy to help.

How did this feel? Did you enjoy the experience? Were you able to get a good erection during the exercise? Did you feel anxious at all? Did your penis fail to respond? Were you able to use fantasy to help?

Feedback, now and in the later stages, is essential. You and your partner need to share thoughts and feelings about what happens in the sessions in order to learn from the experience. Practise pelvic floor muscle exercises to increase blood flow and sensitivity during the session. Repeat this exercise two or three times (more if you like) until your erection is good and firm.

## Stage 2

- Prepare as before; bath, relaxation and massage.
- When ready, move into the 'rowing boat' position and get your partner to stimulate you to a good erection in the way she knows how.
- When you are fully erect she is to stop stimulating you. Let the erection go down.
- Next, she is to repeat the process, stimulating you to a full erection and then stopping to allow the erection to go down again.
- Repeat this a third time.
- On the fourth occasion, she will stimulate you to a full erection and this time you ejaculate.

How did this feel? Were you able to get a good erection three times? Did you enjoy ejaculating . . . or did you only manage once or twice? Think about what was happening to you. Did you use pelvic floor muscle exercises? Were you in touch with the sensations in your genitals? Did you feel anxious at all? Did your partner feel anxious? Discuss together what happened and learn from the experience. Repeat the whole exercise again two or three times (or more) until you are able to get a good erection three times in the session, ejaculating on the final time. Move on only when you are completely comfortable with stage 2.

## Stage 3

- Prepare in the usual way.
- You partner should move into the female superior (woman on top) position, sitting on the tops of your legs.

- Taking hold of your penis, she should stimulate you to a full erection and then let it go down as before. You may need to stimulate your partner to ensure she is aroused enough for the next step, or use some additional lubricant.
- This time when she restimulates you to a full erection, she can put the penis inside her. She only needs to move enough to keep the erection for a short while.
- When ready, she comes off your penis and stimulates you to orgasm.

How did you get on? Did you have a good enough erection for her to put it inside her vagina? How did that feel? If you found you lost your erection as she tried to insert it, she needs to restimulate your penis and try again. Did your penis fail due to anxiety? Think about what made you anxious; this will help you avoid anxiety next time. Did you think about fantasy? Were you concentrating and enjoying yourself? Discuss together what you each observed and learned from the exercise. Give her lots of cuddles and hugs for being there for you. Repeat two or three times (or more) until you have successfully managed the whole of stage 3.

## Stage 4

- Repeat all of stage 3.
- This time, if you would like to thrust then do so.
- If you feel good about how things are going, ejaculate inside her vagina.

How did that feel? Were you able to thrust and keep your erection? Better still, did you ejaculate? If the answer is yes, repeat the exercise two or three times (or more) to consolidate what you have achieved and to build up pleasurable experiences. If you lost your erection at any point during the process, go back to being stimulated outside the vagina a few times, and then move on to putting your penis inside again. Repeat the exercise until all of stage 4 is satisfactorily completed.

*Stage 5*

• Now your erection is reliable try experimenting with different positions. Have fun!

If your partner becomes dry during the exercises (it is hard to stay fully aroused for long periods) you might like to apply a lubricant to help with insertion. You can use it directly on the penis or vagina, or both.

If you have found the above program difficult to complete, you may need to think about why that was. Do you feel exposed? Do you still think you are going to fail? Talk to your partner about your concerns. She can't help you if you don't share what is going on. Do you think negatively about your body? The body awareness program can help increase your confidence. Why not give it a try, and then go back to sensate focus and work through the exercises again.

If you have experienced problems with masturbating you may find it useful to follow the self-help program for erectile dysfunction in Chapter 9, 'Self-Help for Singles'.

## Premature Ejaculation

The aim of this program is to help you to identify your 'point of inevitability': that is, the point of no return after which you will ejaculate no matter what you do or don't do. In order to do this you need to be aware of what your body is doing prior to orgasm. Premature ejaculation is often accompanied by anxiety and performance fears. The following exercises will help to reduce your anxiety and increase your confidence in your ability to stay in control.

### Getting Started

Follow the instructions for sensate focus (Chapter 8) and incorporate the pelvic floor muscles exercises into the first week of that program. Enjoy 'fun week', and discuss together all the good things you are learning. When you have completed all the tasks over the 5 weeks and created the right atmosphere to proceed you will be ready to begin working on your premature ejaculation. In order for the following exercise to work, you need to be relaxed. Relaxation techniques can be carried out while your partner is in the bath/shower. Allow an hour for the exercise and make sure you will not be disturbed or interrupted by the phone. After your bath/shower lie down together and massage in the usual way. By now you will know what you each like.

As your partner will be doing much of the actual work during these sessions it is a good idea to think about her pleasure and when she has an orgasm (if she would like that). Some men prefer to give pleasure first, especially if their desire drops after they have had an orgasm so that they lose interest in further sex play; for others it makes no difference. Discuss together how and when you will include this before you start. If you both know beforehand the order in which you are going to do things, this will keep to a minimum any interruptions in the flow of the session. It is also useful to have a box of tissues handy. Some people are uncomfortable with bodily fluids. Being able to mop up soon after ejaculation can avoid this becoming a problem.

*Stage 1*

- Prepare for the session with a bath, relaxation and massage.
- When you are both ready you should lie on your back while your partner sits on the top of your legs, or next to you, depending on what feels best for her.
- She can then stimulate you in the way she knows you like best while you concentrate on what you are feeling at the base of your penis. When you feel close to ejaculation, indicate that you would like her to stop (you can either say 'Stop' or give some other prearranged signal).
- When the feelings have died down, ask her to continue stimulation while you concentrate again on your bodily sensations. When your orgasm is close, indicate for her to stop again.

- Repeat this a third time. Then, the fourth time, allow yourself to enjoy the experience and carry on to orgasm.

Discuss the session and what worked? How did it feel? Did you manage to go all the way to the fourth time . . . or did you come on the first, second or third occasion? If you did, then share with your partner what you were feeling and what you learned. If you asked her to stop too late, remember this for next time. If you found it difficult to focus on your bodily sensations, use the pelvic floor muscle exercise to help remind you of the muscles you need to concentrate on. Repeat the whole exercise two or three times (or more) until you have completed the task fully.

*Stage 2*

- Repeat all of stage 1.
- This time ask your partner to use a lubricant on her hands while stimulating you.
- Do the exercise three times, ejaculating on the fourth occasion.

How did this feel? What was your experience of her 'wet' hand? Did this make it harder to stay in control? Did you come on the first, second or third attempt . . . or were you successful in waiting for the fourth? Repeat this stage two or three times (or more) until you are fully in control of your ejaculation. Once you are confident that you can recognize your point of inevitability, move on to stage 3.

*Stage 3*

- Prepare as before, with bath, relaxation and massage.
- When you are both ready, ask your partner to sit on you in the female superior position (woman on top).
- Ask her to stimulate you to erection and tell her when she needs to stop.

- On the second stimulation (she may also need some stimulation to ensure she is aroused and lubricated) she sits over your penis and slowly helps you inside her. Allow her to stay still for a short time before withdrawing.
- She can then stimulate you to orgasm with her hand.

Were you able to stay inside your partner without ejaculating? If you did, then well done. If you ejaculated, then think about what happened. Did you allow your initial feelings to build up but not let them subside enough before entry? Discuss progress with your partner about what you have learned, and how you can use that learning in your next session. Give her lots of cuddles and hugs for being there for you. Repeat this exercise two or three times (or more) until you are confident you can be inside her vagina without ejaculating.

## Stage 4

- Repeat stage 3 to vaginal entry.
- This time your partner can move gently up and down until you tell her to stop.
- When your feelings have died down again, ask her to continue with gentle thrusting.
- This time ejaculate when you feel you are ready.

How did this exercise go? Were you able to enjoy intercourse . . . or did you come a little too soon? Practice is all you need now as you are nearly there. Repeat this exercise two or three times (or more) to consolidate the learning and gain in confidence.

## Stage 5

- Try different positions, leaving the one that you used to find most likely to cause PE to the very last.

You have now come to the end of the program. Have you been able to complete all five stages? If not, what happened to prevent you? Did you feel anxious, or concerned your partner might be bored, annoyed, or reluctant? Did you ensure she had a good time too? Were you able to talk about the experience openly and honestly? Did negative thinking play a part? If so, then you may need to work on this (refer back to the exercise in Chapter 6). Did you feel embarrassed, nervous, or unhappy with any aspect of your body? If so, then the body awareness exercise in Chapter 8 might help you. Work through that program before trying these exercises again. If you have a problem with PE during masturbation, you may find it helpful to work through the exercises for that problem in Chapter 9 on 'Self-Help for Singles'.

A word of caution: it is always useful to go on practising the stop/start technique from time to time even after you have conquered your PE. This is because certain situations can increase the likelihood of PE returning, for example a period of time without masturbation or sexual intercourse, or if you have been ill or unwell and not felt like sex for a while. It could also recur as a result of stress, either at home or at work. Whatever the reason, repeat the self-help exercises after any period of abstinence to avoid worry and frustration later on.

## Male Orgasmic Dysfunction

Taking a long time to ejaculate or failing to ejaculate at all seems to be a much more common problem nowadays than it used to be. This may be in part because more men are prepared to admit to the problem. Again, as with all the sexual problems discussed here, the reasons underlying this are numerous, including faulty learning, poor relationships, and a negative self-image, to name just a few. Whatever the reason in your case, the program here is designed to enable you to accept and enjoy the pleasure you can have from your own body.

### Getting Started
Before you start it may be helpful for you to work through the body awareness exercises first (see Chapter 8). If your problem stems from negative feelings about your body, guilt or shame

212

to do with sexual activity, or performance anxiety (including 'spectating' or watching your own performance), body awareness will help to minimize these feelings and increase your own knowledge and awareness before you start working with your partner.

You may also find the sections on masturbation and fantasy in Chapter 8 helpful. Difficulty having an orgasm is often associated with a fear of 'letting go'. Fantasy can really help to distract thoughts away from watching yourself and 'spectating'. If you feel guilty or ashamed about masturbation, see if you can identify where these thoughts or feelings are coming from. Pelvic floor muscle exercises are designed to help you get in touch with the sensations within your genital area. The sooner you can start working on these, the better for the joint program. As with all the programs, relaxation is crucial. Relaxation techniques can really help reduce anxiety and give you a positive start to self-help.

You should now be ready for sensate focus with your partner. Follow the instructions to week 5 (see Chapter 8), then move on to the exercises outlined below. As your partner will be doing a lot of the 'hands-on' work during this stage, it is good to think about her pleasure and when that will be incorporated into the work you are doing together. You could choose to include an orgasm for her (if that is what she would like) after the massage session and before you start on your self-help exercises. Alternatively, you could decide to pleasure her after your exercises, if you feel this would lower your anxiety or help your concentration. The time you put into good planning now could really make a different to the outcome of your session.

You need to plan three sessions a week, restricting your sexual activity to these times only. Being affectionate or kissing and cuddling between sessions is OK, but intercourse and masturbation will be on hold for a short time. This is to reduce anxiety and pressure to perform. Allow yourselves an hour for the exercise itself and some time for preparation. You both need to bath or shower first, prepare the room you have chosen (create a nice atmosphere, have enough pillows/cushions for support), and relax.

213

*Stage 1*

This session is about learning to enjoy your erection and the pleasurable sensations produced through stimulation.

- Lie on your back with your partner next to you or sitting across the top of your legs (whichever suits her best).
- Take hold of your penis and stimulate yourself to erection. Ask your partner to put her hand over yours. Stimulate yourself again so that she can feel the type of pressure, strokes, and speed you prefer.
- Swap hands so that her hand is holding your penis with yours on top of hers. She continues to stimulate you in the way you have just shown her.
- When you are ready, take your hand away and let her continue on her own. Concentrate on how you are feeling. If you need to adjust her technique, put your hand back over hers or say what you would like her to do.
- Once you are happy with what she is doing, close your eyes and enjoy your erection. Let your mind wander to a fantasy of your choice. Enjoy the pleasurable sensations your partner is producing for a little while, and then stop.

How did that feel? Did you experience positive sensations? Did you feel your excitement grow? If not, then what got in the way? Does your partner's stimulation technique need further work? Did you find it hard to concentrate or fantasize? Discuss the session with your partner. Open and honest feedback is essential if you are going to be able to move on. Repeat this session two or three times (or more) until you feel completely comfortable with your erection and the feelings being produced.

*Stage 2*

- Repeat all of stage 1.
- This time allow your partner to keep stimulating you in the way you like until you begin to feel close to orgasm.

- Focus on a fantasy and allow yourself to enjoy the feelings building up inside you.
- When you are at the peak of arousal try not hold back. Allow yourself to enjoy the experience of ejaculation.

How did you feel? Were you able to ejaculate? If so, celebrate with your partner. If you were close but still unable to ejaculate, think about this. What stopped you enjoying yourself? Were you anxious, tired, or distracted? Again, talk to your partner about the experience. Are you or your partner concerned about ejaculate? Does it feel messy? Make sure you have a box of tissues handy to mop up. Learn from the experience and move on. Repeat this exercise two or three times (or more) until you are able to ejaculate regularly.

*Stage 3*

- Repeat stage 1.
- Lie on your back as before, with your partner sitting across the tops of your legs. Make sure that your partner is also aroused and lubricated. (Have some extra lubricant ready in case you need it.)
- Your partner should stimulate you until you are close to orgasm. Concentrate on the sensations in your genital area (pelvic floor muscle exercises can help here).
- Your partner is to sit on your penis, gently lowering herself on to you. She should then thrust in a way that you both enjoy. Focus on your feelings and use fantasy to reach orgasm.
- If the feelings have subsided, ask your partner to lift herself off and use her hand to restimulate you to near orgasm before inserting your penis again.
- Your partner can be as vigorous as you and she would like. Enjoy being inside her, concentrate, and allow your orgasm to come.

If you were unable to achieve orgasm this time, then think about what got in the way. Were you distracted or anxious? Did you need more pressure on your penis? If this is the case then your partner could squeeze her pelvic floor muscles in order to tighten them around your penis. Alternatively, she could hold the base of your penis between her thumb and fingers while thrusting. This could give you the additional pressure you need. Experiment with what feels best. Talk this over with your partner to see how she feels. Repeat two or three times (or more) until you have learned to orgasm in her vagina.

*Stage 4*

• Once you are ejaculating regularly, experiment with different positions.

If you find that you are still unable to ejaculate with your partner, you may find it helpful to work on the problem on your own. Follow the male orgasmic dysfunction masturbatory program outlined in Chapter 9 on 'Self-Help for Singles'. After you have been able to experience orgasm regularly by yourself, you can take your new learning back into your relationship and revisit the program above. With patience and practice you will overcome the problem.

## Female Problems

### Vaginismus

Vaginismus occurs for many reasons. The problem may be a primary problem (you have never had penetrative intercourse) or a secondary one (the problem has arisen after a sex life that was once OK). This program is designed to help you take control of your vaginal muscles, to reduce anxiety about penetration, and to enable you to have intercourse. How long you have had the problem will have some bearing on how long it takes for you to overcome your vaginismus, but if you follow the instructions carefully and only move on when you feel completely comfortable you can succeed.

216

Before you start on this program you may like to work through the body awareness program (Chapter 8) to help you feel more comfortable about your body. This can give you added confidence before working with your partner. Pelvic floor muscle exercises (Chapter 8) are also very important as they not only increase your awareness of sensations in the genital area but help you to relax the muscles as well. Checking out motivation and negative thinking (Chapter 6), and the use of fantasy (Chapter 8) may also give you added confidence in your ability to conquer the problem.

It goes without saying that relaxation is crucial. You will be unable to do any of the exercises if you are tense and anxious. Practise relaxation during your body awareness exercises and at other times until you are familiar with the technique and know automatically what to do. (Refer back to Chapter 7 for a reminder on relaxation technique.) Your partner may like to do some of these exercises as well. Discuss together what may be useful. You need to organize things so that you can have undisturbed time. Help each other to achieve that.

When you have worked through all the preparatory exercises, either together or by yourself, you will be ready to start on sensate focus. These exercises (Chapter 8) are designed to help couples relax and learn to enjoy gentle touching together. They are also about having some fun (see the instructions for week 2). If you have not had sexual contact for a while it may seem a bit strange. Don't worry; you will soon get used to the routine. If you feel uncomfortable about being naked in front of your partner, then use a towel or keep your bra and briefs on. It is important for you to feel comfortable for your first joint session. You will need to get to week 5 of sensate focus before you begin on the vaginismus program. If you need extra time to feel completely comfortable with sensate focus, that is fine.

Before your first joint session it is a good idea to have some time on your own to go back to body awareness and revisit stage 4 (genital touching).

In the vaginismus program, you will do some tasks yourself, and your partner will be asked to join in others. In essence, you will go through a sequence where you practise a task until you are quite comfortable with it, and then repeat it with your partner joining in. Then you move on to another task, first on your own, then with your partner. You will need to arrange your joint sessions around your progress; sometimes you may need more time to become comfortable with a particular individual task before you move on to the corresponding shared task.

Ensure that both you and your partner have cut your fingernails and filed them smooth before either of you tries inserting a finger in your vagina.

*Individual Task 1*
You will need about 30–45 minutes to complete this session.

- Have a bath and relax before following the body awareness exercise to stage 4 (genital touching).
- Towards the end of the exercise, put the tip of one finger inside the entrance to your vagina. Practise your pelvic floor muscle exercises while your finger is inserted. Can you feel the muscle tighten? Can you feel it relax? Take your time. If you feel anxious or tense, stop now.

Go over the exercise in your mind. How did it make you feel? Did you think negative thoughts? If so, what were they about? Try a fantasy next time you do the exercise. Repeat two or three times (or more) until you can put a whole finger inside your vagina. You may like to use a lubricant on your finger to help entry.

It is important to know that your vagina is not an actual space, but a potential one. The insides of the vagina lie close together and the skin is not smooth and flat, but ridgy and bumpy. During sexual arousal the vagina opens and lengthens. In fact, it becomes penis-shaped. Moisture is released from the sides of the vagina to lubricate it and make penetration easier. If you are not fully aroused this will not happen. In these

218

circumstances it is not surprising that penetration can be difficult or even painful.

## Shared Task 1

For this first joint task, each session should take about an hour. Create the right atmosphere in the room you have chosen. You both need to bathe or shower and relax. Before you begin, discuss your partner's pleasure. When will you include an orgasm for him (if he would like this): either before or after this session, or during sensate focus? Do what feels best.

Massage in the usual way, following the instructions for sensate focus. You know how to please each other by now.

- When you are ready move into position, ask your partner to sit propped up against some pillows/cushions with his legs apart. Sit between his legs and lie back against his chest. (If for some reason you are unable to adopt this position, find one that suits you better.)
- Close your eyes and enjoy the closeness of the position. Your partner can caress and stroke your body in the way he knows that you like.
- When you feel aroused, part your legs to allow him to gently stroke your inner thighs, tummy and pubic hair.
- Allow yourself to enjoy his touching and feel your body responding. He can then put the palm of his hand gently on your pubic bone (the hard area you can feel under your pubic hair) and, when you say you are ready, gently put his smallest finger into the entrance of your vagina. If you begin to tense up, then practise your pelvic floor muscle exercises on his finger and ask if he can feel the pressure.
- When you are ready, stop and discuss how you both felt. Trust is a very important factor in overcoming vaginismus. Your partner must only go as far as you are completely happy with.

Repeat this task two or three times (or more) until you feel completely comfortable.

## Individual Task 2

- Repeat individual task 1 and work on arousal.
- This time, try to insert the whole of your finger, taking into account the fact that your vagina is not a 'straight line'. You may need to move your finger gently to find the way inside. Practise your pelvic floor muscle exercises. Insert your finger a little further while relaxing the muscles.
- Continue until your can insert your whole finger.

How did that feel? Were you able to get your whole finger inside? If not, then what got in the way? Did you feel uncomfortable? You may need more lubrication. Did your thoughts get in the way? Remember to use fantasy to help. Repeat this two or three times (or more) until you can comfortably complete the task.

## Shared Task 2

- Repeat shared task 1, working on arousal and fantasy.
- When you are fully aroused, your partner can insert his finger slowly and gently. Do your pelvic floor exercises so that he can go further inside you while you relax your muscles.
- Once he has inserted his finger fully, let it stay there for a short while. Repeat your pelvic floor muscle exercises; while you are relaxing the muscle he can remove his finger.

How did this feel? Were you comfortable? Did you tense up or feel anxious? You may need to experiment with this exercise a few times before you feel completely at ease. You may need some additional lubrication. Repeat this exercise two or three times (or more).

## Individual Task 3

- Repeat tasks 1 and 2 working on insertion of one finger, focusing on arousal and fantasy.

- Next try to insert two fingers. Try the tips of your fingers first. Tense up and relax the muscles before insertion.
- Slowly and gently (using extra lubricant if needed), ease your two fingers inside your vagina. Stop and tense your muscles again, before relaxing and going as far as you can.
- A variation on this is to do the exercise in the bath. The water helps keep the vagina open and you may find this makes it easier to put your two fingers inside. You will still need to work on arousal, though.

How did you feel? Was it difficult? Depending on how big or small your fingers are – and on how confident you are feeling at this stage – you might want to try three fingers. If you do, repeat this exercise two or three times (or more) before trying a third finger.

*Shared Task 3*

- Repeat stage 2 as before.
- This time your partner is going to insert two fingers, slowly and gently, in the same way as he inserted one finger.
- Use additional lubrication and make sure you are fully aroused and relaxed. If your partner has big fingers you might not need to go on to three fingers. This may be all the reassurance you need that you can have something inside you.
- However, if you think you would feel more confident if he were able to put three fingers inside, practise this, using the same technique as for one and two fingers.

If you have succeeded in having two or three fingers in your vagina, that is excellent. You are doing really well. If you are finding it hard, don't worry. Time and patience will pay off. Repeat these exercises until you have completed the task fully. Do not attempt to move on to the next task until you are ready. Continue with the individual tasks to help identify any blocks that you can then share with your partner.

## Shared Task 4

- This exercise is about getting friendly with your partner's penis. Repeat shared task 3 to arousal and finger insertion. Use your new knowledge of what works and what feels good to prepare for this next step.
- Ask your partner to lie down and sit across the top of his legs. Stimulate him to a good firm erection. When ready, raise yourself on to your knees (use extra pillows under your knees if you need support or extra height) and tease your vagina with the end of his penis. Can you feel your vagina responding? Are you opening up?
- Rub your clitoris with the end of his penis. Enjoy the sensation. When you are ready you may like to bring him to orgasm from this position.

How did you feel? Were you tense or nervous . . . or did you enjoy it? Think about how much you have achieved. Discuss your progress with your partner. Repeat this session two or three times (or more).

## Shared Task 5

- Repeat shared task 4, making sure you are fully aroused and well lubricated for this important next step. You may like to lubricate your partner's penis at the same time.
- Sit across your partner as you did before, only this time after stimulating him to a good firm erection, instead of playing with his penis you can start to insert it into your vagina. Raise yourself up until you can put the end into the entrance of your vagina. If you start to tense up, practise your pelvic floor muscle exercises.
- So long as you are aroused, your vagina will be wet, open, and ready to receive him. Sit slowly down on to his erection until you have gone as far as you can on this first attempt. Tense your muscles and relax them before lifting yourself off.

How far did you get? Were you able to stay in control? Did you keep your arousal levels high by using fantasy and stimulation? If not, what happened? Did you feel too anxious? What else may have distracted you from the task? Discuss the session together and learn from the experience. Repeat this task until you are able to put the penis in the whole way.

## Shared Task 6

- Once you have achieved full penetration, try gentle thrusting. Experiment with what feels good. Stop when you are ready.
- You may like to experiment with different positions. When you feel ready, allow your partner to do some thrusting as well.
- Always make sure you are properly aroused before penetration. This will ensure maximum comfort and enjoyment for you both.

Some women are uncomfortable with the thought of putting fingers inside themselves. If so, you may prefer to use vaginal trainers. Two suppliers are given in Appendix 1. You can follow the instructions set out in the section on vaginismus in Chapter 9 for singles, starting from stage 4. Replace fingers with trainers in both your individual and your shared sessions, and work through the program, adapting the instructions to fit the trainers. There are four trainers in each pack. You will need to begin with the smallest one and work through each size until you can put the largest one comfortably inside you. As the last one is penis-size, it can really help allay any anxiety you may have about being able to accommodate a penis. After you have inserted the final trainer, go back to shared task 5 for guidance on inserting the real thing.

## Dyspareunia

Dyspareunia (painful sex) is caused by many things. One of the most common causes is insufficient lubrication. A dry vagina is not going to give a comfortable sexual experience. This can be due to hormonal changes, as in the menopause, or lack of arousal, where foreplay is inadequate. Other common reasons include pelvic inflammation, endometriosis and diabetes, to name but a few. Whatever has caused you to suffer the problem, this program is here to help remedy the situation. However, it is important that if your pain is severe and persistent you see your doctor first. Only when you have the all-clear, and are signed off as medically fit and well enough for sexual intercourse, should you attempt this program.

It is often difficult to resume intercourse after severe pain and discomfort. The memory of pain can linger long after the original problem or cause has gone away. This program will enable you to relearn what pleasurable sex is and enjoy sharing this with your partner. Partners can suffer as well, as it is no fun having sex with someone who is in pain. If you have been left with a negative body image as a result of the problem, you may like to work through the body awareness exercises first (see Chapter 8) to help you feel good about yourself. Pelvic floor muscle exercises (also described in Chapter 8) will help you become familiar with your genital sensations as well as increase arousal. Start working on these as soon as you can. Relaxation is essential and fantasy (Chapter 8) can also be helpful. Try out the relaxation technique provided in Chapter 7, or use your own method (meditation, yoga or whatever works for you).

You and your partner will need an hour for each session. Create a nice, cosy atmosphere, with soft lighting or candles. Each of you will need to have a bath or shower and relax before you start. Follow the instructions for sensate focus to get to know each other again. Enjoy 'fun week' (week 2) by experimenting with different oils or lotions, material, food, or drink . . . whatever smells nice or tastes good. Often couples stop having sex or any intimate time together when there is a problem. This can go on for weeks, months, or longer. If this is the case for you, then sensate focus can help to bridge the gap between doing nothing and doing everything again. As you will see from the program

(Chapter 8), there is no pressure at this time as intercourse and masturbation are put on hold for a short while. Focusing on relaxation and pleasure will put you in a good frame of mind and body to begin overcoming the problem.

The exercise asks for you both to be naked. If that is difficult for you, for whatever reason, don't let it put you off. Start with some underwear or a towel until you become familiar with the work and with each other again. With practice it will become easier.

Work through sensate focus to week 5. The program is based on the assumption that couples will do three sessions a week for 5 weeks. However, this is not always possible. If you end up taking longer to complete each stage, that's fine. Just try to ensure that you don't allow too big a gap between sessions or stages. Building on new learning requires continuity and commitment. Gaps can allow your motivation to slide and negative thoughts to intrude.

During the first stage of the program, your partner will be asked to insert a finger into your vagina. (Make sure his fingernails are short and smooth before you attempt this.) If you feel unhappy about this, you may like to look at the individual tasks given for vaginismus in the previous section. If you prefer, work through the instructions there before you start on your shared work here. Also, discuss pleasuring your partner to orgasm (if that is what he would like). Decide when would be a good time: before or after this session, or during sensate focus?

*Stage 1*

- Repeat sensate focus week 5.
- Enjoy touching and stroking each other. Work on what you have learned about what you each like.
- Ask your partner to lie on the bed propped up against some pillows or cushions. Sit in between his legs so that you can lie back against his chest. He can caress, touch and cuddle you.

- When you feel nice and relaxed, let his hand move down to your genital area. Part your legs for him so he can touch your clitoris and your vagina.
- Use a fantasy while he is doing this. Let your body go with the flow; your vagina will open up when you are aroused. Enjoy the sensations.
- Now your partner should gently insert one finger into your moist vagina. See how far you can let him go. Practise your pelvic floor muscle exercises while his finger is inside you. Can he feel the pressure? When you are ready, tense up on his finger. When you relax the muscles tell him he can withdraw slowly.

How did that feel? Were you relaxed? Did you use fantasy to help? Did you feel any pain . . . or was it slightly uncomfortable? This could be due to lack of lubrication and not feeling fully turned on. Work on pleasuring a bit more together before finger insertion, and use some additional lubricant on your vagina and your partner's finger. Talk to your partner about the session: how was it for him? Repeat the exercise two or three times (or more) until you can comfortably accommodate his full finger inside you.

## Stage 2

- Repeat all of stage 1.
- This time your partner can put two fingers inside you. Practise your pelvic floor exercises to help him. How does that feel? Make sure you are fully aroused and relaxed.

What was the experience like for you? Were you able to have two fingers inside you comfortably, or was there some discomfort? Discuss progress with your partner. Work on overcoming this through repetition of stage 1, relaxation, good lubrication and full arousal. When you feel comfortable he can insert three fingers, following the same routine. Repeat the exercises two or three times (or more) to consolidate the learning. When this has all been achieved with absolutely no pain you can move on to the next stage.

## Stage 3

- Pleasure each other in the way you both know how.
- When you are fully aroused, ask your partner to lie down. Sit across the tops of his legs. Stimulate his penis to a good firm erection (he can stimulate your clitoris with his hand at the same time). Use a lubricant on his penis for added comfort. When you are ready, sit up and put his penis inside the entrance to your vagina.
- Lower yourself gently on to his penis as far as you can. Sit still and practise your pelvic floor muscle exercises on his penis. When you are ready, sit up and take his penis out. You can stimulate him to orgasm now if this is what you would both like.

How did you get on? Were you able to complete the task fully? Did you feel any discomfort at all? If you did, what caused the pain? Were you lubricating enough? Did you use additional lubrication? Did you allow yourself to become distracted so that your arousal levels dropped? Was the position difficult? Maybe you need pillows or cushions under your knees to give you extra height. Think about these things and talk to your partner about them. Repeat the exercise two or three times (or more) until you can get the whole of his penis inside you. Build on what you have learned.

## Stage 4

- Repeat all of stage 3.
- Lower yourself onto your partner's penis, but this time move gently up and down.
- Move as slowly or as fast as feels comfortable to you.
- Allow him to have an orgasm if he wishes.

What was that like? Did you feel in control? Was it pain-free moving gently? Were you able to experience pleasurable sensations? Talk to your partner about your progress. Repeat two or three times (or more) until you are moving freely.

## Stage 5

- Now you are comfortable with penetration, your partner can also thrust, still with you in the on-top position. Make sure you are well lubricated and fully turned on.
- Experiment with other positions to ensure all are pain-free. Your partner can ejaculate inside you once you are ready.

When trying different positions, be aware of the direction of the penis inside you. Some positions are best avoided. For instance, if your uterus (womb) is lying towards your back passage instead of over your bladder, deep penetration can hit the cervix (neck of the womb), causing some discomfort. You can find out for sure if this applies to you by having a medical examination – or just choose positions that are not troublesome.

If, during any of these exercises, you find your pain has come back, be sure to consult your doctor straight away to see what is happening in case there is a medical problem to be sorted out. You can return to the program once you are pain-free again.

## Orgasmic Dysfunction

The inability to have an orgasm can cause much distress in a relationship. Unfortunately, this is often accompanied by lots of pressure to succeed. It's important to know who is putting on the pressure. Are you putting it on yourself? Or do you feel it from your partner (who may well be questioning his ability as a lover)? Sometimes, childhood messages to do with sex can leave you feeling guilty or ashamed of your body and about feeling sexy. Masturbation can be a taboo subject: many women never feel able to try it for themselves. Occasionally, the problem is related to a fear of letting go or of being out of control. Anxiety can build up and culminate in questions like 'Will I look stupid?' or, worse, 'Will I take too long and will he get bored?' For older women in particular, a fear of letting go can be linked to slight stress incontinence (leaking of urine from the bladder at orgasm). This can be very inhibiting.

Whatever the reason, the program outlined here is designed to help you overcome inhibitions, reduce tension and anxiety, and help you take control of your own body. Body awareness is essential to help overcome negative feelings about your body, and pelvic floor muscle exercises will put you back in touch with pleasurable sensations in your genital area and aid arousal. Refer back to Chapter 8 for guidance on these preparations. Many women with this problem do experience high levels of excitement and arousal, but find that these are then not translated into orgasmic release. It is the mind–body connection here that is the key. Check out the section on fantasy in Chapter 8 to help you identify what arouses you and turns you on. If you can have an orgasm on your own, but not with your partner, you will need to explore what this is about. Is it to do with guilt, or a lack of confidence in your appearance or body? Are you afraid to tell him how you like to be touched?

## The Phases of the Female Orgasm

For those of you who have never experienced an orgasm, the following will help you understand a bit more about what an orgasm is.

There are four distinct phases to an orgasm – arousal, plateau, orgasm and resolution:

- *Arousal*: Within 10–20 seconds of starting to feel turned on, your vagina will start producing natural lubrication from the inner walls and blood will flow into the pelvic area (your pelvic floor muscle exercises will enhance this process). Your temperature will start to rise, creating a redness or flushing over your tummy, chest, and neck. The vulval area and your vaginal lips will become engorged (full) with blood, making them appear darker in colour. Inside your vagina lengthens and widens, extending beyond the cervix (in effect, becoming penis-shaped), while your uterus (womb) tilts backwards and upwards in readiness for intercourse.

- *Plateau*: During this phase your vagina expands further, and the clitoris stiffens, swells, increases in size, and moves under the clitoral hood. During stimulation the movement of the clitoral hood adds to the pleasurable sensations. Your body is working harder, so your blood pressure increases, as do your heart rate and breathing. At this point you will be longing for release and satisfaction through orgasm.

- *Orgasm*: At the very peak of stimulation your body will tense and stiffen as you experience orgasmic contractions at 0.8-second intervals. These will vary in length and intensity before they gradually fade away. Part of the final trigger into orgasm comes from a reflex in the brain, and if you are inhibited, nervous or anxious the normal orgasmic response can be blocked. Under these conditions you will not achieve an orgasm.

- *Resolution*: When all your contractions have faded away, the blood will drain away from the genital area and the feelings of 'puffiness' will go. The 'sex flush' will fade and your heart rate, breathing and blood pressure will return to normal levels.

Woman have also reported that certain actions or triggers can help them to have an orgasm. These 'orgasmic triggers' are strategies that you can use during your body awareness exercises (in stage 4, genital touching). Don't worry if you feel a bit silly at first: nobody is going to see you. First, arch your back, tense up your tummy and thigh muscles, and hold your head back (over the edge of the bed is a good position). Second, practise the pelvic floor muscle exercises while fantasizing. Third, *pretend* to have an orgasm: breathe rapidly, pant, make noises while stimulating yourself. Feel your way into what an orgasm might be like. Put these all together in a way that suits you.

## Getting Started

Work through sensate focus to week 5. Don't be put off if you take longer than 5 weeks to get to this point: this is only a rough guide based on couples doing three sessions a week. Sometimes life gets in the way and you need more time. However, try not to let too much time lapse between sessions as they are designed to build up your confidence steadily as you successfully work through the program. Allow an hour for each session, with time for preparation added on. Create a nice, cosy atmosphere, have a bath or shower, and, most importantly – *relax*!

By week 5 you will have learned lots of new things about yourself and your partner. You will have had some fun during week 2 using oils, lotions, and other items or substances to make the sessions more interesting. Most importantly, you will have been talking with your partner about what feels good and how you like to be touched. By this time you know that you can both give and receive pleasure.

## Stage 1

- Make sure you are nice and relaxed before you begin.
- Prepare and work through sensate focus week 5 until you are both feeling aroused and turned on. Discuss when your partner would like his orgasm.
- Ask your partner to sit propped up against some pillows or cushions, sit between his legs with your back to him, and lie back against his chest.
- Pull his arms around you until you both feel nice and relaxed in this position. When ready, your partner can begin to caress and stroke you.
- Using your hand to touch yourself, gently stimulate your clitoris until your body is responding by opening up (arousal). Turn yourself on by concentrating your mind on the pleasure you are experiencing, or focusing on a fantasy.
- Ask you partner to put his hand over yours so that he can feel how you like to be touched. Let him feel the pressure, speed, and motion that give you pleasure.

- When you are ready, let him try your technique himself. Give him lots of encouragement and feedback on what is good. If he doesn't get it quite right, put your hand on top of his and guide him gently. Let him try again on his own until you are happy with the result. Then let your orgasm come and enjoy it.

How did that feel? Did you both enjoy it . . . or did your partner find it hard to get the technique right? Don't worry, it is bound to feel a little strange to start with. Practice and familiarity will help overcome these feelings. The important thing is that you are open and honest with each other. If you have ever pretended to have orgasms in the past, the last thing you should do now is pretend that his touching is hitting the spot when it isn't. Repeat the exercise two or three times or as many as you need in order to feel comfortable with each other.

If you're happy with manual stimulation only, you can skip stage 2 and go straight to stage 3. If you have used a vibrator in the past, and/or if you both feel comfortable with the idea of trying it now, do the exercise again, but this time, instead of your hand, use the vibrator.

## Stage 2: Using a Vibrator

- Follow the instructions as in stage 1, but using a vibrator instead of your hands.

Many women find that the adjustable speed and constant stimulation will enable them to climax. A vibrator should never replace other forms of touch. It is just another way of achieving satisfaction. Continue with manual stimulation as well. (If you would like to buy a vibrator, reliable sources are listed in Appendix 1 under 'Sex Aids'.)

How did that feel? Were you both comfortable with the vibrator, or did you find it too intense? Too quick? Or not as pleasant as stimulation by hand? Discuss this fully with your partner. The goal here is to find out what works best for you.

Don't forget to use fantasy. Additional lubrication can help stimulation if it takes a while to get to orgasm. Repeat two or three times (or more).

## Stage 3

- Repeat stage 1 to arousal.
- When you are both ready, ask your partner to lie down and sit across the tops of his legs so that you can arouse each other easily.
- Use additional lubrication on his penis if you wish. Sit up and put his penis inside your vagina and slowly lower yourself on him. (Use cushions under your knees if you need extra height.)
- You or your partner can stimulate your clitoris at the same time as you gently move up and down on his penis.
- Use the orgasmic triggers: hold your head back, arch your back, tense your muscles. Increase your speed to increase stimulation.
- This position is excellent for achieving orgasm. Move yourself around to maximize sensation and pleasure, continue until you feel your vaginal muscles start to tighten, then allow your orgasm to come.
- You may like to stimulate your partner to orgasm now if you haven't already done so.

How did that feel? Were you able to orgasm? If not, don't worry as you were probably very close. As long as you focus and don't allow yourself to become anxious or distracted, with practice you can be orgasmic. Repeat this exercise two or three times or more – as many as you like. Have fun learning how to make your body respond. Encourage your partner to tell you how he feels.

## Stage 4

- Experiment with different positions and different ways to stimulate your clitoris. Your partner can begin thrusting as well.

- If you have not been orgasmic during penetration, discuss how and when you would like to be stimulated to orgasm.

Many women do not experience orgasm through penetration alone. If that is the case then learn to enjoy your orgasm manually, using a vibrator, or orally. Repeat this exercise two or three times (or more) until you are regularly enjoying your sexual relationship together.

If you have experienced any problems during the program, there are other things you can try. If you have never masturbated, you may find it helpful to refer to the section on orgasmic dysfunction in Chapter 9, 'Self-Help for Singles'. If you follow the instructions, they will help you learn how to let your body respond. Once you are orgasmic on your own, you can share the information gained with your partner and then work through the above program again. As with many things, it will take trial and error, patience, and help and support from your partner to overcome your sexual problem. Remember, do not put yourself under pressure. Go at your own pace and you will get there in the end.

## Loss of Interest/Desire

Many couples lose interest in sex. When this affects them both it is often not a problem. Knowing you are not having sex but understanding why and being absolutely confident that you can get sex back whenever you want to does not really constitute a problem. Problems only arise if one or both of you is/are not happy with the situation. The problem can be made worse if the one who wants to have sex starts thinking that their partner has gone off them, or that their partner might be having an affair. If sex has suddenly gone out of the relationship it is important to think about why that might be. Have you been together a long time and just got used to each other? Have your children and/or your jobs taken over? Are you just too busy? Is there a sexual problem neither of you wants to confront, so that losing interest has helped you avoid the problem?

Has your partner gained or lost a lot of weight so that you don't fancy them in the same way any more?

There are many reasons that can lie behind loss of sexual desire. You and your partner need to sit down and talk about what has happened in your relationship to put one or both of you off sex. It may be that you feel hostile or resentful at being taken for granted . . . or you may have been ill and got used to not having sex. Whatever the cause, the fact you are reading this is a good indication that you want to change this situation.

You will then need to ask yourselves what you want from sex and set some goals to work on (refer back to Chapter 6 for guidance). If you are sure that no sexual dysfunction exists, then the treatment program itself (see below) is quite straightforward. What will be harder is the part outlined above: understanding the reasons for the problem. Before starting any joint work, make sure you are both in agreement with the goals and desired outcomes. You will need to be highly motivated, especially if the problem has been going on for a long time. Plan some rewards for when progress is good. Praise and support each other, and offer encouragement when things don't go according to plan.

## Getting Started

You will need an hour for each session plus extra time for preparation (bath, shower, and relaxation). Refer back to Chapter 8 and follow the instructions for sensate focus up to week 5. The program is based on a couple doing three sessions a week for 5 weeks. If you are not able to do all three sessions in any one week, don't worry. Try to get them completed in just over a week. However, try to avoid long gaps in between sessions as these will not help you feel you are making progress towards your goal. Also, it is easy to become demotivated if one or both of you seems to be reluctant to initiate a session. If this should occur, discuss together what is happening and why.

Sensate focus is about getting to know each other again and involves gentle touching exercises to help you feel close and intimate. Should you experience any anxiety or concerns, then share them with your partner. For instance, if it has been a while since you have been naked together, start with underwear on, or use a towel to cover yourself while still giving your partner access to your body. During these exercises you may find it helpful to do some body awareness exercises on your own so as to build up a more positive self-image. You should never move on a stage until you are entirely comfortable with the one before. This could prolong the time you spend on the program, but that doesn't matter. It will take as long as it needs to take.

When you have completed all of sensate focus, and you both know what you each like and enjoy, you can resume intercourse and masturbation again. Experiment with different positions; have manual or oral sex. Use what you learned during week 2 (fun week) to keep things interesting. Using oils, lotions, fabric, feathers, chocolate, beer or whatever you like to massage each other can bring excitement back into the relationship. Bath or shower together rather than separately. Perhaps the reason why you went off sex was that it had become predictable and uninspiring? You now have the tools to avoid such problems in the future. Sensate focus is for all of your life. Perhaps one day, when you are both old and grey, sensate focus may be all that you can manage. Fortunately, you will know how to get the very best out of sexual togetherness to the benefit and pleasure of you both.

## Dual Dysfunctions

What does this mean? Literally it means two sexual problems in the relationship, but there may be more. It is perfectly possible to learn how to manage two or more problems at the same time. Difficulties occur in many different combinations, but some go together more often than others. For example, PE can lead to erectile dysfunction (ED), and then on to loss of interest or desire. Vaginismus and dyspareunia can often be associated with ED. Men in these relationships often feel bad about their partner's problem, and by losing their erection they are taking the pressure off them by not having sex. Also, a woman may not be orgasmic because her partner has PE.

How does a dual dysfunction program work? You will need a bit more time than in the case of a single dysfunction program to discuss the practicalities. Body awareness can help you both overcome any issues around body image, or negative feelings about sex in general. This may be a good place to start. Each of you can take responsibility for your own problem and do everything you can to work by yourself through some of the preparatory exercises outlined in Chapters 6 and 8. These might include pelvic floor exercises, relaxation, masturbation, fantasy, or tackling negative thinking. Check out what you think would be helpful in your situation. Lifestyle and stress management may be worth a look, too, as these play a big role in contributing to sexual problems. (Refer to Chapter 7 to remind yourself about this.)

When you begin to work together, you will need to start with sensate focus and progress through to week 5. During this time you will be exploring what you both like and enjoy without pressure to have intercourse. Masturbation, too, is off-limits for a short time. Week 2 is about fun and can help reduce anxiety and increase confidence. As you move further on through the sequence you will see how sensate focus helps improve your communication: this is essential for dealing with dual dysfunctions as you will need to be flexible and to negotiate what happens, when it happens.

Look at the program for your particular problem, and then go through what is required with your partner. Discuss how the processes for overcoming both problems can be dovetailed together. If your partner has gone off sex because of your problem, look at how his/her interest can be revived by following the loss of desire program. Once he/she is involved again, you can move on to the exercises provided for your sexual problem.

If the dual problems are painful sex (dyspareunia) and ED, then of necessity you will need to work on the ED first. However, you can include the earlier exercises in the program for dyspareunia alongside those for ED. If you plan well, the ED will be much improved before the need for penetration in the sequence for tackling dyspareunia. The same applies to vaginismus. If you or your partner has PE and ED, then work on the ED first. When the erection is back, move on to the instructions for PE. Sometimes two people with orgasmic problems come together. Working on this together can be very productive, as both of you share a difficulty with letting go, so, provided the motivation to overcome the problem is high, the treatment programs can complement each other as you both learn not to suppress your sexual feelings.

The general rule, then, when working as a couple, is always to go through sensate focus first. Following on from this, think logically about which problem you need to start work on first, then include the second problem into the program when the time is right. If there is a third or fourth problem, explore how these can be included too. For example, imagine a couple in which the woman is vaginismic with orgasmic problems, and her partner has ED and PE. Begin with the ED and vaginismic programs. Treatment for her orgasmic problems can be fitted into the vaginismic program quite easily. Once his erection is established, they can move on to his PE to enable penetration. It may seem like a lot of work, but it's worth it to reclaim a good sex life.

# 11

# *Conclusion*

Having got this far, you may well be thinking: What next? If you have succeeded in overcoming your sexual problem – well done! For you, further help might involve looking at how you can spice up your love life now that you are back on track. This may include exploring different positions, using sex toys, or simply finding out about alternative ways to enjoy yourself or each other. There are many ways of keeping your sex life alive and vibrant. Most important is making sure you find quality time now that you have put sex back into your life. It is all too easy to allow other things to intrude and take over again, especially if part of the reason for having no sex or no good sex in the first place was a busy lifestyle, children, or stress at work. Having worked through the book to alleviate the resulting problems, it's crucial that you stay in control. Having fun can make all the difference now you are no longer worried about performance. Check out the suggested further reading in Appendix 1.

But what do you do if still it isn't working? There may be many reasons why you have not succeeded yet. Have you read all the relevant parts of this book that address your problem? Have you taken enough time over the preparatory exercises laid out in Chapters 6 and 8, and given thought to the issues related to lifestyle and stress discussed in Chapter 7? In the specific programs, have you followed all the instructions fully? If you are in doubt, go back and consider again exactly what your problem is. Check through all the exercises to see which ones apply to you, and see if you have missed out any important elements. If you still find yourself not reaching your goal, it may well be that you will need to consider further help from a trained professional. Having the space to ask questions and check out instructions with a sex therapist suits some people. Or you may be able to get more specific help in overcoming your particular problem without face-to-face sessions, if that is what you prefer. Listed in Appendix 1 are some organizations that can offer help, with contact details including telephone numbers and websites.

# Appendix 1: Useful Organizations and Resources

For contact details of organizations outside the UK, turn to pages 245–50.

## Beaumont Society

27 Old Gloucester Street, London WC1N 3XX Tel. (24-hour infoline): 01582 412220; email: enquiries@beaumontsociety. org.uk; web: www.beaumontsociety.org.uk

National membership organization providing support for all transvestite/cross-dressing/transgender people, spouses, and partners.

## The British Association for Counselling and Psychotherapy (BACP)

Web: www.bacp.co.uk; tel.: 0870 4435252; fax: 0870 4435161.

Can help those of you seeking counselling or psychotherapy. BACP is recognized as the upholder of professional standards in counselling and psychotherapy.

## The British Association for Sexual and Relationship Therapy (BASRT)

E-mail: info@basrt.org.uk;web:www.basrt.org.uk;tel.:020 8543 2707 (normal office hours).

BASRT can give you general help in finding a therapist in your area. The association also accredits and offers continuing professional development to psychosexual therapists to ensure professional standards and quality of care.

### Citizens Advice Bureau (CAB)

Web: www.adviceguide.org.uk; tel. freephone: 0800 367222. Alternatively, look in your local phone directory for your nearest branch.

CAB offers help and advice for all sorts of problems including debt. Legal advice is available through qualified solicitors.

### Cruse

E-mail: helpline@crusebereavementcare.org.uk. For local branches see your telephone directory or contact voluntary services through your local council.

Offers bereavement care for anyone dealing with the loss of a loved one.

### Eating Disorders Association

Web: www.edauk.com (for general information). Tel. helpline for adults (over 18): 0845 634 1414; e-mail: helpmail@ edauk.com. Youth helpline (for those aged under 18) : 0845 634 7650; youthline text service: 07977 493 345; e-mail: talkback @edauk.com.

### FPA

National helpline: 0845 310 1334; also in your local directory under 'Health'.

Formerly the Family Planning Association, the FPA works to improve sexual health and reproductive rights for all. It offers free advice and guidance on contraception. All sexual health concerns are dealt with in a caring and confidential environment.

## International Stress Management Association UK

Web: www.isma.org.uk

## National Council on Sexual Addiction and Compulsivity

Web: www.sexcriminals.com

Gives help to those worried they may be suffering from sexual addiction.

## Parentline Plus

Tel. helpline: 0808 800 2222; web: www.parentlineplus.org.uk

For parents under stress or anyone wanting to consult on parenting issues.

## Relate

Web: www.relate.org.uk. Telephone numbers for a branch in your area can be found in your local telephone directory.

The premier agency in relationship therapy, Relate offers counselling for couples, counselling for individuals with relationship issues, and psychosexual therapy, as well as many other services. They publish many guides, sold in their bookshop; see 'Suggested Further Reading' for a selection that may be relevant.

## SPOD (Association to Aid the Sexual and Personal Relationships of People with a Disability)

286 Camden Road, London N7 0BJ. Web: www.spod-uk.org. Tel.: 020 7607 8851.

SPOD is a national organization which provides a range of advice and information on sexual and relationship issues for disabled people.

## The Stroke Association

Helpline (Monday–Friday 9 a.m.–5 p.m.): 0845 30 33 100; web: www.stroke.org.uk

## Terrence Higgins Trust (THT)

Direct helpline: 0845 1221 200; web: www.tht.org.uk

For help and advice with HIV/AIDS.

## Vulval Pain Society

Web: www.vul-pain.dircom.co.uk

A confidential service for women who suffer from vulval pain due to vulval vestibulitis and vulvodynia.

## Women's Aid

Helpline: 0808 2000 247; web: www.womensaid.org.uk

Offers help and support to anyone suffering from domestic violence. Alternatively, contact your local police station for help and guidance with this issue.

## Additional Telephone and Internet Resources

### Gay/Lesbian/Bisexual Helplines

These can be found in your local telephone directory or by logging onto Gay Switchboard on the internet. This should lead you to your own local service.

*Useful Organizations and Resources*

## Genito-Urinary Medicine Clinics

For advice and guidance on sexually transmitted diseases, contact your local genito-urinary medicine (GUM) clinic. This is normally located in your nearest hospital or sexual health clinic. The number can be found in your local telephone directory.

**www.bullyingonline.org** is a resource for those suffering from workplace bullying and related issues.

**www.surfonthesafeside.com** is a website for parents wishing to protect their children's use of the Internet.

**www.soberrecovery.com** is a website offering help in coping with addiction, covering problems with drugs and alcohol, and also eating disorders.

## Seeking help in Australia

### Anxiety & Stress Management Service of Australia

Web: www.socialanxiety.com.au/asmsa.htm; e-mail: contact@anxietyhelp.com.au; tel: +617 5456 1296 or 0409 898 828.

### Australian Association for Cognitive Behaviour Therapy

Web: www.aacbt.org/

### Citizens Advice Bureau of the ACT (Canberra, Australia)

Web: www.citizensadvice.org.au/; tel: (02) 6248 7988.

### Domestic Violence and Incest Resource Centre (Victoria, Australia)

Web: www.vicnet.net.au/~dvirc/; e-mail: dvirc@dvirc.org.au; tel: (03) 9486 9866 (Monday–Friday 9 a.m.- 5 p.m.); fax: (03) 9486 9744.

## The Eating Disorders Association Inc.
### (Queensland, Australia)

Web: www.eda.org.au. The Association also runs the Eating Disorders Resource Centre. To contact the resource centre, e-mail: eda.inc@uq.net.au; tel: (07) 3876 2500 or fax: (07) 3511 6959.

## FPA Health

Web: www.fpahealth.org.au.

Formerly known as Family Planning, the website lists the location of all the FPA centres in Australia as well as sexual health centres and AIDS councils.

## Hope Bereavement Care

Web: www.bereavementsupport.com; e-mail: bpbp@barwon health.org.au; tel: (03) 5226 7269; fax: (03) 5246 5186.

Provides support and advice for families suffering from the loss of a child.

## National Stroke Foundation

Web: www.strokefoundation.com.au; stroke helpline: 1800 787 653 (1800-stroke).

## Parentline (Victoria, Australia)

Tel: 13 22 89 (8 a.m. –12 p.m. Monday–Friday, 10 a.m.–10 p.m. weekends); web: www.parentline.vic.gov.au

Provides professional advice on parenting of children up to 18-years of age.

## *Sexual Health & Family Planning Australia*

Web: www.fpa.net.au; e-mail: fpa@fpa.net.au; tel: (02) 8752 4348; fax: (02) 9716 7234.

# Seeking help in Canada

*Bereavement Self-Help Resources Guide (Ontario, Canada)*

Web: www.bereavedfamilies.net/guide

## *Canadian AIDS Society*

Web: www.cdnaids.ca/

## *Canadian National Clearinghouse on Family Violence*

Web: www.hc-sc.gc.ca/hppb/familyviolence; tel: 1 800 267 1291 or (613) 957 2938; fax: (613) 941 8930.

## *Canadian Psychoanalytic Society*

Web: www.psychoanalysis.ca; e-mail: cpsqeb@qc.aira.com; tel: 514 342 7444; fax: 514 342 7444.

## *Heart and Stroke Foundation*

Web: ww1@heartandstroke.ca; tel: (613) 569 4361; fax: (613) 569 3278.

## *The National Eating Disorder Information Centre (NEDIC) (Toronto, Canada)*

Web: www.nedic.ca; e-mail: nedic@uhn.on.ca; national toll free line: 1 866 NEDIC 20 (1 866 63342 20) or 416 340 4156; fax: 416 340 4736.

## *Planned Parenthood Federation of Canada (PPFC)*

Web: www.anac.on.ca/sourcebook/resource_planned.htm;
e-mail: admin@ppfc.ca; tel: (613) 241 4474; fax: (613) 241 7550.

Resources for stress management can be found at www.crha-health.ab.ca/hlthconn/items/StressMgmt.htm#resources

## Seeking Help in New Zealand

### *Family Planning Association New Zealand*

Web: www.fpanz.org.nz; tel: 00 64 4384 4394 (international);
tel: (04) 384 4349 (national).

### *Headspace*

Web: www.headspace.org.nz/family.

A useful website offering help on many issues including eating problems, sex, stress management and depression.

### *HIV/AIDS Information/ Resources*
### *(Ministry of Health website)*

Web: www.moh.govt.nz/aids

### *Preventing Violence*

Web: www.dvc.org.nz; e-mail: enquiries@preventingviolence.org.nz; tel: (09) 303 3938; fax: (09) 303 0067.

A useful resource for those suffering from domestic abuse.

### *Skylight Trust*

Web: www.skylight.org.nz; e-mail: info@skylight-trust.org.nz;
national helpline: 0800 299 100 (freephone).

Bereavement support for all ages.

## Seeking Help in South Africa

*Domestic Violence Service Providers' Directory*

Web: www.hotpeachpages.net/africa/southafrica.htm

A useful site full of information and helplines for organizations across South Africa.

*Family and Marriage Association of South Africa*

Web: www.swd.co.za/ngo/famsa.html; tel: 044 874 5811; fax: 044 874 7026.

This organization offers counselling and therapy as well as training and support groups.

*Heart Foundation South Africa*

Web: www.heartfoundation.co.za; e-mail: heart@heartfoundation.co.za; tel: (021) 447 4222; fax: (021) 447 0322.

*Planned Parenthood Association of South Africa*

Web: www.ppasa.org.za; e-mail: admin@ppasakzn.org.za

## Seeking Help in the USA

*American Domestic Violence Crisis Line*

International toll free crisis line: 866 USWOMEN (866 879 6636); web: www.awoscentral.com; e-mail: geninfo866uswomen @866uswomen.org; fax: (503) 907 6554.

*American Heart Association*

For information on strokes and other heart diseases, visit www.americanheart.org or tel: 1 800 AHA USA 1 or 1 800 242 8721.

*The American Psychoanalytic Association*

Web: www.apsa.org

## The Body: the Complete HIV/AIDS Resource

Web: www.thebody.com/hotlines/other.html

## Family Planning Councils of America

Web: www.fpcai.org/; e-mail: info@fpcainc.org

## International Stress Management Association (ISMA)

Web: www.isma-usa.org; e-mail: info@isma-usa.org

## The Irvine Health Foundation (IHF) (California, USA)

Web: www.ihf.org; e-mail: requests@ihf.org; tel: 949 253 2959; fax: 949 253 2962.

## National Eating Disorders Association (NEDA) (USA)

Web: www.nationaleatingdisorders.org

## New Hope Center for Grief Support (Michigan, USA)

Web: www.newhopecenter.net/; e-mail: griefhelp@aol.com; tel: (248) 348 0115.

## The Society for the Advancement of Sexual Health (USA)

Web: www.ncsac.org; e-mail: sash@sash.net; tel: (770) 541 9912; fax: (770) 541 1566.

The society provides help and advice for tackling sexual addiction.

## Imago Relationships

Web: www.imagorelationships.org/.

This useful website also has links to many other relationship therapy sites in many other countries.

## Suggested Further Reading

### Underlying and Related Problems

Other titles in the *Overcoming* series may help with underlying problems. *Overcoming Depression* by Paul Gilbert (revised edition, Robinson, 2000), and *Overcoming Anxiety* by Helen Kennerley (Robinson, 1997), are just two of the really helpful guides available.

*Abused Men: The Hidden Side of Domestic Violence* by Philip W. Cook (Greenwood Press, 1997). ISBN 0 2759 5862 0.

*The Book for People Who Do Too Much* by Bradley Trevor Greive (Andrews McMeel, 2004). ISBN 0 7407 4183 7.

*Building a Culture of Respect: Managing Bullying at Work* by Noreen Tehrani (Taylor & Francis, 2001). ISBN 0 415 2468 2.

*Creating a Balance: Managing Stress* by Stephen Palmer, Cary Cooper, and Kate Thomas (British Library, 2003). ISBN 0 7123 0892 X.

*Debt Advice Handbook* (CPAG, 2004). ISBN 1 9016 8966 1.

*The Emotionally Abusive Relationship: How to Stop Being Abused and How to Stop Abusing* by Beverly Engel (Wiley, 2002). ISBN 0 4712 12970.

*The Good Sleep Guide* by Michael Van Straten (Trafalgar Square, 2004). ISBN 1 8562 6539 0.

*Healing the Addictive Mind* by Lee L. Jampolsky (Celestial Arts, 1991). ISBN 0 8908 7623 1.

*How to Get Out of Debt, Stay Out of Debt and Live Prosperously* by Jerrold Mundis (Bantam, 2003). ISBN 0 7732 8396 0.

*Living with Bereavement* by Alex James (Elliot Right Way Books, 2004). ISBN 0 7160 2166 8.

*Men Who Beat the Men Who Love Them: Battered Gay Men and Domestic Violence* by David Island (Harrington Park Press, 1991). ISBN 0 9189 397 3.

*Natural Solutions to Infertility* by Marilyn Glenville (Evans, 2004). ISBN 0 7499 2059 9.

*New Pregnancy and Birth Book* by Dr Miriam Stoppard (Ballantine, 2004). ISBN 0 7513 3627 0. This practical guide includes a section on sex during pregnancy and after childbirth.

*Violent No More: Helping Men End Domestic Abuse* by Michael Paymar (Hunter House Inc., 2000). ISBN 0 8979 3268 4.

## Useful Relate Guides

*After the Affair: How to Build Trust and Love Again* by Julia Cole (1999). ISBN 0 09 182515 6.

*Stop Arguing, Start Talking* by Susan Quilliam (1998). ISBN 0 09 185669 8.

Other useful topics in the series include *Better Relationships*, *Loving in Later Life*, *Second Families*, and *Starting Again*. For details on how to obtain any of these, see contact details for Relate on page 243.

## Sexual Health

*The Endometriosis Sourcebook* by Mary Lou Ballweg (Contemporary Books, 1995). ISBN 0 8092 3263 4. Very useful book for anyone suffering from this distressing condition.

*The MANual: The Complete Man's Guide to Life* by Mick Cooper and Peter Baker (HarperCollins, 1996). ISBN 0 7225 33187.

*The New Male Sexuality* by Bernie Zilbergeld (Bantam, 1999). ISBN 0 553 38042 7. Excellent all-rounder and very readable.

*Painful Sex: A Guide to Causes, Prevention and Treatment* by Michele Goldsmith (Thorsons, 1995). ISBN 07225 3104 4. Out of print, but worth searching the internet for a copy.

*Sexual Health for Men: At Your Fingertips* by Dr. Philip Kell and Vanessa Griffiths (Class, 2003). ISBN 1 85959 011 X. Looks at erectile dysfunction and its many causes in straightforward question-and-answer format.

*The Vulvodynia Survival Guide: How to Overcome Painful Vaginal Symptoms & Enjoy an Active Lifestyle* by Howard I. Glazor and Gae Rodke (New Harbinger, 2002). ISBN 1 5722 4291 4.

## Enhancing Your Sex Life

*The Art of Erotic Massage* by Dr. Andrew Yorke (Cassell, 2000). ISBN 0 7137 1988 5.

*Becoming Orgasmic: A Sexual and Personal Growth Programme for Women* by Julia R. Heiman and Joseph LoPiccolo (Piatkus, 1998). ISBN 0 8618 8798 0.

*Best Fetish Erotica* edited by Cara Bruce (Cleis Press, 2002). ISBN 1 5734 4146 5. For those interested in unusual sex.

*Better Than Ever: Sex for People in Their Later Years* by Bernie Zilbergeld (Crown House, 2004). ISBN 1 9044 2436 8.

*The Busy Couple's Guide to Great Sex* by Rallie McAllister (Running Press, 2004). ISBN 0 7624 1832 X.

*The Joy of Sex* by Dr Alex Comfort (Quartet, 2003). ISBN 1 84000 785 0.

*Massage Secrets for Lovers: The Ultimate Guide to Intimate Arousal* by Dr. Andrew Stanway (Quadrille, 2002). ISBN 1 9038 4587 4.

*The Multi Orgasmic Man: The Sexual Secrets That Every Man Should Know* by Mantak Chia and Douglas Abrams Arave (HarperSanFrancisco, 1996). ISBN 0 7225 3325 X.

*Relate Guide to Sex in Loving Relationships* by Sarah Litvinoff (Vermillion, 1999). ISBN 0 09 185668 X.

*Sex for One: The Joy of Selfloving* by Dr Betty Dodson (Crown, 1987). ISBN 0 517 58832 3. Out of print but well worth seeking on the internet.

*Sexy Mamas: Keeping Your Sex Life Alive While Raising Kids* by Cathy Winks and Anne Semans (Inner Ocean, 2004). ISBN 1 9307 2227 3.

## Appendix 1

## For Gay and Lesbian People

*The Intimacy Dance: A Guide to Long-Term Success in Gay and Lesbian Relationships* by Betty Berzon (E. P. Dutton, 1996). ISBN 0 5259 4234 3.

*The Joy of Gay Sex* by Charles Silverstein and Felice Picano (HarperResource, 2004). ISBN 0 0600 1274 9.

*Out of the Closet and Nothing to Wear* by Lesléa Newman (Alyson Publications, 1997). ISBN 1 5558 3415 9.

## Fantasy

*Joy of Sexual Fantasy* by Andrew Stanway (Carrol & Graf, 1998). ISBN 0 7867 0582 5.

*Joy of Sexual Fantasy: Understanding and Enriching Your Fantasy Life* by Andrew Stanway. (Headline, 1992). ISBN 0 7472 7932 2.

*Women on Top* by Nancy Friday (Arrow, 1991). ISBN 0 09 946239 7. Also *My Secret Garden* and *Men in Love* by the same author.

## Sex Aids

### Beecourse

Beecourse Ltd, PO Box 1824, Andover, Hampshire SP11 7ZJ. Tel.: 01264 358 853; web: www.beecourse.com; e-mail: info@beecourse.com

A discreet service catering for all your sensual needs including Amielle vaginal trainers.

### Owen Mumford

Brook Hill, Woodstock, Oxford OX20 1TU. Tel.: 01993 812021. Fax: 01993 813466.

Supplier of Amielle vaginal trainers.

## Sh! Women's Erotic Emporium

39 Cronet Street, London N1 6HD. Tel.: 020 7613 0020; web: www.sh-womenstore.com; e-mail:info@sh-womenstore.com.

This excellent organization is purely for women. The company is run by women and staffed by women. Men can enter if accompanied by a woman but not otherwise. This gives women the freedom to browse in comfort.

# Appendix 2: Drugs Table

| Generic Name | Brand Name | Remarks |
| --- | --- | --- |
| Sildenafil | Viagra | Take one hour before sex. Effects last 2–3 hours. It is recommended not to eat a meal before use as it slows the process down. |
| Tadalafil | Cialis | Effects can last up to 36 hours, thereby giving back some spontaneity. Also Cialis is not affected by consumption of food. |
| Vardenafil | Levitra | Unaffected by food (unless very fatty) or drink. Lasts 3–4 hours, but works best in first hour. |

None of the above drugs are suitable for those of you taking nitrates or Nicorandil (associated with heart-related illnesses).

| | | |
| --- | --- | --- |
| Apomorphine | Uprima | As this drug works in a different way from the above it can be taken with nitrates but discuss with your G.P before taking. Absorption of drug not affected by food. |

## Appendix 2

| Generic Name | Brand Name | Remarks |
| --- | --- | --- |
| Alpostadil | Caverject or Viridal duo<br>OR | Injected into the penis |
|  | MUSE system | Inserted into the penis (via the urethra) in the form of a pellet. These are both useful alternatives to those unable to take tablets. |

It is claimed that none of these drugs are affected by alcohol, but it would be sensible to limit its use whilst taking any of them. A word of caution for those of you using amyl-nitrate poppers: do not use with any of the above drugs. For more information check out *Sexual Health for Men* in the further reading section.

Other drugs, for example antidepressants, psychotropics (used for mental health-related illnesses) and those related to the heart, blood pressure and indeed many other commonly treated health issues, can affect sexual function in some cases. If you have reason to believe your treatment is affecting your sex life adversely, the best person to discuss this with is your doctor.

# Index

259

# Order further books in the *Overcoming* series

| No. of copies | Title | Price | Total |
|---|---|---|---|
| | Anger and Irritability | £9.99 | |
| | Anorexia Nervosa | £7.99 | |
| | Anxiety | £7.99 | |
| | Bulimia Nervosa and Binge-Eating | £7.99 | |
| | Childhood Trauma | £7.99 | |
| | Chronic Fatigue | £9.99 | |
| | Depression | £7.99 | |
| | Low Self-Esteem | £9.99 | |
| | Mood Swings | £7.99 | |
| | Obsessive-Compulsive Disorder | £9.99 | |
| | Panic | £9.99 | |
| | Relationship Problems | £9.99 | |
| | Social Anxiety and Shyness | £7.99 | |
| | Traumatic Stress | £7.99 | |
| | Weight Problems | £9.99 | |
| | Your Smoking Habit | £9.99 | |
| | P&P & Insurance | | £2.50 |
| | **Grand Total** | | £ |

Name: _____

Address: _____

_____ Postcode: _____

Daytime Tel. No.: _____

E-mail: _____

Three ways to pay:
1. **For express service telephone the TBS order line on 01206 255 800 and quote 'CRBK2'. Order lines are open Monday–Friday 8:30a.m. – 5:30p.m.**

2. I enclose a cheque made payable to **TBS Ltd** for £_____

3. Please charge my ❑ Visa ❑ Mastercard ❑ Amex ❑ Switch (switch issue no. .......... ) £_____

    Card number: _____

    Expiry date: _____ Signature _____
    (your signature is essential when paying by credit card)

Is/ are the book(s) intended for personal use ❑ or professional use ❑?

**Please return forms (*no stamp required*) to, Constable & Robinson Ltd, FREEPOST NAT6619, 3 The Lanchesters, 162 Fulham Palace Road, London W6 9BR. All books subject to availability.**

**Enquiries to readers@constablerobinson.com**
www.constablerobinson.com

Constable & Robinson Ltd (directly or via its agents) may mail or phone you about promotions or products. Tick box if you do not want these from us ❑ or our subsidiaries ❑.